Woolf Studies Annual

Volume 7, 2001

PACE UNIVERSITY PRESS • NEW YORK

Copyright © 2001 by
Pace University Press
One Pace Plaza
New York, NY 10038

All rights reserved
Printed in the United States of America

ISSN 1080-9317
ISBN 0-944473-54-7 (pbk: alk.ppr.)

Member

Council of Editors of Learned Journals

♾ ™ paper used in this publication meets the minimum requirements of
American National Standard for Information Sciences–Permanence of Paper
for Printed Library Materials,
ANSI Z39.48–1984

Editor

Mark Hussey — *Pace University*

Editorial Board

Tuzyline Jita Allan	*Baruch College, CUNY*
Eileen Barrett *(Book Review Editor)*	*California State University, Hayward*
Kathryn N. Benzel	*University of Nebraska-Kearney*
Pamela L. Caughie	*Loyola University Chicago*
Wayne K. Chapman	*Clemson University*
Patricia Cramer	*University of Connecticut, Stamford*
Beth Rigel Daugherty	*Otterbein College*
Anne Fernald	*Purdue University*
Val Gough	*University of Liverpool*
Sally Greene	*University of North Carolina, Chapel Hill*
Leslie Kathleen Hankins	*Cornell College*
Karen Kaivola	*Stetson University*
Jane Lilienfeld	*Lincoln University*
Toni A. H. McNaron	*University of Minnesota*
Patricia Moran	*University of California, Davis*
Vara Neverow	*Southern Connecticut State University*
Annette Oxindine	*Wright State University*
Beth Carole Rosenberg	*University of Nevada-Las Vegas*
Bonnie Kime Scott	*University of Delaware*

Consulting Editors

Nancy Topping Bazin	*Old Dominion University*
Morris Beja	*Ohio State University*
Louise DeSalvo	*Hunter College, CUNY*
Carolyn G. Heilbrun	*Avalon Foundation Professor in the Humanities Emerita Columbia University*
Jane Marcus	*Distinguished Professor CCNY and CUNY Graduate Center*
Lucio Ruotolo	*Stanford University*
Brenda R. Silver	*Dartmouth College*
Susan Squier	*Pennsylvania State University*
Peter Stansky	*Stanford University*
J. J. Wilson	*Sonoma State University*
Alex Zwerdling	*University of California, Berkeley*

Many thanks to readers for volume 7: Ann Gibaldi Campbell (Lake Forest Academy), Emily Dalgarno (Boston U), Suzette Henke (U of Louisville), Georgia Johnston (St. Louis U), Ellen Carol Jones (St. Louis U), Krista Ratcliffe (Marquette U), Diana Swanson (N Illinois U).

Woolf Studies Annual is indexed in the *American Humanities Index, ABELL* and the *MLA Bibliography*.

The Society of Authors has been appointed to act for the Virginia Woolf Estate. Inquiries concerning permissions should be addressed to:

Mr. Jeremy Crow
The Society of Authors
84 Drayton Gardens
London SW10 9SB

Fax: 0171-373-5768
Tel: 0171-373-6642

Contents

Woolf
Studies
Annual

Volume 7, 2001

	vii	Abbreviations
Naomi Black	1	Letter to the Editor
Anca Vlasopolos	3	Focalization, the Cinematic Gaze, and Romance in Meredith and Woolf
Catherine Craft-Fairchild	23	"Same Person...Just a Different Sex": Sally Potter's Construction of Gender in *Orlando*
Judith Greenberg	49	"When Ears are Deaf and the Heart is Dry": Traumatic Reverberations in *Between the Acts*
Kristina Busse	75	Reflecting the Subject in History: The Return of the Real in *Between the Acts*
David Porter	103	*Orlando* on her Mind? An Unpublished Letter from Virginia Woolf to Lady Sackville

GUIDE

115   Guide to Library Special Collections

REVIEWS

| Eileen Barrett | 129 | *Virginia Woolf: The Novels* by Nicholas Marsh; *Virginia Woolf:* To the Lighthouse, The Waves Ed. Jane Goldman |
| Mark Hussey | 133 | *Virginia Woolf Icon* by Brenda R. Silver |

Sally A. Jacobsen	136	*The Dialogic Self: Reconstructing Subjectivity in Woolf, Lessing, and Atwood* by Roxanne J. Fand; *Heralds of the Postmodern: Madness and Fiction in Conrad, Woolf, and Lessing* by Yuang-Jung Cheng.
Georgia Johnston	142	*Other Sexes: Rewriting Difference from Woolf to Winterson* by Andrea L. Harris
Phyllis Lassner	146	*No Room Of Their Own: Gender and Nation in Israeli Women's Fiction* by Yael S. Feldman
Annette Oxindine	150	*Outsiders Together: Virginia and Leonard Woolf* by Natania Rosenfeld
Beth Carole Rosenberg	155	*Virginia Woolf Essays: Sketching the Past* by Elena Gualtieri
Diana L. Swanson	159	*Virginia Woolf: Public and Private Negotiations* by Anna Snaith
J. J. Wilson	164	*The Measure of Life: Virginia Woolf's Last Years* by Herbert Marder
Stephanie Zappa	167	*Granite and Rainbow: The Hidden Life of Virginia Woolf* by Mitchell Leaska
Janet Winston	171	*The Feminist Aesthetics of Virginia Woolf: Modernism, Post-Impressionism and the Politics of the Visual* by Jane Goldman
Notes on Contributors	174	
Policy	175	

Abbreviations

AHH	A Haunted House
AROO	A Room of One's Own
BP	Books and Portraits
BTA	Between the Acts
CDB	The Captain's Death Bed and Other Essays
CE	Collected Essays (4 vols.)
CR1	The Common Reader
CR2	The Common Reader, Second Series
CSF	The Complete Shorter Fiction
D	The Diary of Virginia Woolf (5 vols.)
DM	The Death of the Moth and Other Essays
E	The Essays of Virginia Woolf (6 Vols.)
F	Flush
FR	Freshwater
GR	Granite & Rainbow: Essays
JR	Jacob's Room
L	The Letters of Virginia Woolf (6 Vols.)
M	The Moment and Other Essays
MEL	Melymbrosia
MOB	Moments of Being
MT	Monday or Tuesday
MD	Mrs. Dalloway
ND	Night and Day
O	Orlando
PA	A Passionate Apprentice
RF	Roger Fry: A Biography
TG	Three Guineas
TTL	To the Lighthouse
TW	The Waves
TY	The Years
VO	The Voyage Out

To the Editor

What an excellent idea to print in the *Woolf Studies Annual* [Vol. 6 2000] the texts of the letters that Virginia Woolf received about *Three Guineas*. Anna Snaith has done a prodigious amount of work; I am sure that readers unfamiliar with the letters will find them fascinating and will be grateful for the detailed annotations.

I have not gone over the transcriptions in detail, but I think there is a significant, if small, mistake that readers should know about. This is at the end of Pippa Strachey's letter (#3 in Snaith, p. 20), which is a very legible long-hand, and I have its xerox before me. What Pippa in fact wrote was "unmitigated by hares and stockings," which must be a reference to Woolf's statement on p. 152 of the first English edition that one of her interlocutors (probably in the part based on Pippa herself) should be let alone "to give the finishing touches to your bazaar, arrange the hare and coffee-pot. . ." The stockings come from the request Woolf cites for the clothes to be sold at a bazaar, by implication the same one (see the first note to chapter 2).

The whole story of the bazaar is a little more complicated than it seems; I've written it up for the forthcoming Shakespeare Head edition of *Three Guineas* and won't go into it here.

Sincerely,
Naomi Black
Halifax, Nova Scotia

Focalization, the Cinematic Gaze, and Romance in Meredith and Woolf

Anca Vlasopolos

For a critic to revaluate aspects of Woolf's relation to literary history via *Men, Women, and Chain Saws* and "When the Looker Becomes a Bitch" may seem eccentric, but a century of cinematic art and three decades of intense feminist theorizing have led literary criticism to a new vision of narratology. I use the word "vision" advisedly, for my argument uses the idea of focalization in narrative studies and of the gaze in theories of the cinema, and traces Virginia Woolf's affinity for George Meredith and her continuation of his experiments to the way in which visual power operates in their novels. In this respect my analysis differs from studies of point of view, which center on vocalization, speech acts, and metaphoric distances between the narrator as speaker and expression by or about characters. Using the lens offered by Carol J. Clover in *Men, Women, and Chain Saws* and by Lisa Disch and Mary Jo Kane in "When a Looker Becomes a Bitch," I examine implicit and explicit assumptions about power relations in the deployment of such terms as focalization and the cinematic gaze, and I interrogate their relevance to a revision of narrative history via Meredith's and Woolf's romance plots.

I have selected *The Egoist* (1879) because it is the novel that echoes throughout Woolf's body of work and, more importantly, because in this novel Meredith's challenge to social illusions about gender relations achieves its first emphatic articulation through his innovative use of focalization. In *To the Lighthouse* (1927) Woolf adopts and refines Meredith's experiments with focalization, unmanning the power implicit in point of view, in order to revisit the site of the traditional West-European romance plot so as to express its destructiveness and, ultimately, its growing irrelevance to women's lives. Woolf's affinity for Meredith, and her technical amplification and ideological expansion of his experiments inform us about the way in which visual power, a narrative parallel to the cinematic gaze, can operate within the medium of fiction.

Revisiting literary history via influence studies can, as Pamela Caughie cautions, lead to "an ideal standard of values" whose timelessness and universality implies a unified subject. My argument, however, is precisely that Meredith and Woolf strategically subvert the concept of a unified subject, Meredith briefly and interruptedly, Woolf consistently and thematically. Woolf seizes upon Meredith's innovations and pushes them toward an ideological end that Meredith was incapable of imagining. Hence, his use of intense subjectivity remains provisional, caught within the parameters of the realist genre and ideologically within Victorian respectability, whereas Woolf's uses of subjectivity make *To the Lighthouse* a highly experimental novel, whose themes undermine heterosexual monogamy and general pieties about British culture.

The invention of the cinema and the increasing use of experimental photography provided modernist writers with patterns for seeing that were unavailable to their Victorian counterparts. As the grand-niece of the distinguished portrait photographer Julia Margaret Cameron, whose soft-focus, idealized studies of Victorian womanhood occasionally used Woolf's own mother as subject, Woolf may well have seen the need to envision differently, to cut through what she called the "nondescript cotton wool" of "non-being," of ordinary living and traditional representations of daily life, to the "revelation," coming with "sledge-hammer force" to overthrow ordinary ways of seeing (*MOB* 72). More significantly, the collapse of illusions in the wake of World War I about principal aspects of European civilization gave Woolf the freedom not only to push experimentation with focalization but to use it as a lever against a re-entrenchment of power. These experiments with narrative subjectivity allow Meredith and Woolf to use focalization to reverse traditional power; focalization is a more technical deployment of point of view that allows for a reversal in narrative authority from omniscient and traditional viewpoint to a *vue d'en bas* (the cat looking at the king). These experiments also propel both authors toward a narrative parallel to what Clover calls the "reactive" cinematic gaze: a view of the villain through the would-be victim's eyes, whose gaze confronts and thus transforms the agent of power into the victim's specular object, thus diminishing the agent's status. Meredith begins to make use of the reactive gaze, and Woolf fully exploits it in order to destabilize narrative/ideological authority based in a single or a dominant viewpoint, whose subjectivity is taken as normative.

Studies of continuities or literary influence between Meredith and Woolf, which center on issues such as biographical and feminist connections, on the two authors' use of comedy, and on theme and imagery, have failed to note the extraordinary technical similarities in focalization and in the use Meredith and Woolf make of the cinematic gaze as a means of interrogating and disrupting established power (Margaret Comstock, David McWhirter, Jane Marcus, Gillian Beer). Critics commenting on Woolf's technique emphasize the importance of the visual field in her narrative by drawing analogies from painting, but never from film. Molly Abel Travis and Allen McLaurin, for instance, compare Woolf with post-Impressionist painters, Travis by arguing that Woolf gives no authority to knowledge acquired through a consuming gaze, McLaurin by contrasting Mrs. Ramsay's Impressionistic myopia with Lily Briscoe's seeing whole. Conversely, H. Porter Abbot insists that Woolf found "free self-invention" in exercising tight control of characterization as classical delineation rather than imitating the diffuseness of late-nineteenth-century painting (402). Rebecca Saunders restates the postmodern praises of Woolf for indeterminacy in point of view, which creates "a self that can not only multiply, but can unify, can assimilate . . . the non-self, the Other, the phenomenological world, and make it self" (210), but she also argues that Woolf achieves this revolutionary diffusion within the bounds of traditional syntax; in other words, the revised, indeterminate post-Impressionist vision or postmodern self can co-exist with traditional prose.

In single-author analyses, however, critics independently arrive at conclusions about the two novelists' relations to language that hint at Woolf's and Meredith's discontent with their chosen medium and thus their desire to push against its limits. Martha Nussbaum, in her essay on language and knowledge in *To the Lighthouse*, and Susan Morgan and J. Hillis Miller, in their studies of Meredith, persuasively argue that Woolf and Meredith are in a fundamental way betrayed by language, their very tools as writers (Nussbaum 733; Morgan 174-77; Miller 100-43). Perhaps our own *fin-de-siècle* perspective on the inadequacies of language and the ever-growing power of visual technologies makes us turn to the cinema as a mediating discourse between culture and art. Narratologists currently give more attention to point of view in fiction than to more traditional areas such as plot development and characterization, and they define it in cinematic terms: "camera angle," "focalization" (Erlich 4). Bal makes this connection clear when she writes, "[focalization] is a term that looks technical. It is derived from photography and film; its technical nature is thus emphasized" (102). Despite Bal's theoretical claim for visual technologies and the other critics' insights into the way the traditional language of fiction fails to bear the burden of experiment that Meredith and Woolf demand of it, no critic so far has applied theories of cinematic technology to the two novelists as a means of examining their narrative affinities.

Focalization in narratology and the gaze in film theory raise questions of gendered power relations that bear directly on Meredith's attempts to represent a more balanced partnership in the romance plot and on Woolf's insistence on demolishing the centrality of that plot altogether. Yet focalization, despite its technical, camera-like angle, seems to do no more than reverse the authority of power. Bal defines the role of focalization in the creation of power, as well as in the manipulation of the reader's vision (reader sees what the character with the greater scope of focalization sees) and thus her/his sympathetic response to one side in the conflict. She concludes, "Consequently, the focalization has a strong manipulative effect" (109-110). If we look at Meredith's use of focalization in *The Egoist*, we see precisely the shift in power that Bal declares to be the effect of focalization, from witty aperçus that uphold the authority of imperial rights and the landed gentry to the intense subjective gaze of the protagonist, a very young woman trying to escape that authority. And perhaps this mere reversal of power gives us a clue to the failure of focalization as a technique with which to challenge entrenched authority. Even though Meredith's protagonist manages to convert most characters in the novel, and of course the readers, to her viewpoint on her intended, she cannot carry the entire burden of narrative authority in a novel in which the displacement of power remains mostly in the province of comedy, where we may covertly laugh at power but conspire to keep it pacified.

But what if, as Saunders suggests, there is an "ethics of discourse" (196) in which the question of who has the right to focalize on whom and for whom is precisely the issue? Both Meredith and Woolf work toward redirecting the gaze by making their female protagonists agents of focalization as well as traditional objects of the male characters' (often implicitly the reader's and narrator's) focalization; thus, they are able to challenge representations of power relations between men and women. Woolf, however, moves from the confines of the realist comedy—in which the young woman needs to marry somebody—to the novel in which the gaze shifts, flashes backward and forward, moves from subjectivity to angles from which we see people from the viewpoint of objects, we see people as objects, and we find subjectivity itself scattered through its multifarious perspectives.

Two recent revaluations of the cinematic theory of the gaze provide the most useful lens through which to examine Meredith's and Woolf's struggles to encompass visual experience in the language of fiction. Ever since Laura Mulvey's seminal essay, the gaze has been read as a technology of masculine power and control. In Clover's *Men, Women, and Chain Saws* and in Disch and Kane's essay "When the Looker Becomes a Bitch," however, the ownership of the gaze, its power over the object of the gaze, and its effect on the audience receiving the narrative become sites of contestation, not assertions or reassertions of power. Clover argues that in the contemporary horror film, which is a transgressive, liberating genre that appeals to a new audience—not unlike the modernist novel—the gaze is not allowed to maintain voyeuristic possession over its object:

> Such gazing [assaultive or predatory] is repeatedly associated with the camera ... and it is resolutely figured as male.... What is striking about this male gaze, however, is how often it remains at the level of wish or threat—how seldom it carries through with its depredations, and, even when it does succeed, how emphatically it is then brought to ruin (204).

Not only is the assaultive male gaze unable to "focalize" (in Bal's terms) for the viewer, but it cannot maintain control since a "reactive gaze," gendered as female and taking "pride of place in the scopic regime of horror . . . as the look that sees the truth," supersedes it (205). That conventional notions of gendered power are disrupted rather than reinstituted by such focalization, that the reader/audience becomes hostile to the focalizor and sides with the "reactive" gaze when the object of the gaze returns it or registers the assault as violence, opens the way to a revaluation of both focalization and the gaze in narratives other than the cinematic, as Bette London and Ruth D. Johnston have shown in their revisions of Romantic texts.

Disch and Kane expand the analytic use of the gaze and its power from narratology and cinema theory to actual gendered exchanges in their discussion of a recent event in which a woman sports reporter was charged with sexual harassment by athletes and counter-sued. Again, the "reactive" gaze in a woman's narrative challenges power prerogatives. In their case study, the contested site is neither the cinema nor a book, but the locker room, where female sports reporters have only recently gained access and where they struggle for authority with newsmaking male athletes. Disch and Kane contend that,

> By calling her a dick-watching bitch, Olson's antagonists disclose the woman sports reporter's potential to break up [the logic of "natural" heterosexuality]: by her intrusion into the locker room, she destabilizes the opposition between masculinity as that which is both penetrating and impenetrable and femininity as that which is receptive and deferential . . . . The charge of looking [made by the players against Olson] is deployed to contain this excess [of professional authority she enjoys as a woman] by turning her look of appraisal and her authoritative critical voice into a crime (330-31).

Feminist theories have enabled Disch and Kane to read the real-life conflict between the players' charge of sexual harassment and Olson's counter charge as a challenge to the authority of looking and judging. Woolf's feminine mirror in *A Room of One's Own* and its role of reflecting a flattering, magnified image of masculinity, the "specular economy of patriarchy" that presents women not only as objects of the gaze but mirrors that produce an inflated sense of patriarchal importance, provides a basis for analysis of a contemporary event. In the Olson vs. the Patriots case, however, Disch and Kane also detect the reactive gaze discussed by Clover, the act of "peeking excessively" that disrupts this economy and makes the mirror look back through the Other's eyes (335).

Disruptions in traditional representation may not lead to radical social reforms, but they allow us to envision other ways of seeing, which in turn may translate into the kind of challenge to gendered power exemplified by Disch and Kane's case study. Both Meredith and Woolf choose looking and gazing as crucial acts of gender reversal and as ways of asserting women's focalizing authority. Meredith was looking for a way to disclose the problematics of relations between men and women in "civilized" society through a disruption of the use of gazing that Western tradition had inherited from courtly love, in which the power of the gaze appears to reside in the woman, but only inadvertently, and in which the man compensates for his subordinate position through his art: the woman merely glances at the receptive passer-by, invariably the sonneteer-lover, who is stricken by the power of her beauty, physical and spiritual; the lover, who generally cannot possess the woman either because she is married and/or indifferent to his desire, sublimates his love and gains access to the beloved's body through a corpus of writing, which embodies, creates, the beloved strictly in terms of the lover's vision of her. As Ramona Ralston shows, Petrarchan tropes were revived in the late eighteenth century through new, popular translations of *Le rime* and a slew of sonnet sequences, and they were put to use by the Romantic poets. By Meredith's time, however, these tropes could no longer satisfy the demands of the novel genre and its readership for recognizable social content, however sentimentalized. For Meredith, the vocabulary of love falsified power relations in courtships and marriages solidly based on market-place calculations in which the woman and her chastity were commodities; in which men were neither subordinate to their love nor artists dedicating their talents to the celebration of the beloved's qualities; but in which both men and women pretended about the woman's power of choice and the man's subordination to her wishes. However, arriving at a new language about gender, neither that of courtly love nor that of crude naturalism with which Meredith occasionally flirted but which was not acceptable to a Victorian readership, meant taking risks within the form Meredith chose, the realistic novel.

As a critic, Woolf acknowledges Meredith's innovations, but denies him greatness because of his failure to pursue the insights into the possibilities of narrative that his experiments open up. As a writer, however, she recognizes her debt to him for the risks he took to expand the range of the realist novel. Insistently, Woolf focuses on Meredith's "intermittent brilliancy" through metaphors of vision: "For pages all is effort and agony; phrase after phrase is struck and no light comes. Then, just as we are about to drop the book, the rocket roars into the air; the whole scene flashes into light; and the book, years after, is recalled by that sudden splendour" (*CE*1 228). Blending criticism and admiration, she continues: "though we may be able to see these people, very brilliantly, in a moment of illumination, they do not change or grow; the light sinks and leaves us in darkness . . . . with Meredith there are no touches; there are hammer-strokes only, so that our knowledge of his characters is partial, spasmodic, and intermittent" (*CE*1 229). Meredith ranks among the "imperfect novelists largely because they insisted upon introducing qualities, of thought and of poetry, that are perhaps incompatible with fiction at its most perfect"; yet what the imperfect novelists have done for a writer like herself is to have opened up the confines of fiction, which, "had [it] remained what it was to Jane Austen and Trollope, . . . would by this time be dead" (*CE*1 231). Those qualities and their incompatibility with perfect fiction not only bring to mind Woolf's own search for a way out of the bind of fictional form but point to the growing inadequacy of traditional novels to make room for technical innovations, "poetry," and for sociopolitical innovations, "thought."

Woolf's analysis of Meredith's technique offers comparisons with her own both in her assessment of his relation to the realist tradition and in terms of his effects, again expressed through visual metaphors. Meredith attempts to escape the straitjacket of realism in his use of synecdoche, but the trope functions through intensity of focalization:

> Let us suppose that he has to describe a tea party; he will begin by destroying everything by which it is easy to recognize a tea party—chairs, tables, cups, and the rest; he will represent the scene merely by a ring on a finger and a plume passing the window. But into the ring and plume he puts such passion and character and such penetrating rays of vision play about the denuded room that we seem to be in possession of all the details as if a painstaking realist had described each one of them separately . . . . That is the way, as one trusts at such moments, that the art of fiction will develop. (*CE*1 235)

Meredith's introduction of poetic tropes has a cinematic effect of deep focus—"penetrating" rays; the intensity gives the appearance of clarity through a non-realistic technique whose effects seem to capture "all the details" while eschewing the ordinary descriptions of realism. Yet Woolf, awake to her own needs for expressive freedom and a new view of gender, sees Meredith's shortcomings: "A touch of realism—or is it a touch of something more akin to sympathy?—would have kept the Meredith hero from being the honourable but tedious gentleman . . . . It would have charged the high mountain air of his books with the greater variety of clouds" (*CE*1 236).

In Woolf's critique of Meredith, we perceive the openings that her own fiction was to create, as well as her sense of indebtedness to the "brilliant and uneasy figure [that] has his place with the great eccentrics rather than with the great masters" (*CE*1 232). These assessments of 1918 and 1928 remain unchanged almost a decade later, 1937: "I began Lord Ormont & his Aminta, & found it so rich, so knotted, so alive, & muscular after the pale little fiction I'm used to, that, alas, it made me wish to write fiction again. Meredith underrated" (*D*5 72). Woolf's judgment remains applicable to our contemporary reception of Meredith. Efforts like Meredith's "to escape plain prose," to compress description in realistic narrative to the illustrative trope, to achieve characterization through brilliant "vision," however ill-assorted with the conventions of fiction in his time, as well as ours, allow Woolf an entry into her own experimental fiction, nowhere more visual than in her novel of light and darkness, *To the Lighthouse*.

Meredith's experiments in *The Egoist* challenge Victorian truisms about gender. His focalizing techniques, which at moments illuminate for the reader the prison of gender conventions from a subjective, female point of view, anticipate Woolf's technical experiments, without, however, reaching the virtuosity of Woolf's multifaceted subjectivities. It is also clear that *The Egoist* preoccupied Woolf as a critique of gender relations; she uses the mirror image and the shadow of the over-inflated male "I" she gleaned from *The Egoist* in *A Room of One's Own* (104), and she alludes to Meredith's text in an egoist's exposure in *The Years* (361). *The Egoist*, moreover, contains a characterization based on Leslie Stephen, her father, a depiction Woolf obliquely dissents from in *To the Lighthouse* by conflating the forthright Vernon and the egoist Willoughby in the character of Mr. Ramsay, thereby exposing the structures of heterosexual power rather than exchanging one player for another, as Meredith does.

In *The Egoist*, more technically innovative than the more feminist *Diana of the Crossways*, Meredith begins dismantling the discourse of courtly love with its emphasis on sight as origin and locus of heteroerotic attraction. Mrs. Mountstuart's celebrated sayings, based on her aperçus of personality, haunt the novel with the inadequacy of romantic language and vision. Described as "the remembered, if not the right, thing," they nonetheless attach themselves to beings and lead to misapprehensions and reversals that dethrone both the acuity of perception, "She looked at you, and forth it came," and the notion of stable identity (10). Willoughby's metonymic leg, in particular, misleads both Willoughby and a number of characters around him as to his erotic and socioeconomic desirability. The emphasis on desirability—"Such a leg . . . will walk straight into the hearts of women. Nothing so fatal to them" (12)—might mislead even the reader, had not the narrator in Chapter 1 armed the reader against a unitary view of the presumed hero.

In courtly love, the lovers gaze in amorous combat, in which the male is wounded by the beloved's accidental look, armed with arrows and other weaponry. Yet the wounded becomes the hunter, seeking to possess the soul of the beloved as it peeps through the eyes. In *The Egoist*, Meredith self-consciously uses the contradictions, as well as the outdated conventionality of neoplatonic tropes, to ground his critique of Victorian courtship by making the gaze into a truly contested site of power instead of an artifice of contestation; he does so through two principal departures from courtly love: first, he places the gaze firmly within the conscious control of the woman looking or looking back; two, his focalizor, the one whose perceptions guide the sympathy of the reader, is consistently female in this novel. In the exchange of glances between Willoughby and

Laetitia, he looks at her to make sure that she remains devoted to him, despite his two engagements and his hinted-at affairs. Laetitia looks in turn, "up to the brightest," i.e. Willoughby (18). Initially, the two gazes are engaged in the predictable trajectory of "specular economy," wherein Laetitia serves as magnifying mirror to the male ego: "The anxious question permitted him to read deeply in her eyes. He found the man he sought there, squeezed him passionately, and let her go" (24). Laetitia, however, is convinced that Willoughby sees her, for she consoles herself about his engagement to Clara because, she reasons, "What is in me, he sees on her" (29). Through this shift in focalization, in which the reader sees not only the man's construction of the woman's gaze but her own focalization, Meredith exposes the delusions of romantic sight, in which each partner seeks him/herself in the other's gaze.

In his relations with Clara, Willoughby is gradually reduced in her eyes. From the first, his gaze is robbed of its power of control: "He looked on her, expecting her to look at him. But as soon as he looked he found that he must be in motion to win a look in return" (33). In fact, Willoughby makes himself the object of Clara's selective gaze by displaying, as a male bird would: "He looked the fittest; he justified the dictum of Science" (35). But even his preening, which he assumes captured Clara's gaze, proves useless; for Clara's gaze gains in power to the point where Willoughby sees himself diminished not only in her eyes and in the eyes of those around him but in his own esteem, in the literal reflection of his own looking-glass. He begins by seeing Clara as "essentially feminine . . . a parasite and a chalice" (38), but, not satisfied with her "heart" and uncertain of possessing her "soul," he attempts to own it without looking into it: "he would have seen that she had a spirit with a natural love of liberty . . . . Those features, unhappily, instead of serving for an introduction to the within, were treated as the mirror of himself" (39). What the mirror begins projecting, however, is an image that not only does not flatter, but minimizes, almost annihilates, Willoughby. A difference of opinion about Crossjay makes him look for acquiescence in Clara; instead, "He found himself addressing eyes that regarded him as though he were a small speck, a pin's head, in the circle of their remote contemplation. They were wide; they closed. She opened them to gaze elsewhere" (66).

In addition to Clara's resistance to play mirror to him, Willoughby has to contend with her as the object of other male gazes and, as such, the aggressor of courtly-love tradition. She remains throughout "a dazzling offender," "insufferably fair," her beauty "striking out to a distance," "one of the women who are dead shots with men" (139, 284). The military descriptions of Clara's attractions are the stock in trade of sonneteer conventions about the assaultive power of female beauty to the susceptible male. But, whereas in the courtly tradition the beloved is the object at which the lover gazes at least with the pretense of hopelessness about possession if not with actual despair, in Meredith's fiction, as during his life, the beloved is watched for signs of frailty since she is also the "repository and fortress of [male] honour" (139). Thus, Willoughby finds himself prey to jealousy: "an image of surpassingness in the features of Clara . . . gave him the . . . mace-blow" (189). His conquering gaze is reduced to jealous watchfulness prompted by fear of exposure as jilted lover. From "leg" marching into women's hearts and fittest male displayer, Willoughby descends to eyeless arachnid: "he was isolated, yet consciously begirt by the mysterious action going on all over the house . . . . His blind sensitiveness felt as we may suppose a spider to feel when plucked from his own web and set in the centre of another's. Laetitia looked her share in the mystery" (243).

Described through the masculine image and pronoun as "the hawk on stretched wings over the prey he spies," Clara's reactive gaze sees the monster in Willoughby and gradually "takes pride of place," in Clover's phrase, through Meredith's use of focalization. We are told her hawk-like eyes "were steady when thoughtfulness was awakened" (36). Thus, Willoughby's attempt to absorb Clara, to reduce her to "the female image of himself" is doomed to fail in the light of her awakened gaze. Clara begins her focalization by questioning her own perception: "Had she seen him with the eyes of the world, thinking they were her own? That look of his, the look of 'indignant contentment,' had then been a most noble conquering look, splendid as a general's plume at the gallop. It could not have altered. Was it that her eyes had altered?" (47). She then moves to an interior illumination that seems an isolated and isolating insight; for the reader, however, Clara serves as focalizor:

> "Beware of marrying an Egoist, my dear!" He bowed gallantly; and so blindly fatuous did he appear to her, that she could hardly believe him guilty of uttering the words she had heard from him, and kept her eyes on him vacantly till she came to a sudden full stop in the thoughts directing her gaze. She looked at Vernon . . . at her father, and at the ladies Eleanor and Isabel. None of them saw the man in the word, none noticed the word; yet this word was her medical herb, her illuminating lamp, the key of him. . . . Egoist! She beheld him—unfortunate, self-designated man that he was!—in his good qualities as well as bad under the implacable lamp, and his good were drenched in his first person singular. (82)

From being the only one to see Willoughby in the clarity of close-up—"implacable lamp"—Clara in the course of the novel becomes the informant on Willoughby's true nature. Both Mrs. Mountstuart, the worshiper of the leg representing the attractions of English landed gentry, and Laetitia, the worshiper of a Willoughby of medieval romance, come round to Clara's perceptions. From the pinnacle of adulation that the young Willoughby received with "the composure of Indian gods undergoing worship" (14) at the time of Mrs. Mountstuart's encomium, he descends to native malefactor scrutinized by colonial overseer. Mrs. Mounstuart's husband taught her the power of the gaze: "Mountstuart told me that the muscles of the mouth betray men sooner than the eyes, when they have cause to be uneasy in their minds" (285). Thus, when she beholds the man with a leg, she comments, "You show your under-teeth too at times when you draw in a breath, like a condemned high-caste Hindoo my husband took me to see in a jail in Calcutta" (284). Less radically but as unwaveringly, Laetitia focalizes on a Willoughby no longer metonymic by virtue of his leg but dis-membered: "She admired him still: his handsome air, his fine proportions, the courtesy of his bending to Clara . . . excused a fanatical excess of admiration on the part of a woman in her youth, who is never the anatomist of her hero's lordly graces. But now she admired him piecemeal. When it came to the putting him together, she did it coldly" (269). The distant star has become an assemblage of parts to the awakened woman's gaze; seeing Willoughby as he is, Laetitia can withstand his proposal of marriage and, when she accepts, make conditions based on "coldly" appraising him.

In *The Egoist* focalization, used to dismantle the pretense of romance in view of the socioeconomic, gendered realities of Victorian courtship and marriage, also advances the possibilities of the realistic novel toward a charged interiorization anticipating modernism. Despite the pun on her name, Clara's view of Willoughby does not serve the transparency of realism. Rather, it transforms him into a monster akin to horror-film stalkers, whose menace to women combines sexual predation with murder. Clara's horror of the physical intimacy Willoughby demands begins gradually: "He whispered, 'Come.' In the hurry of the moment she did not examine a lightning terror that shot through her" (49). We perceive her aversion to the inevitable consummation in images of stalking: "she retreated more and more inwardly; . . . she invoked the frost to kill her tenderest feelings. She was in revolt, until a whisper of the day of bells reduced her to blank submission; out of which a breath of peace drew her to revolt again . . . and once more the aspect of that singular day of merry blackness felled her to earth. It was alive, it advanced, it had a mouth, it had a song" (79). The reader sees Willoughby from Clara's vantage point, a tightly controlled, focused, subjective focalization such as the view in a subjective camera shot: "The gulf of a caress hove in view like an enormous billow hollowing under the curled ridge. She stooped to a buttercup; the monster swept by" (107).

By temporarily switching subjective focus from Clara to Willoughby, Meredith establishes that the metamorphosis from man to monster has a sociopolitical, not just a psychological, basis. He thus avoids eroticizing a young woman's sexual reticence. We see Clara from Willoughby's perspective, typical of men of his class and time, as a flower, a fruit, a confection, a lesser self, to be not just possessed but devoured and, if not possessed, then destroyed. After a disquisition on men's demand for purity in women, which turns them into "market produce" for male "gluttony," we see Clara in Willoughby's eyes as the morsel all the more delectable for its inertness: "his design was to conduct her through the covert of a group of laurels, there to revel in her soft confusion. She resisted . . . . He rejoiced in his disappointment." He mistakes her dislike for "her production of the article he demanded of her sex," the frigidity of purity (93). He responds to her plea to be released by an inner explosion of possessiveness: "She shone for him like the sunny breeze on water . . . . Ten thousand Furies thickened about him at a thought of her lying by the roadside without his having crushed all bloom and odour out of her which might tempt even the curiosity of the fiend, man" (186). His desire, at all times inflamed by her beauty, leads him to imagine her "a discarded weed" and to do violence to her in his thoughts: "An illness, fever, fire, runaway horses, personal disfigurement, a laming . . . . And then a formal and noble offer on his part to keep to the engagement with the unhappy wreck" (244).

Yet despite his deployment of focalization to uncover the horror plot of sexual relations between a predatory male and a woman kept unnaturally chaste, Meredith cannot escape the demands of his own time and the confines of genre. Setting out to write a comedy in an era no longer tolerant to overt victimization of comedy's blocking agent, he reduces but does not expel Willoughby; he is also forced by the demands of the Victorian novel to confine Clara to a union spiritually elevating rather than erotically satisfying. Yet even in confirming the formulaic conclusion favoring the "honourable but tedious" gentleman to whom Woolf objects, Meredith ascribes to his heroine the power of the gaze, consequently of choice (*CE*1 236). Meredith solves the problem of allowing a proper Victorian heroine to gaze on a man by bringing Clara upon a Vernon asleep. She focuses first on him, then on the double-blossomed cherry tree, then back on him: "she turned her face to where the load of virginal blossom, whiter than summer-cloud on the sky, showered and drooped and clustered so thick as to claim colour and seem, like higher Alpine snows in noon-sunlight, a flush of white. From deep to deeper heavens of white, her eyes perched and soared." When she returns "to earth," she retains a permanent vision of Vernon: "'He must be good who loves to lie and sleep beneath the branches of this tree'" (95). Clara, however, feels the attraction of the erotic as well as the virtuous, but, to remain respectable, she must dismiss the erotic. Just as the vision of the cherry tree moves the novel forward toward the charged subjective focus of modernist prose, so the imagery of the erotic anticipates Woolf's description of Mrs. Ramsay's artesian flow, seen in erotic terms by her jealous child. In conversation with De Craye, Clara for the first time "bathed in mirth. A boy in a Summer stream shows not heartier refreshment of his whole being" (144). To Clara, De Craye appears as the image of life-giving relief: "Issuing out of torture, her young nature eluded the irradiating brain, in search of refreshment, and she luxuriated at a feast in considering him—shower on a parched land that he [De Craye] was" (167). In Meredith's world, however, De Craye's erotic plenitude needs to give way to Vernon's dryness in order for the novel to preserve its propriety.

Freeing herself from the constraints still governing Meredith, Woolf moves toward a less compromising and compromised exposure of the depredations of heterosexual relations, as well as toward a rejection of romantic love as the denouement. Too, in *To the Lighthouse* she sets out to write an elegy, not a comedy, and thus answers to different generic requirements, both in terms of plot and character. In this novel, Woolf deploys focalization so as to destabilize gender conventions and gendered power in a way informed by her predecessor's freeing experiments with subjectivity. *To the Lighthouse* memorializes what seems to be the last Victorian marriage at the same time that it exposes its failures and points to its obsolescence in a new century in which certainties had already been rent by the Great War. Men's sphere—"deference and chivalry, . . . the Bank of England and the Indian Empire" (7)—that Mrs. Ramsay happily relinquishes to them in return for "her protection" (6) suffers a dissolution from which no builders, no cleaning women, can save it; as Lily muses in her apostrophe to Mrs. Ramsay, "It has all gone against your wishes. . . . Life has changed completely," so that "all her [Mrs. Ramsay's] being, even her beauty, became for a moment, dusty and out of date" (175).

From varied focalizations—at times rivaling, at others harmonizing—of "The Window," we are led to the single authoritative gaze of the unmarried woman artist in "The Lighthouse," a gaze that not only arrives at an informing moral vision like Clara's, but one that replaces the blown-up grid of commerce and empire sustaining the world with the "fabric" of artistic creation that "must be clamped together with bolts of iron" (171). Yet Lily Briscoe's "vision," the concluding word of the novel, remains provisional, eschewing conquest, domination, or traditional narrative closure, for, as Lily modestly reflects, notwithstanding her faith in the lasting power of art, her picture will probably "be hung in the attics . . . rolled up and flung under a sofa" (179). Woolf gives Lily's "reactive" gaze authority without having her replicate male egoism about her work.

"The Window," the opening section that exposes the reader to the greatest number of shifting points of view, combines the pictorial quality of a moment fixed on the painter's canvas with the technique of cinematic flashbacks, a point in time repeatedly revisioned. Opening on the family romance—mother and son sitting together, father and disciple walking outside, other children and guests within radius of family influence—"The Window" also serves as frame for Lily's painting, to be superimposed or flashed back to in the latter two sections of the book. Lighting, as well as people looking, gazing, perceiving, dominates the narrative. In the twilight that abstracts mother and son as pictorial objects to a "purple shadow" (52) for Lily's gaze, characters struggle for power and at the same time are haunted by thoughts of light and dark. From inside the frame with its view of the family romance—the "all this" (19) with which Lily is in love—Mr. and Mrs. Ramsay's dispute about the weather for a morrow that we never see discloses the limitations of marriage, as well as the cruelty to others it requires, such as the "sacrifices" of unrelated people like Tansley (16). In the discussion about mother-son paintings between Bankes and Lily, Woolf points to the traditional artistic idealization overlaying the reality of family life. Domestic acts of violence—the Ramsays' quarrel, the hurt to James's hopes by his father's and Tansley's weather predictions, Tansley's dismissal—take place under Lily's eye. While watching to make sure that Mr. Ramsay "would not stand still and look at her picture" (17), Lily undergoes her own psychodrama of looking "at the mass, at the line, at the colour" of the window, protecting herself from the violence of others' gaze in order to exert the authority of her own vision.

Like Willoughby's, Mr. Ramsay's gaze exercises a power derived from the weight of a tradition of gender expectations and behaviors, a power inimical, almost murderous to Lily's painterly efforts, as later to his children and to Lily as a woman. Mr. Ramsay, too, is a stalker whose appearance strikes despair in the hearts of his victims, and Woolf, even more than Meredith, places the focalization with its "reactive gaze" in the would-be victims' consciousness. While Lily struggles to "clasp some miserable remnant of her vision to her breast" (19), Mr. Ramsay glares at people without seeming to see them, making them feel like intruders on his privacy and inadequate in regard to his own manufactured emotion, his excessive self-pity: "His eyes, glazed with emotion, defiant with tragic intensity, met . . . their normal gaze"; he leaves Lily Briscoe and William Bankes "looking uneasily up into the sky" (25). Ten years later, Mr. Ramsay without his wife's mediation has perfected the exploitive gaze of his "tragic intensity" to monstrous proportions:

> As Mr. Ramsay stood there, . . . his gaze seemed to fall dolefully over the sunny grass and discolour it, and cast over the rubicund, drowsy, entirely contented figure of Mr. Carmichael . . . a veil of crape, as if such an existence, flaunting its prosperity in a world of woe, were enough to provoke the most dismal thoughts of all. Look at me, he seemed to be saying, look at me; and indeed, all the time he was feeling, Think of me, think of me. (152)

Only when Lily refuses the gender role of magnifying mirror of his woe by escaping his gaze and redirecting it so as to deflect his own away from controlling her, does she gain a measure of equality with Mr. Ramsay that allows her to feel sympathy for him. Taking control of the gaze by "looking down" at his boots, away from the demand of his "sickly look," Lily steers him to "the blessed island of good boots" (153-54). This moment of absurd comedy enlarges Lily's vision of Mr. Ramsay but does not erase his egoism, which, like Willoughby's, turns him into "a lion seeking whom he could devour" (156).

Unlike Meredith, Woolf deals with marriage and its aftermath, not merely with the romance plot. As such, she chooses to represent aspects of family that Meredith only hints at. Whereas Meredith centers mostly on a young woman's struggle to escape from an engagement grown loathsome, Woolf looks beyond courtship to the marriage itself and the entrapment of some of its participants. Mr. Ramsay's other victims, James and Cam, try to free themselves from their father's rapacious gaze, all while they crave his parental attention; unlike Lily, they cannot fully shrug off their father. A power struggle of gazes occurs on the boat toward the lighthouse. Mr. Ramsay startles his daughter with one of his bursts of quotation; he deflects the reproach implicit in her bodily reaction by ordering the children to look at the island; his daughter resists passively: "But Cam could see nothing," could only gaze "vaguely," making her father by turns angry with her womanly "vagueness" and tender toward her weakness. As Mr. Ramsay exercises his power over Cam by trying to get her to smile, James remembers his mother's surrender to his father's demands: "She'll give way, James thought, as he watched a look come upon her face, a look he remembered. They look down .... Then suddenly they look up... then somebody... surrendered" (166-68). James recalls his own gaze on his father's egoism ten years before, when he "felt all her [Mrs. Ramsay's] strength flaring up to be drunk and quenched by the beak of brass, the arid scimitar of the male, which smote mercilessly, again and again, demanding sympathy" (38). However, caught between her father's efforts to charm and James's indignation, Cam remains aware even under her father's spell of "that crass blindness and tyranny of his" that informs the children's pact not to give in; like Lily, she chooses to gaze elsewhere, "doggedly and sadly at the shore" (170).

Only when Mr. Ramsay reaches quiescence and becomes an object of others' focalization does he stop being the stalking monster. In the boat as on the island of boots, Mr. Ramsay is either manipulated or distracted into abdicating his devouring gaze. As Cam argues in her mind with James's view of their father as tyrant, she urges him, "But look! she said, looking at him. Look at him now. She looked at him reading"; being able to look at him allows Cam to see him as fatherly, "for she was safe, while he sat there" (190), and to see the island in proper proportion: "She gazed back over the sea, at the island. . . . It was very small; it was very distant. The sea was more important now than the shore" (191). Similarly, she focalizes for the reader on James's equal need for his father, on the boy's own coming to terms with the male parent who for once spontaneously offers the praise "James had been wanting," thus freeing him from the oppressive gaze so James, too, can look away from father and sister (206).

While the adult Ramsays' romance replicates at moments of intensity the contest of gazes of courtly love, in Woolf as in Meredith heterosexual romance itself can appear as the monster of egoism. However, for Woolf, but not for the Meredith of *The Egoist*, love of a different kind informs the concluding vision of the novel, from Lily's and the children's reawakened tenderness for Mr. Ramsay to the love of woman for woman, man for boy, and the friendship of woman and man. In *The Egoist* Meredith struggles to create a narrative that can explode courtship conventions, but he remains fettered by conventions of genre and gender. Clara begins her career not by ambitions to be well married, but by having "dreamed of love as one of the distant blessings of the mighty world, lying somewhere in the world's forests, across wild seas, veiled, encompassed with beautiful perils, a throbbing secresy . . . . Her chief idea of it was, the enrichment of the world by love" (34). Meredith ends his novel with two pairs of well-suited lovers, and perhaps a hint of the possibility of friendship between women and love of a child not related to the characters who most care for him. The circle of love barely expands beyond convention. Woolf, however, enlarges the precedents set by Meredith to the point where heterosexual romance is perhaps the most flawed relationship, and other loves bring fulfillment beyond marriage, leading to wholeness of vision.

The love of the Ramsays, represented as symbolic of married union, as well as of marriage as the wreck of men's careers and of women's well-being, appears through exchanges of gazes more than through words. Mrs. Ramsay sees herself rising to Mr. Ramsay's need in visual images of plenitude: "Mrs. Ramsay . . . braced herself, and, half turning, seemed to raise herself with an effort, and at once pour erect into the air a rain of energy, a column of spray, looking at the same time animated and alive as if her energies were being fused into force, burning and illuminating" (37). She becomes the fountain, the "spray of life" that "created drawing-room and kitchen, set them all aglow," as if indeed her reactive gaze to Mr. Ramsay's need turns into a spotlight, a camera sweep that illuminates reality with its own power, making it accessible to her husband. When Mrs. Ramsay becomes herself in her solitude, she feels exposed by Mr. Ramsay's gaze: "Had she known that he was looking at her . . . she would not have let herself sit there, thinking" (68); for his gaze requires that she be not only magnifying mirror to his ego but validation of his life. Yet she senses that her remoteness hurts him as he looks at her, and she gives him "of her own free will what she knew he would never ask," namely, the illusion they both sustain of his protecting her (65). The last sight we are given of the Ramsays is a continued contest between their gazes; once more, Mr. Ramsay wants to possess his wife by watching her, wants to force her into uttering the conventions of love. She returns his desiring look but withholds the verbal reassurance he craves; instead, she allows him to be right about the weather, and with that deflection wins through her reactive gaze: "And she looked at him smiling. For she had triumphed again. She had not said it: yet he knew" (124).

If the Ramsays' marriage reaches moments of extraordinary accord, won against daily struggles, incipient romantic love appears monstrous through Lily's eyes, and it is she who focalizes for the reader on the romance plot. Left out of the glow of the just-engaged Paul and Minta, Lily impulsively desires to "be included among the sailors and adventurers" who embark on the risks of romance. Paul's response is not individuated; Lily focalizes on it as type: "He turned on her cheek the heat of love, its horror, its cruelty, its unscrupulosity. It scorched her, and Lily, looking at Minta . . . flinched for her exposed to these fangs, and was thankful" (102). At the dinner table Paul metamorphoses from "a nice young man" to "a bully with a crowbar" (102-3), yet ironically it is he who will be exposed to the "fangs," since the marriage founders through their incompatibility and he is the one to suffer; the couple finds accord only as they cooperate to fix their car. Lily does justice to heterosexual love, recognizing it as "beautiful and necessary" (103) to the world, but not to her. By exposing the monstrous egoism promoted by the romance plot and by exploding its generic requirements of happy pairings, Woolf is able to create a heroine who can participate in "the enrichment of the world by love" dreamed of by Meredith's Clara. Turning away from devouring love, Lily focuses on her artistic vocation: "For at any rate, she said to herself, catching sight of the salt cellar on the pattern, she need not marry, thank Heaven: she need not undergo that degradation. She was saved from that dilution. She would move the tree rather more to the middle" (102).

Yet in order to have her "vision," Lily must reconstruct her own earlier focalizations. She needs the illuminated moments in "The Window," the cumulative sight made possible by a narrative technique that allows us through the use of flashbacks the "fifty pairs of eyes to see with" that re-create the past in its complexity. "The Lighthouse" section ending in Lily's completed painting moves toward that resolution through scenes visualized, mostly by Lily, of Mrs. Ramsay, of Lily's friendship with William Bankes, of Mr. Carmichael's grief for Andrew. To her earlier sense that "she was in love with them all, in love with this world" (22), Lily adds the acuity of focus on the past and present: "She went on tunnelling her way into her picture, into the past" (175).

Taking risks with focalization, Woolf has Lily ultimately play mirror to no animate gaze, but rather to her canvas. This switch in point of view, in which the canvas becomes the camera eye gazing on Lily, possessing her, is perhaps the most daringly cinematic in the novel (106). From this vantage point, the reader becomes the canvas, watching Lily: "She saw her canvas as if it had floated up and placed itself white and uncompromising directly before her. It seemed to rebuke her with its cold stare for all this hurry and agitation" (156). This time Lily, who resisted playing the mirror to Mr. Ramsay's grief, to Tansley's need to assert himself, even to Mrs. Ramsay's irresistible impulse toward matchmaking, mirrors her empty canvas: "She looked blankly at the canvas, with its uncompromising white stare" (157). It is the canvas, and no man, that makes the fountain, the "delicious fecundity" (37) of creation rise within Lily: "as she lost consciousness of outer things, and her name and her personality and her appearance . . . her mind kept throwing up from its depths, scenes, and names, and sayings, and memories and ideas, like a fountain spurting over that glaring, hideously difficult white space" (159). To what Lily perceives as the canvas's pressing need—"it seemed to rebuke her"—she responds with a plenitude of images that, unlike Mrs. Ramsay's illumination of reality, gives the effect of a cinematic montage: "scenes, and names, and sayings," etc.

The amorous contest of gazes subverted in Meredith and placed in a context of grief and loss by Woolf is replayed by the artist and her canvas. Mr. Ramsay's self-aggrandizing heroic combats and Mrs. Ramsay's domestic sacrifices, of herself and others, give way to the contest between the artist's eye and the pressure of reality: "It was a miserable machine, an inefficient machine, she thought, the human apparatus, for painting or for feeling; it always broke down at the critical moment; heroically, one must force it on" (193). At the same time, Woolf deliberately subverts the heroic quest as well as the amorous combat. Like James, who concludes that the lighthouse is both "tower, stark and straight" and "the eye opening and shutting" (186), so Lily concludes that "love had a thousand shapes," that any triumph, even in art, is provisional: "The great revelation perhaps never did come. Instead there were little daily miracles, illuminations, matches struck unexpectedly in the dark." Lily arrives at her creation neither through the isolated quest of the hero nor the consuming contest of erotic love, but rather from her encompassing love in its "thousand shapes"—that generous vision of love that Clara can only dream of—so that "Mrs. Ramsay making of the moment something permanent (as in another sphere Lily herself tried to make of the moment something permanent)—this was of the nature of a revelation. In the midst of chaos there was shape" (161).

In classifying Meredith with the great eccentrics whose experiments enlarged the possibilities of the novel, Woolf is no doubt reflecting on her own attempts to combine traditional narrative with the vitality of other genres. Both Meredith and Woolf deploy focalization to destabilize power relations, especially between men and women. Both achieve a degree of subjectivity that anticipates sophisticated uses of subjective camera angles that create the now-famous cinematic gaze. Each submits to the requirements of the genre each chooses, comedy for *The Egoist* and elegy for *To the Lighthouse*, but Woolf is not only the freer to experiment because of her historical circumstances and her feminism, she is freer because of the risks taken by Meredith. I would concur with one of Woolf's last recorded judgments of Meredith, that he remains underrated; and I hope that her prediction about his novels, that they "must inevitably rise from time to time into view" (*CE*1 232), will prove justified, if for no better reason than for his contribution to the experiments of modernist fiction like Woolf's, which enlarge the scope of narrative so as to demystify heterosexual conventions and to take in the "thousand shapes" of love.

Works Cited

Abbott, H. Porter. "Character and Modernism: Reading Woolf Writing Woolf." *New Literary History* 24 (1993): 393-405.

Bal, Mieke. *Narratology: Introduction to the Theory of Narrative*. Trans. Christine van Boheemen. Toronto: University of Toronto Press, 1985.

Beer, Gillian. "The Victorians in Virginia Woolf: 1832-1941." *Dickens and Other Victorians: Essays in Honour of Philip Collins*. Ed. Joanne Shattock. London: Macmillan, 1988. 214-235.

Caughie, Pamela. *Virginia Woolf & Postmodernism: Literature in Quest & Question of Itself*. Urbana: University of Illinois Press, 1991.

Clover, Carol J. *Men, Women, and Chain Saws: Gender in the Modern Horror Film*. Princeton: Princeton University Press, 1992.

Comstock, Margaret von Szeliski. "George Meredith, Virginia Woolf, and Their Feminist Comedy." Diss., Stanford University, 1975.

Disch, Lisa and Mary Jo Kane. "When the Looker Becomes a Bitch: Lisa Olson, Sport, and the Heterosexual Matrix." *The Second Signs Reader: Feminist Scholarship, 1983-1996*. Eds. Ruth-Ellen B. Joeres and Barbara Laslett. Chicago: Chicago University Press, 1996. 326-56.

Ehrlich, Susan. *Point of View: A Linguistic Analysis of Literary Style*. London: Routledge, 1990.

Johnston, Ruth D. "Dis-Membrance of Things Past: Re-Vision of Wordsworthian Retrospection in *Jane Eyre* and *Villette*." *Victorian Literature and Culture* 22 (1994): 73-102.

London, Bette. "Mary Shelley, *Frankenstein*, and the Spectacle of Masculinity." *PMLA* 108 (1993): 253-67.

Marcus, Jane. *Art & Anger: Reading Like a Woman*. Columbus: Ohio State University Press, 1988.

McLaurin, Allen. *Virginia Woolf: The Echoes Enslaved*. London: Cambridge University Press, 1973.

McWhirter, David. "Meredith, Woolf, and Comic Distance." *Look Who's Laughing: Gender and Comedy*. Ed. Gail Finney. Amsterdam: Gordon and Breach, 1994. 189-204.

Meredith, George. *The Egoist*, ed. Robert M. Adams. New York: Norton, 1979.

Miller, J. Hillis. *Ariadne's Thread: Story Lines*. New Haven: Yale University Press, 1979.

Morgan, Susan. *Sisters in Time: Imagining Gender in 19th Century British Fiction*. New York: Oxford University Press, 1989.

Mulvey, Laura. "Visual Pleasure and Narrative Cinema." *Screen* 16 (1975): 6-18.

Nussbaum, Martha. "The Window: Knowledge of Other Minds in Virginia Woolf's *To the Lighthouse*." *New Literary History* 26 (1995): 731-754.

Ralston, Ramona Marie. "Wordsworth and the Feminized Sonnet: A Suppression of Eighteenth-Century Poetic Influences." Diss., University of Southern California, 1987.

Saunders, Rebecca. "Language, Subject, Self: Reading the Style of *To the Lighthouse*." *Novel* 26 (Winter, 1993): 192-213.

Travis, Molly Abel. "The Modernist Tease of Textual Intimacy and the Erotics of Reading in Woolf," *Virginia Woolf: Emerging Perspectives: Selected Papers from the Third Annual Conference on Virginia Woolf*. Eds. Mark Hussey and Vara Neverow. New York: Pace University Press, 1994. 77-82.

Woolf, Virginia. *Collected Essays*. London: The Hogarth Press, 1966.

———. *The Diary of Virginia Woolf*. Ed. Anne Olivier Bell. San Diego, New York and London: Harcourt Brace Jovanovich, 1984.

———. "A Sketch of the Past." *Moments of Being*. London: Harcourt Brace, 1976.

———. *To the Lighthouse*. London: Harcourt Brace, 1927; rpt. 1989.

"Same Person...Just a Different Sex": Sally Potter's Construction of Gender in *Orlando*

Catherine Craft-Fairchild

Sally Potter—for there could be no doubt of her intention—filmed Virginia Woolf's *Orlando* with an eye toward emphasizing its gender-bending elements. In interviews, Potter insists, repeatedly, that her film is about an "essential self" that transcends gender. Yet, what strikes and fascinates about *Orlando* is the way in which, despite its auteur's professed aim, gender ideology unavoidably permeates the celluloid text: Potter's film accurately traces the historical development of gender identities and their solidification along modern lines during the eighteenth-century. The movie's visual and verbal trifling with gender—its fracturing of diegesis through use of the first-person controlling female gaze, its creative play with costuming, its repeated triangulations of sexual relations—diminish when Orlando confronts the mirror, not as a man entering the symbolic order, but as a woman excluded from it.

Although postmodern literary critics have announced the "death of the author," auteur scholarship remains alive and well in film studies. In her recent book, *High Contrast: Race and Gender in Contemporary Hollywood Film*, Sharon Willis suggests that it is, in part, film's status as mass-market commodity that "sustain[s] our reinvigorated interest in auteurs. . .[T]he persistence and frequent renewal of the auteur has to do with anchoring filmic production to a social location through its point of enunciation" (7). The "point of enunciation" for *Orlando* is its screenplay writer/director Sally Potter. Numerous interviews attest to the fact that, given the surprising popular success of her "arthouse" film, Potter's statements about her own intentions carry weight with the cinema-going public.

There are, however, dangers in taking the director's words as gospel; Potter, perhaps as a form of political maneuvering, often sidesteps key issues about her work. Speaking to Scott MacDonald for *Camera Obscura*, Potter acknowledges that "There's a tendency for a 'historical drama' to become a spectacle," but goes on to say that, "*Orlando* is *not* a costume drama, *not* a period film, no matter how much it may appear so: it's really about the present moment" (211). Earlier, Potter had said much the same thing to Penny Florence for *Screen*: ". . .this is not a costume drama, this is not a historical film, it's a film about now that happens to move through these periods" (276-7). The issue that Potter raises in these sound bites concerns the relationship between the "now" and the historical past. Potter implies that a work of art can somehow reflect history, pass through historical moments, without being touched by them—that *Orlando*, in short, can remain in some kind of eternal present.

This belief allows Potter to insist that "all this masculinity/femininity stuff is really a dressing up of an essential self. They're identities that you can choose or not choose" (MacDonald 219). Stepping outside of history, it seems, enables one also to refuse gender identity. Potter's comments about the existence of an "essential self" in her film pose the question of whether or not a work of art can transcend history and create a space for the individual "outside" his/her own cultural constraints. Potter claims, in interviews, that it can, but what her film actually illustrates is that even avant-garde creations cannot get above or beyond the ideologies of the periods in which they are created—the most they can do is to point up ideology *as* ideology.[1] In addition, by choosing to film *Orlando*, a piece about history itself, one based upon an early twentieth-century novel by Virginia Woolf, Potter inevitably took on as well the concerns both of those earlier times the work portrays and of the particular author it issued from. By tracing the film's recreation of the history of sexuality, I hope to prove that Sally Potter's Orlando is not at all, as Potter would have us believe, "the same person" when she becomes "a different sex."

Midway through Virginia Woolf's novel/biography/picaresque/parody/ what-you-will, *Orlando*, the hero awakes to find he has become a heroine. This transformation, appearing as it does around the second-hundredth year of the central character's four-hundred-or-so-year life-span, occurs in the midst of the eighteenth century. Among the many questions left to plague the reader of *Orlando* are the questions of plot and of timing: why make the pivotal event a shift in gender and why situate that gender-switch in the Enlightenment?

---

[1]Both critics and scholars who write about Potter's film tend to muddle this question of whether or not there can be an "essential self" divorced from historical period and particular culture. Kathleen Doty seemingly takes Potter's remarks about her work at face value, writing, "Like the novel, the film *Orlando*...is positively utopian in its vision of how the imagination and the power of language can free us from the tyranny of sexual dualities and social constraints" (921). Julianne Pidduck tries to have it both ways, asserting that Orlando can somehow remain a stable core in a world where historical change does, in fact, make a great deal of difference: ". . .Orlando moves through the film virtually unchanged. What transformation occurs does not change the 'essence' of Orlando/Tilda Swinton, but registers at the level of costume and hairstyle, or, in the case of the sex change, is etched on the body surface. . .Woolf and Potter remind us that gender is superficial and matters not a whit. At the same time, however, the film's irony arises from its constant demonstration that gender is made to matter very, very much

Woolf's *A Room of One's Own*, which she was writing simultaneously with *Orlando*, offers possible answers to both questions. The crossing from one gender to another within *Orlando* may emerge from Woolf's notion that the true artist must have an "androgynous" mind. In *A Room of One's Own*, Woolf insists,

> . . .a great mind is androgynous. . . .it transmits emotion without impediment. . .it is naturally creative, incandescent and undivided. . . .
>
> [I]t is fatal for any one who writes to think of their sex. It is fatal to be a man or woman pure and simple; one must be woman-manly or man-womanly. . . .Some collaboration has to take place in the mind between the woman and the man before the act of creation can be accomplished. (98, 104)

Given Woolf's allegiances, if *Orlando* was to be in part about writing, then *Orlando* also had to be about masculinity, femininity, and androgyny—the first two qualities receive equal time and their dialectic within the person of Orlando allows Woolf to explore how a writer might include male and female in a harmonious intellectual blend.

Locating Orlando's sex change in the Enlightenment seems the logical outcome of Woolf's assertion that "towards the end of the eighteenth century a change came about which, if I were rewriting history, I should describe more fully and think of greater importance than the Crusades or the Wars of the Roses. The middle-class woman began to write" (*AROO* 65). *Orlando*, which is framed as a rewriting of history, particularly literary history, does describe fully Woolf's greatly important event: the rise of the woman writer in the "Age of Reason." Admittedly, she rises rather literally and startlingly from the body and mind of the Elizabethan male poet, but what else could she do?—Shakespeare's sister was already dead, having languished miserably for the want of a publisher who would print the product of a female pen before 1682.[2]

---

through absurd social convention" (182-3). Only one other critic, Susan Watkins, finds "something disturbing about the implications of Potter's belief in an essentially gender-free self" and she argues that "[t]he linguistic complexity and ambivalence of Woolf's novel when compared with Potter's film makes it clear that the former is a more radical text..." (54, 56).

[2]Mary Jacobus remarks, "Orlando's gender shift from masculine to feminine occurs during the reign of Charles I [sic] at approximately the moment when (according to Woolf's literary-historical scheme) it was possible for the first time to become a woman writer and not the suicidal Judith Shakespeare of *A Room of One's Own*. . ." (21-2). For explorations of Woolf's choice of period with relation to the topic of British Imperialism, see the work of Kathy Phillips and Jaime Hovey.

Eschewing, to a large extent, Woolf's theme of the historical growth of the poet's mind, Sally Potter's film adaptation of *Orlando* (Adventure Pictures 1992) focuses heavily on the androgyny. This is the theme Potter culls from her reading of the novel: "I think Virginia Woolf's hypothesis—that we're all born simply as human beings who are then shaped one way or the other, masculine or feminine, and that mostly it's how we're perceived by others that makes the difference, rather than what we are—that hypothesis really holds good" (Dowell 16). Potter muses, "I don't think the book so much explores sexual identities as dissolves them, and it's that kind of melting and shifting where nothing is ever what it seems for male or female that I think is the strength of the book and which I wanted to reproduce in the film" (Florence 283).

What Potter grabs hold of in Virginia Woolf's *Orlando* is the sense that sexual identity is imposed upon the individual. But instead of recognizing that such societal constructions themselves constitute identity, a recognition that Woolf was one of the first to explore, Potter asserts that there can be an "essential" self that exists behind or apart from the constructed self. On the interview circuit, Potter insisted that "*Orlando* is a very gentle, very passionate look at the blurring of sexual identity and the nonsense of femininity and masculinity as constructions. . . . It's about the claiming of an essential self. . ." (Ehrenstein 5, 7). According to Potter, such an "essential human self. . .transcends genders" (Corliss 63) and "goes beyond. . .the property line, inheritance and so forth . . .[revealing] that those are in a sense masks or irrelevances" (Florence 284). This is Potter's mantra; for *Sight and Sound*, she summed it up by saying, "For me. . .*Orlando* is not so much about femininity and difference as about Woolf's notion of an essential self that lies beyond gender" (Glaessner 14).[3]

But did Woolf have any notion of an "essential self that lies beyond gender"? Many Woolf scholars have said so,[4] perhaps because there is something appealing about the idea that Orlando's androgyny enables him/her to escape the

---

[3] See also Potter's remarks to *Interview*'s Manohla Dargis, "It's a love poem to the essential self" (42) and to *Vogue*'s Mira Stout, "I'm trying to restore to people that sense of themselves which has nothing to do with gender, time, or circumstance" (140).

[4] See, for example, Maria DiBattista's assertion that "Sex in *Orlando* is never treated as an indisputable fact of biological and social life....Male and female are roles sanctioned by society, roles one may adopt or dismiss at one's whim—or hazard" (117, 120-1). Sandra Gilbert offers a more emphatic phrasing: "costume, not anatomy, is destiny....[Orlando] inhabits a world where almost anyone can change his or her sexual habits at any time....[Orlando is] an eternally living doll whose wardrobe of costume selves enables her to transcend the constraints of flesh and history" (206-8).

constraints of gender, to transcend roles shaped by the ideologies of the ages he/she passes through. Yet, although tempted by the idea of an "essential self" in *Orlando*, Woolf finally refuses to depict Orlando as a transcendently free being.

Woolf's narrator comes closest to asserting that Orlando's gender identity is a social and external affair, easily manipulated by the individual, shortly after Orlando's return to England. Orlando seemingly can change her gender identity merely by donning a "change of clothes," and such changes seem to have "much to do with" the shifts in her tastes, emotions, and values as he/she moves from male to female (*O* 187). Orlando "found it convenient at this time to change frequently from one set of clothes to another. . . . She had, it seems, no difficulty in sustaining the different parts, for her sex changed far more frequently than those who have worn only one set of clothing can conceive" (220-21). The narrator sums up this strand of Woolf's narrative by arguing that "it is clothes that wear us and not we them. . .they mould our hearts, our brains, our tongues to their liking" (188). Had men and women "worn the same clothes, it is possible that their outlook might have been the same too" (188). In the very next paragraph, however, the narrator contradicts this viewpoint that gender identity is simply outer display; here, the narrator inclines to the essentialist view that "The difference between the sexes is, happily, one of great profundity. Clothes are but a symbol of something hid deep beneath" (188).

Several scholars have noted these contradictions in the text of *Orlando* and attempted to interpret Woolf's intentions. Pamela Caughie, in "Virginia Woolf's Double Discourse," sees the fluctuating viewpoints as Woolf's strategy for showing "how sexuality and textuality perform in the world" (48). Caughie insists that critics who read Orlando as "a pure, free ontological essence which we can locate and define prior to its insertion into language, society, culture" are misreading Woolf's character because "[p]roving the contrary is precisely the point of the vacillating rhetoric and epicene protagonist of Woolf's novel. . . .To put sexual identity and textual meaning into confusion, as Woolf does in *Orlando*, is to disclose the dependence of sexual traits. . .on certain kinds of discourse" (46-7).[5]

---

[5]Caughie's work has been highly influential; several critics, writing about the topic of androgyny in *Orlando*, have tended to follow in Caughie's wake, arguing that Woolf's protagonist highlights, rather than transcends, the historical constructedness of gender identity. For example, Avril Horner asserts, "Orlando's panoramic view across history enables Woolf not only to consider the creation of the subject within specific historical moments, but also to exercise her own attitudes to historical periods, historiography, and the relationship between literature and history" (73). Ruth Parkin-Gounelas writes, "And yet, in the last resort, Orlando as a woman *does* stake all her hopes in love for a man...along with the traditional feminine concerns of motherhood..." (147). Kathy

In "Re-Dressing Feminist Identities: Tensions Between Essential and Constructed Selves in Virginia Woolf's *Orlando*," Christy Burns argues that "[t]his question of whether some innate human essence can surmount historical effects or whether the only 'essence' we know as personality is fully shaped by the world around one" (343) is the central issue of Woolf's text. Burns sees the competing theories getting "sorted out as the novel progresses," with "the notion of an essential self being comically reduced to a belief that Woolf's less than competent narrator struggles to defend, while the parody of the narrator's attempt results in the realization of the modern, constructive figuration of subjectivity" (346). Yet Burns does not view the character of Orlando as being without any choice or freedom whatsoever; she argues that "Woolf's conception of Orlando's identity holds within it the possibility for participation in social and self construction," but a self-construction that remains "embroiled in the problematics of historical change and sexuality" (346).[6]

Burns's sense that Woolf presents an ongoing tension between personal autonomy and ideological forces seems a richer and more accurate reading of the text of *Orlando* than Potter's insistence that the character illustrates the existence of an "essential self" standing apart from history. As *Orlando* progresses, Woolf eschews the two oppositional versions of gender identity that she began with—the first, that gender identity is an external, self-controlled quality ("it is clothes that wear us," 188), the second, that gender identity is something innate that arises from the sexual body ("Clothes are but a symbol of something hid deep beneath," 188)—in favor of a third notion, the sense that the age and the self collaborate in gender construction. Although Orlando struggles to maintain some continuity in his/her sense of self—strives, for example, to maintain an ongoing

---

Phillips echoes this: "Nevertheless, if Orlando sometimes avoids her society's prescriptions for women, gradually she acquiesces. Her partial capitulation suggests that no one can entirely evade the ideology of the age" (193). Balancing Woolf's work against Potter's, Susan Watkins argues that the novel "is a more radical text precisely because it understands gender identity performatively, and because such an understanding is more available to Woolf, working with words, than it is to Potter, working with visual images....We do not have a 'free choice' of genders: some are more socially acceptable than others" (56-7).

[6]Adam Parkes offers a similar "compromise" position, urging that "the process of theatrical self-transformation offers potential freedom from the historically assigned social roles....[However] Woolf still suggests that Orlando's apparently limitless freedom may be qualified....If clothes wear us, then we are constructed, and potentially censored, by some external agency—for instance, by the sexual hierarchy that assigns particular clothes to the male and female roles" (451-52).

commitment to writing poetry—what Orlando finally finds is that he/she cannot avoid the influences of the historical times he/she is part of. Woolf labels these forces the "spirit of the age," and shows Orlando having particular difficulties with the nineteenth century:

> Such is the indomitable nature of the spirit of the age however, that it batters down anyone who tries to make stand against it far more effectually than those who bend its own way. Orlando had inclined herself naturally to the Elizabethan spirit, to the Restoration spirit, to the spirit of the eighteenth century, and had in consequence scarcely been aware of the change from one age to the other. But the spirit of the nineteenth century was antipathetic to her in the extreme, and thus it took her and broke her, and she was aware of her defeat at its hands as she had never been before. (244)

Hence, Orlando's capitulation to matrimony (through her union with Shelmerdine) and to motherhood (as she bears his son) is dictated by Victorian ideology; Orlando cannot escape the spirit of the age, although she can resist it to some degree by making an unconventional marriage.[7]

With regard to Woolf's text, then, Potter's tolling of the death knell of gender—her insistence that *Orlando* blurs sexual identity, reduces the masculine and feminine to sameness or to nonsense, and allows for a sense of self apart from gender, time, and place—is more than a little premature. Yet, in her film, by following the outlines of Woolf's fiction and rendering historical periods with care, Potter does what she claims she does not: *Orlando* actually recapitulates the construction of gender that it sets out to demolish and does so in historically accurate terms. Modern gender identity—in film, fiction, and fact—begins to take shape in the eighteenth century and solidifies in the nineteenth.

As Thomas Laqueur illustrates in his landmark, oft-quoted study, *Making Sex: Body and Gender from the Greeks to Freud*, medical, legal, and social thinking about human sexuality changed form around the middle of the eighteenth century. Laqueur writes,

> . . .the female body came to be understood no longer as a lesser version of the male's (a one-sex model) but as its incommensurable opposite (a two-sex model). . . .

---

[7]Burns writes, "Although she conforms by virtue of marrying Shelmerdine, Orlando resists the particular demands of Victorian marriage and womanly roles. . . .That is, Orlando takes the category that is forced upon her (marriage), but she subverts it by negating many of its more traditional constraints" (355).

. . .the old model, in which men and women were arrayed according to their degree of metaphysical perfection, their vital heat, along an axis whose telos was male, gave way by the late eighteenth century to a new model of radical dimorphism, of biological divergence. . . .

Sometime in the eighteenth century, sex as we know it was invented (viii, 5-6, 149).[8]

The one-sex model, which dominated medical and social thought until the end of the seventeenth century, allowed for rather permeable boundaries between male and female identities. Laqueur continues, "in the world of one sex, the body was far less fixed and far less constrained by categories of biological difference than it came to be after the eighteenth century" (106).

Laqueur points out that, "in the absence of a purportedly stable system of two sexes, strict sumptuary laws of the body attempted to stabilize gender—woman as woman and man as man" (124-25). In short, you were what you wore—visible markers were intended to signal both class and gender status. Even in clothing, however, while differences between male and female dress existed, they were by no means so clearly demarcated as they would be in the century that followed. Men's clothing during the reign of Queen Elizabeth was every bit as ornate as women's, if not more so; but by the time George III ascended the throne, typical male dress had taken on a cut of severity that left nearly all ornamentation to the woman.[9]

---

[8]Approaching the subject from a different angle—studying the growing intolerance toward the sexual ambiguity of the hermaphrodite and the homosexual within the eighteenth-century—Randolph Trumbach adds weight to Laqueur's argument about the solidification of sexual identity: "By 1800, it was conceived in discussion both of men and women that there were only two types of bodies, male and female. But the variety of sexual acts in which human bodies might engage guaranteed that there were four genders, two of them legitimated, and two stigmatized. Consequently, in the modern western world, there were men and women, and sodomites and sapphists" (135). Changing attitudes toward cross-dressed women and lesbians during the period also lends support to Laqueur's theory that gender boundaries solidified during the Enlightenment; see Craft-Fairchild's "Cross-Dressing and the Novel: Women Warriors and Domestic Femininity" and "'Oh! Sappho, Sappho': Lesbianism and Literature in the Eighteenth Century."

[9]Kaja Silverman, in "Fragments of a Fashionable Discourse," summarizes the changes succinctly: ". . .ornate dress was primarily a class rather than a gender prerogative during the fifteenth, sixteenth and seventeenth centuries, a prerogative which was protected by law. . . .Moreover, the elegance and richness of male dress equalled and often surpassed that of female dress during this period, so that in so far as clothing was marked

Sally Potter's rendering of Woolf's *Orlando* visually recreates a history of sexuality with a trajectory similar to that outlined above; her film highlights the different configurations of gender in the various ages Orlando passes through. The majority of the film's gender playfulness is confined to its Elizabethan-Jacobean sequences, while its treatment of Orlando after the gender switch in the eighteenth century reintroduces the rigidity of sexual difference—a movement from gender fluidity to fixity that is historically accurate.[10]

The film problematizes gender from the start by beginning with a voiceover that insists, "There can be no doubt about his sex." As with the opening of Woolf's written text, this unnatural emphasis on what is generally taken to be obvious serves to defamiliarize the familiar.[11] The uncanniness is increased, not diminished, when Orlando turns conspiratorially to the camera after the narrator begins, "He. . ." to insert, "That is, I. . . ." Potter insists that the direct addresses to the audience are "about connectedness and complicity, not alienation" (Dargis 42). She elaborates in *Sight and Sound*, "Part of the idea was. . .that direct address would be an instrument of subversion, so that set against this historical pageant is a complicity with the audience about the kind of journey we're on. If it worked, I hoped it would be funny; it would create a connection that made Orlando's journey also the audience's journey" (Donohue 12). When asked by the interviewer at *Rolling Stone* how she would "get audiences to accept Tilda

---

by gender, it defined visibility as a male rather than a female attribute.

It was not until the eighteenth century that the male subject retreated from the limelight, handing on his mantle to the female subject. During the second half of that century, the voluminous clothing and elaborate wigs of the nobleman slowly dwindled into what would eventually become the respectable suit and *coiffure à la naturelle* of the gentleman, while female dress and headpieces reached epic proportions.

. . .masculine clothing ceased to proclaim hierarchical distinction and became a harmonizing and homogenizing uniform, serving to integrate not only male members of the same class, but male members of different classes" (139, 141).

In short, clothing as an announcement of class difference gave way (in part, though not entirely) to clothing as a marker of sexual difference, "placing men and women on opposite sides of the great visual divide" (Silverman 147). For further discussion and depiction of sartorial alteration during this period, consult Aileen Ribeiro's *Dress in Eighteenth-Century Europe* and *Dress and Morality*.

[10]Roberta Garrett notes this shift: "...most of the film's 'camp' engagement with gender-play and cross dressing...takes place before Orlando is 'officially' transformed into a woman" (95). But Garrett explains it only as Potter's "glorify[ing] the 'otherness' of femininity" (94).

[11]About Woolf's first sentences, Pamela Caughie writes, "The text of *Orlando* is as unstable as the sex of Orlando. The first words of the novel shake our certainty about

Swinton in the role of a man?," Potter replied, "By taking them into our confidence in the first minutes of the film when Orlando talks to the camera. That establishes a state of suspended disbelief" (Travers 90).

Potter may think so, but few other theatregoers, raised on Hollywood practices of invisible editing, found such blatant ruptures of the diegesis comforting, amusing, or winning. Viewing the film a few days after its local release, I watched the majority of theatre patrons turn away from the film and begin to mutter after Swinton's first aside. Several critics' responses point to this "staginess" of the film as a source of discontent: for example, Michael Levine, assessing the film in *Virginia Woolf Miscellany*, writes, "When Orlando speaks directly to the camera. . .the movie demonstrates a pointless awareness of itself as a movie. . . . From the opening scene, the gesture appears forced, a wink at the audience that is supposed to foster the intimacy that exists between a writer and a reader but instead feels like an admission that images will ultimately fail to illuminate Woolf's words" (3). John Simon, in his column for the *National Review*, complains of the lack of realism: "Tilda Swinton never made me believe her as a man, or respond to her as a woman" (54). Terrence Rafferty, writing with more restraint in the *New Yorker*, seconds Simon: "And surely it wouldn't have killed her [Swinton] (or Potter) to try a bit harder to persuade us that Orlando is male in the early sequences" (97).

To expect or exact modern representations of masculinity in those early sequences of the film is to miss what the film actually accomplishes. The Elizabethan and Jacobean sequences maintain a fluidity of gender entirely appropriate to the systems of representation of that time. They do so, in part, by over-elaborating period costumes. Throughout the film, Orlando's clothing represents the excesses of the forms available for each age. In cut, color, and texture, Orlando's garb causes him to harmonize with some characters—in the first part of the film, typically those whose gender is as indeterminate as his own—yet remain set apart from others, mainly those who inhabit more traditional sexual roles. Tilda Swinton's red-haired, brown-pantalooned, and golden-legged Orlando is closely connected to Quentin Crisp's auburn-tressed and autumnally-brocaded Elizabeth: as a vermilion-clad castrato ushers them in, the young cross-dressed woman faces off against the old cross-dressed queen. Visually, this threesome dominates over the less colorful forms of Orlando's parents and lackeys.

---

anything in this text. We read, 'He—for there could be no doubt of his sex. . .,' and immediately our doubt is aroused. The emphasis on what should be obvious makes it seem unnatural" (42). See also Nancy Cervetti's assertion that Woolf "protest[s] too much, creating the very doubt that her words would deny" (166).

Gender playfulness continues into the Jacobean sequences, where Sasha's closely-tailored, sparkling Russian garments play nicely against Orlando's glittering doublet and hose. Although Swinton's Stuart dress is similar in cut and construction to the outfits of the other courtiers, she remains visually identifiable because luminous pearl beading renders her garb more ornate, while the glistening rich fabric has a noticeably different sheen; the careful work with costuming creates a visual foregrounding of Orlando's and Sasha's gender-ambiguous romance. And although Tilda Swinton engages in an old theatrical convention when she dramatizes an actress's "breeches part," the homo-eroticism of her and Charlotte Valandrey's seductive, open-mouthed kiss in the sleigh scene on the frozen river is not greatly lessened.[12]

Jacobean audiences had grown restive with boys in women's roles because of same-sex tensions such as these—tensions that Potter brings to bear by lingering upon and doubling the image. As Orlando and Sasha kiss, the call of water fowl is heard; soon afterwards, the camera settles on the pair of lovers in an odd V-formation, with Orlando in the foreground leaning to the right, Sasha in the background leaning to the left. One is reminded of the image of wild geese flying and the importance of "V" in Woolf's conception of *Orlando*—references to Vita Sackville-West, to whom the text is dedicated as a "love letter."[13]

Homoerotic threads are picked up again in the subsequent scene, Potter's restaging of Desdemona's death from Shakespeare's *Othello*, which underscores the sexual triangulation previously presented while it emphasizes Orlando's deep jealousy and possessiveness of Sasha. When the man playing Othello passionately embraces the younger man who plays Desdemona, the man to man-woman eroticism echoes the previous woman to woman-man seduction in ways that suggest the polymorphous pleasures available to an earlier age.[14]

---

[12]Like me, Roberta Garrett found the femme-femme coupling of Orlando and Sasha erotically charged, "a specifically lesbian affair" (95). Maggie Humm also comments, "…Potter quite radically and with originality shows same-sex desire between Sasha and Orlando…" (168). Leslie Hankins ("Redirections") and Eileen Barrett ("Response"), however, thought that Potter's film downplayed, even erased, Woolf's lesbian content; Barrett, in particular, asserts that the film "is a gay man's fantasy," and notes that Tilda Swinton "is most convincing as a young gay man" (198).

[13]For analyses of the lesbian themes and elements in Woolf's text, see the work of Sherron Knopp, Elizabeth Meese, Adam Parkes, Marilyn Farwell, Jean Kennard, and Leslie Kathleen Hankins ("*Orlando*: 'A Precipice Marked V'. . .").

[14]In 1680, in "The Disabled Debauchee," Lord Rochester could still write, "Nor shall our love-fits, Chloris, be forgot,/ When each the well-looked linkboy strove t'enjoy,/And the best kiss was the deciding lot/Whether the boy fucked you, or I the boy" (ll. 37-40).

If running time can be used as evidence, Potter must have enjoyed recreating these earlier historical periods. Although Woolf's book allows considerably more space to examining Orlando as a woman writer (roughly two-thirds of her text are devoted to the subject),[15] Potter reverses that emphasis, apportioning 56 minutes of her 90-minute[16] film to Orlando-male. To achieve this new balance, Potter both adds to and subtracts from Woolf's text. Leslie Hankins questions the reason why "Potter add[s] two battlefield scenes and cut[s] the provocative scene in a shop where the woman Orlando and the woman Sasha almost re-meet" ("Redirections" 174). Eileen Barrett notes that Potter includes an entire portion devoted to "bonding between Orlando and the Turkish Khan—a scene that is not in the novel—[but that] exudes the homoerotic....[while] Potter omits the lesbian scenes between Orlando and Nell that are in the novel" (198). What Hankins and Barrett are illustrating are the ways that the lesbian content of Woolf's novel is diminished but, approaching the issue from another angle, one can note that the net effect of Potter's additions and subtractions is to link her film more closely to history. In Woolf's *Orlando*, androgyny and gender-switching are heightened after Orlando becomes a woman—it is at this point, writes Woolf, that Orlando's "sex changed...frequently" and she "enjoyed the love of both sexes equally" (221). Contrary to the claustrophobic domestic confinement many eighteenth- and nineteenth-century women experienced, Woolf's female Orlando cross-dresses and sallies forth to meet lovers, fight duels, captain a ship, and "dance naked on a balcony" (221-22). By contrast, in Potter's film, gender fluidity and playfulness are emphasized for the Renaissance Orlando-male, while the arduousness of conforming to various female roles becomes the predominate theme for Enlightenment/Victorian Orlando-female.

Although longer, the pacing of the early sequences of Potter's film is more spritely than that of the latter portion—a point I shall return to—while the presentation is largely from Orlando's point of view. Orlando addresses the camera directly ten times before his gender change, usually at the end of scenes. These moments, by breaking the narrative flow in strategic ways, allow Orlando to control his own representation.[17] For example, a striking tableau is created when Orlando turns to face the camera after gazing at the painting of his parents; posed in front of the portrait with his fiancée, Orlando's look suggests his appropriation of the property and power of his father, whose place he supplies in the frame.

---

[15] Orlando-female is allotted 196 pages out of 329 in my edition.

[16] Technically, the film is 93 minutes long, but three minutes are devoted to the credits.

[17] Critics have noted the way that Orlando's direct gaze into the camera defeats, to some extent, Tilda Swinton's objectification by the camera. Scott MacDonald writes,

Combined with the visual, Orlando's verbal asides offer commentary on the action preceding them, instructing the viewer on how to perceive the film. From the first intrusion, by which Orlando establishes his personal authority over the voiceover and, presumably, the film ("That is, I"), he goes on to determine our response to the queen ("Very interesting person"). Orlando's nonchalance here puts in perspective the Queen's predatory desire. In Woolf's text, Orlando's body "is specularized and fragmented in much the same way that women's bodies usually are in analogous situations" (Dresner 55). Queen Elizabeth "held him a foot's pace from her and looked him up and down....Eyes, mouth, nose, breast, hips, hands—she ran them over...legs..." (*O* 24). Potter allows Crisp's Elizabeth power—the drag queen's authoritative, desiring glance dominates the banquet scene, which ends with Swinton's nervous gulp. Yet the pastiche that follows, punctuated by extreme close-ups of Orlando's face, mitigates the monarch's control even before the camera finally settles on a long take of Orlando, alone in bed, staring at the ceiling. The way the scene comes to rest restores Orlando's supremacy, as the whole section ends with Swinton's direct address.

Orlando-male's asides present him in a favorable light as lover, poet, and patron. They serve to dismiss our concern over his infidelity ("It would never have worked—a man must follow his heart"); make us take seriously the presentation of Shakespeare's *Othello* ("Terrific play!"), Sasha's betrayal ("The treachery of women!"), Shakespeare's and Nick Greene's poetry ("Ah, poetry!"), and finally Orlando's own magnanimity in his control of assets ("Pay it, quarterly"). In these instances, once viewers have overcome the strangeness of the direct asides, these utterances further understanding of Orlando's character and passions.

"By creating the illusion of an unusually intimate relationship between Orlando and the audience, Potter has found a novel and effective way of responding to the debate about the exploitive, voyeuristic 'male gaze' that has been so important in film studies since Laura Mulvey published her 'Visual Pleasure and Narrative Cinema': our personal intimacy with Orlando causes us to experience him/her, not as an object to be gazed at, but as a complex, sensual friend with whom we empathize..." (190). Cristina Degli-Esposti also sees the technique as subversive: "Potter's cinematically codified interpretation of *Orlando* is not innocent but conscious of the intertextuality of a scopic regime that makes the subject an object of voyeurism. From the beginning of the film the character subverts this expectation....The camera becomes the tool for his/her own intention" (80-1).

Potter also allows Orlando-male traditional cinematic authority by rendering several scenes from Orlando's perspective, identifying him with the filmic apparatus and allowing him subjective control.[18] For example, Orlando's first encounter with Sasha is filmed using conventional forms: the first shot shows Orlando, skating with his fiancée, startled by something he sees offscreen. The next frame reveals that something to be Sasha. The sequence of shots that follow portray Orlando in conference with a male friend about Sasha while his eyes continue to consume her form. When the camera cuts to a closeup of Sasha, her gaze is roving and unfocused, as though she feels herself being stared at, but is uncertain from whence the gaze issues. Unlike Orlando, Sasha here is not allowed to look directly into the camera or have her eyes settle. Orlando's intense, predatory gaze dominates the scene, and offers Orlando the enunciatory power typically granted to a male protagonist.

In an article that specifically treats the issues of point-of-view in the film, "Sally Potter's *Orlando* and the Neo-Baroque Scopic Regime," Cristina Degli-Esposti insists that enunciatory control is also accorded Orlando-female. Degli-Esposti writes that Orlando

> is often portrayed in medium shots or close-ups which work toward the creation of a void, both temporal and spatial, around him/her. . . ..He/she emerges visually alone in space and commands the spotlight from beginning to end. . . .
>
> . . .Orlando. . .is now the authoritative central figure of the narrative, a position, and a privilege that has been traditionally masculine. Potter's film gives Orlando as a woman the chance to hold that privilege and to be equated with a man. Orlando, in his dual identity, exits the frame as "the author of a text," the maker of the word, a male prerogative by tradition (84, 90).

The problem with Degli-Esposti's assertions is that Orlando is not portrayed similarly in the two halves of the film. For one thing, Orlando-female ceases to be "the maker of the word." Tilda Swinton's instances of first-person address dwindle to six and change form: instead of being assertions or interpretations like the earlier stop-actions, they are most often brief glances without words or fragments of speech on traditionally feminine topics. Orlando offers a cryptic look—is it fear, dismay, or anger?—when Alexander Pope says that she is lost; she mutters

---

[18]Kaja Silverman describes the enunciatory power of point-of-view in these terms: "In fact, the only truly productive gaze in the cinema is that of the camera. . . .However, just as a shot of a character within the fiction engaged in the activity of seeing functions to cover over the camera's coercive gaze, so the representation of the male subject in terms of vision has the effect of attributing to him qualities which in fact belong to that same apparatus—qualities of potency and authority"(*Semiotics* 223).

"Spinster!" and "Alone!" in the shrubbery; and cries, "I think I'm going to faint—I've never felt better in my life" as Shelmerdine embraces her. Each of these instances, far from revealing Orlando's particularity, as the earlier "male" asides did, seem highly conventional female responses. The rest of Orlando-female's direct addresses are hardly addresses at all, being entirely mute, pure expressions of "feminine" emotion: she offers a momentary glance at the sky when startled by an airplane; she reveals a transitory expression of bemusement in response to publisher Nick Greene asking her how long it took her to draft her poem; and ends with a trance-like gaze at the camera at the close of the film.

While lingering close-ups that allow Orlando to dominate the frame are frequent when Orlando is male, the primary mode of shooting Orlando-female is full-figure establishing shot and medium shot. In the first part of the film, the facial close-ups diminish the importance of Orlando's clothing and bearing while highlighting the significance of Orlando's words and thoughts. In the second part of the film, the emphasis is placed on Orlando's female body, on her beauty and voluminous attire, rather than her self-expression.

Many more shots are conventionally sutured in the second portion of the film than were in the first, and a significant number of these follow her suitors'—Archduke Harry's (John Wood's) or Shelmerdine's (Billy Zane's)—points-of-view. True-to-period, when Orlando enters the Countessa's salon, she submits to the gazes of the men with downcast eyes. The camera renders the scene almost entirely from the Archduke's perspective, focusing on his look, cutting to an elaborately coiffed and festooned Orlando playing with her fan, then suturing the sequence. Harry's proposal of marriage to Orlando in the garden is similarly structured, and appropriately so, since his insulting words about her lack of respectability and the curtailing of privileges her femininity demands, like the aphorisms of the poets on similar subjects, undercut Orlando's authority as much as the framing of the scene does.

Orlando-female's authority is diminished in another way—through camera angles. Orlando-male was frequently shot low-angle (as when he proudly shows Sasha his estate) or shown atop imposing edifices (as he stands on the bridge watching the ice break up, as he sits astride the tall library ladder, as he walks along the battlements with King Charles II, and as he climbs a tower to receive the Order of the Bath). Admittedly, this shot is used so often and carried to such extremes that it becomes ironic. Potter's intention was probably to use similar irony in depicting Orlando-female from high-angle, but perhaps because the images Potter selects are so familiar or possibly because Billy Zane's Shelmerdine is far more imposingly masculine than his literary and photographic counterparts in Woolf's text, the satiric intent in the second half often fails to register. Whether sitting at Shelmerdine's feet as she presents him a bowl and bathes his ankle, or on the ground looking up at him astride his horse, Orlando is positioned so that the camera, and thereby the audience, must look down at her.

The instance of high-angle camera work that stands out most glaringly occurs immediately after Orlando's sex-change: the black-veiled Orlando moving through the desert on a camel, accompanied by servants, is seen from a steeply high, almost aerial vantage point. The only scene in the film shot from this perspective, it renders Orlando a small speck, no different from the other figures in the procession. This seems a diminishment of the character who had so fully occupied the frame when male, and suggests that Orlando's recent assertion that there is "no difference at all" between male and female is untrue.

Hence, the sex-change appears the pivotal point within the film, an explicit construction of gender that alters completely the treatment of Potter's protagonist. Appropriately, the first view of Orlando's female self is of an image in a mirror. As John Berger wrote in a now-famous passage from *Ways of Seeing*, the function of the mirror is "to make the woman connive in treating herself as, first and foremost, a sight" (51). Seeing herself in the mirror does not allow the female Orlando entry into the symbolic, but instead represents her exclusion from it, denying, rather than enhancing her enunciatory power. As a perceptive student of mine noted, the key-hole shape of the mirror "caresses Orlando's sex,"[19] emphasizing the lack of what was before present—pointing, in effect, to the missing parts. A key-hole also contains within it implications of voyeurism that the rest of the film will bear out: Orlando moves from being a speaking subject to becoming a visually-desirable object. Although her direct address to the camera during this scene—"The same person. No difference at all. [Pause] Just a different sex"—would seem to belie the point, the framing Potter selects for this shot and the remaining scenes of the film affirms that "there could be no doubt about *her* sex."

The differences between Potter's film and Woolf's text crystallize fully when one compares the treatment of the sex-change within the two versions. Unlike Potter's slow-motion glide over Tilda Swinton's body, complete with breathy chanting and display of full frontal nudity, Woolf veils Orlando's transformation with a comic masque where the focus is on the appearance and banishment of the three "muses" of conventional femininity—the Ladies Purity, Chastity, and Modesty (*O* 134-36). As Suzanne Young notes, "The fanfare of the veiled dancers and the trumpets blaring 'Truth' amount to a sort of metaphysical striptease that encourages and then frustrates the mastery of the gaze. . . .[W]e

---

[19] This perceptive student was Craig Rubenzer, who made this observation in his final exam for English 270: The Novel and Film, December 1994.

are . . .refused the truths that the spectacular unveiling has led us to expect" (179). Woolf's Orlando is "ravishing," combining "the strength of a man and a woman's grace," but this androgynous beauty appears to be for the benefit of its possessor, rather than available for the voyeuristic pleasure of viewers; in Woolf's novel, "Orlando looked himself up and down in a long looking-glass, without showing any signs of discomposure, and went, presumably, to his bath" (138). Maybe in part because of the delay in altering pronouns, Woolf's use of the mirror seems Lacanian, offering Orlando a comforting view of herself as a powerful subject.

By contrast, Potter's emphasis on Orlando's beauty, at her first appearance and again during the scenes involving Shelmerdine, could be regarded as a "transformation of the female body into a fetish," an overly eroticized object that allays the anxiety aroused by its visible lack (Silverman, *Semiotics* 224). The soft-focus, sparkling light that haloes her and ornate border of the mirror that surrounds her spectacularize Orlando, rendering Tilda Swinton in painterly terms, framing her as a classical nude. Juxtaposed with Swinton in the shot is a shapely urn holding water, which suggests a feminine economy of fluids as it attracts the eye to the curves of the woman beside it. Although the mirror image is shot from behind Swinton's shoulder, the painterliness is so arresting that the eye is drawn away from the living body in the frame to the imagistic one. Several critics have likened Swinton's pose and framing to Botticelli's *The Birth of Venus*[20]—a work of art that codifies the traditional feminine ideal. Like the figure in that painting, Swinton is robbed of animation and dynamism; Potter's scene is beautiful, but also static and dead.

Similarly, in her love-scene with Billy Zane, which offered the image that became the film's identifying tag (it was turned into posters and the cover for the videocassette), Swinton's nude body is the centerpiece over which the camera slowly glides. In pore-examining close-up, viewers see one thigh, one hip, a portion of the waist and shoulders, then at last one open eye—Swinton's body is fragmented into curvaceous parts. And, while two eyes open to the camera may control the gaze, one—fixed and fixated on the off-screen body of her lover—does not. Orlando's rebirth as a woman again resembles death; as the lawyers who come to seize her estate inform her, death and femininity are akin.[21]

---

[20]See, for example, Garrett, 95; Degli-Esposti, 87; and Humm, 173

[21]The lawyers who approach Orlando in the garden charge: "First, you are legally dead and therefore cannot hold any property whatsoever. Second, you are now a female, which amounts to much the same thing. . ." (Potter's *Orlando*, adapted from Woolf's *Orlando*, p. 168). The diminishment of Orlando's rights and seizure of her property

A *St. Paul Pioneer Press* reviewer perceptively noted, ". . .when Orlando becomes a woman. . . .[e]vents give way to conversations, and, despite some occasionally clever back-and-forth, they invariably move to more predictable ends" (Sheehan 16B). The pacing of the film changes with the sex-change, too. Scenes of Orlando-male shifted swiftly from day to night, from bright to dark, and back again; most centered on movement—running to meet Queen Elizabeth, skating on the Thames with Sasha, perambulating with King Charles II, striding through Eastern streets as an ambassador. Orlando-female's movements are much more restricted—she loiters in one spot for far longer periods. Whether viewed enduring the tedium of the toilet, pacing slowly through a gallery, sitting with wits, or laying with her lover, Orlando-female does not regain much power of motion until she enters the twentieth century. Even in moments when motion is the central event, Orlando-female is usually seen running away from things unpleasant (e.g. an unwanted proposal) or deadly (the two World Wars); unlike Orlando-male, she rarely moves to pursue the things that she desires.

Contributing to the inhibiting of Orlando-female's movements is her clothing. Orlando-male's impatient agitation and refusal to be still while the servants buckle on his Elizabethan flummery finds its counterpoint in Orlando-female's patient resignation and submission to the movements of others when her maids tighten her corset.[22] The *mise-en-scène* is absorbing: the camera closes on hands lacing a corset, then backs away to reveal that the image was a reflection in a mirror. The lens moves up the woman's torso, lingering on her breasts, then finally arrives at her face. Contrary to expectation, Swinton is not looking back at the camera but is gazing downward at—the next frame reveals—a hand-held mirror. This triple specularization of the lens and two reflective glasses multiplies the mirrors of the sex scene, forcing Swinton to connive at her own objectification.

---

when she moves from man to woman parallels the historical case of the Chevalier d'Eon. See Gary Kates's "D'Eon Returns to France" in *Body Guards*, 167-94.

[22]Stella Bruzzi offers a similar parallel: "The recurring action representing the tension between the personal and the social is Orlando hitching up her voluminous eighteenth- and nineteenth-century skirts and trying to run, an uneasy movement which ironically recalls the opening sequence of the film in which the male Orlando, late to greet Elizabeth I to his family home, is able to gallop towards the house with unfettered strides" (195). Again, Potter's emphasis on the tyranny of female fashion forms a marked contrast to Woolf, who writes, "...it was this mixture in her of man and woman, one being uppermost and then the other, that often gave her conduct an unexpected turn. The curious of her own sex would argue how, for example, if Orlando was a woman, did she never take more than ten minutes to dress? And were not her clothes chosen rather at random, and sometimes worn rather shabby?" (189).

That objectification is aided by the period style of dress. Joseph Addison's description of woman in *The Tatler*, offered in part within the film's dialogue, applies to Orlando:

> ...Woman [is]...a beautiful Romantick Animal, that may be adorned with Furs and Feathers, Pearls and Diamonds, Ores and Silks. The Lynx shall cast its Skin at her Feet to make her a Tippet; the Peacock, Parrot, and Swan, shall pay Contributions to her Muff; the Sea shall be searched for Shells, and the Rocks for Gems; and every Part of Nature furnish out its Share towards the Embellishment of a Creature that is the most consummate Work of it (no. 116, 5 January 1710).

Such burdensome embellishments require Orlando to learn to walk anew; the eye of the camera remains fixed on Orlando's ungainly promenade down the long Georgian gallery. The huge hip bolsters of Orlando's wedgewood-blue gown and the massive bustle and large leg-o'mutton sleeves of her Victorian ensemble hamper her movements, constraining and curtailing Orlando's level of activity and contributing to her more static presence in the second half of the film.[23]

Action giving way to inaction, scopic control to exhibitionism—such terms accurately describe not only the trajectory of Potter's movie, but also the construction of femininity within the eighteenth century. Sexual fluidity no longer characterizes gender ideology by the end of the period, and Potter's film bears this out. Orlando's relationship with Shelmerdine is, as one critic noted, "the least perverse of Orlando's dalliances" (Hoberman 43). This "dashing American revolutionary" (Hoberman 43) or "Byronic American adventurer" (Ansen 65), as the reviewers styled him, falls off his horse and into Orlando's life in a scene that parodies Mr. Rochester's meeting with Jane Eyre in Charlotte Brontë's novel. Based upon this paradigmatic middle-class hero of the domestic novel, and unlike the sexually ambiguous figures of the first part of the film, Billy Zane comes across as a "real" man.

Potter, far more than Woolf, tries to define what constitutes a "real" man. Unmotivated and unprepared for in the novel, Woolf's treatment of the sex

---

[23] Julianne Pidduck studies movement and visual composition within the film, noting that "the sheer crippling unmanageability of Orlando's bourgeois female attire speaks volumes to the 'structure of feeling' of upper-class British womanhood—the limits on physical and social mobility. The newly-corseted Orlando in her voluminous stiff white gown minces with difficulty around the dust-draped furniture....Similarly, in the 'Society' parlour scene, Orlando is immobilized like one elaborate, frosted blue cake on a love seat. Complete with an unlikely sculpted headdress, she becomes a porcelain figurine, hampered equally by costume and convention from moving or responding to the routine snubs of the male 'wits'" (176).

change mocks "the whole sex-psych industry of her day" by refusing to define the female Orlando as a castrated man and thereby leaving Orlando's gender identity in flux (Hankins, "Redirections" 173). Potter, expressing herself dissatisfied with Woolf's ambiguous treatment, explained to *Mirabella*'s B. Ruby Rich that she purposely revised the scene: "The sex change was too arbitrary in the book. I made it more motivated—by war. To kill or be killed: that's the end of the line for masculinity" (42). Orlando, unable, it appears, to stomach the brutality of war, bails out first by entering a lengthy, trance-like sleep and then by awaking as a woman; Potter's treatment reinscribes the notion that the movement from male to female is a diminishment.[24]

In her exchange with Manohla Dargis of *Interview*, Potter was more expansive about her thoughts on the gender shift:

> **MD:** The one thing I take exception to is that Orlando changes gender after he experiences war.
> **SP:** I felt it important that the change be motivated. What Orlando is doing as a man at that point is facing the ultimate test every boy grows up holding somewhere in his psyche, that he may have to go to war, fight, kill or be killed. That is the moment Orlando realizes he cannot, will not, be a man in the sense he is being asked to.
> **MD:** My problem with that is Orlando's big moments fall along such classic gender lines.
> **SP:** But that's accurate in the history of the world. It doesn't mean, therefore, that men are designed as battle machines and women as birth machines, but that's where our identities are constructed (42).[25]

Contradicting her many claims about the "essential self," Potter here more accurately describes what her film does: highlight the historical constructedness of gender. Potter recognizes that "[i]n the book, Woolf was able to be arbitrary, to play with arbitrariness in a rather arch way.... But the Godliness of the author is not in the film; my presence is not the same.... I had to make each step credible in its own terms..." (MacDonald 214).

One might ask, credible for whom? Leslie Hankins raises the issue of whether or not, in her rhetoric about *Orlando*, Potter wasn't engaged in "dumbing down her politics for the mass audience she desired," especially since Potter's interview commentary about her earlier films was quite theoretically

---

[24]Susan Watkins, commenting on this scene, says that, "in Potter's version, femininity can be seen as an *evasion* of masculinity" (55).
[25]Potter offers similar remarks in *Rolling Stone* (Travers 90) and *Cineaste* (Dowell 16).

savvy ("Redirections" 182, note 9). Roberta Garrett refers to Potter's posturing as "strategic" (94). Indeed, many of Potter's and Swinton's remarks on the publicity circuit mimic the current craze of "post-feminism"—the belief that eurocentric cultures have gotten beyond the need to explore feminist concerns. This view is reflected in comments like Swinton's, "I'm beginning to think that gender politics in principle have become a distraction" (West 20). If Potter's remarks represent mere trendiness, an effort to align her film with popular taste, then it makes perfect sense that they offer such poor interpretation of her own work.

For, while Potter claims that she "can't play God" as Woolf does, there are moments in her film that do resist ideological pressures. Stuart Klawans hit upon something in his review for *The Nation* when he wrote, "Tilda Swinton manages to look as if she's in drag as both the male *and* female Orlando" (78). Swinton agrees, saying of her role, "our film is about a young man played by a woman who becomes, in essence, a woman played by a man" (West 20). As so many critics pointed out, Orlando-male doesn't look particularly manly; until the late twentieth century, however, Orlando-female seems equally uncomfortable and unreal. The exaggeration of costume has much to do with producing this effect. For example, like the "splendid and ample Canopy" or "Silken Rotunda" Addison writes about in *Tatler*, no. 116, Orlando's hoop petticoat takes its historical model to an absurd extreme, while her ungainliness in manipulating it gives the lie to notions of inherent female grace. Such exaggeration de-naturalizes gender identity by highlighting its arbitrary, learned, and performative elements. As Judith Butler points out, "*[i]n imitating gender, drag implicitly reveals the imitative structure of gender itself—as well as its contingency. . . .* [W]e see sex and gender denaturalized by means of a performance which avows their distinctness and dramatizes the cultural mechanism of their fabricated unity" (137-8).[26] Sally Potter's film and Tilda Swinton's performance in it are most successful when they make viewers see the historical construction of gender for what it is—a construction.

---

[26]Several recent critics have utilized the theories of Judith Butler to focus on how the fantastic elements of Virginia Woolf's *Orlando* highlight the performative nature of gender identity. No one, as yet, has offered an extended treatment of Potter's film from this vantage point, although Susan Watkins has used Butler's work to analyze the ways Potter fails to be as radical as Woolf, pointing out that, "[i]n the film, anatomical sex, gender identity and gender performance are closer than they are in the novel, partly as a consequence of Potter's decision to include a nude scene—specifically a female one" (51). Regarding the novel, Talia Schaffer, for instance, writes of Woolf's character, "Orlando's sex change destabilizes the idea that anyone has a 'real' gender identity,

So, although stepping outside historical or present-day ideology to get to an "essential self" remains impossible, the act Potter's film actually engages in—pointing up the constructions with which it works—is both satisfying and useful. By denying that male and female roles are "natural" and remain constant throughout time, *Orlando* opens up spaces for negotiation. For while no individual can elect to exist without gender, individuals in a society may decide to alter the parameters of the roles they occupy. What is constructed can be reconstructed, reconfigured—perhaps that's what the millennial singing angel at the end of the film is trying to tell us. In short, what Potter does in filming *Orlando* remains more compelling than what she says she does.

---

while Orlando's comic difficulties with femininity puncture the notion of 'natural' gender roles. Rather, gender becomes an endlessly shifting intersection of sartorial signs that have no relation to any genital referent" (29). For other readings of *Orlando* along these lines, see essays by Lisa Haines-Wright and Traci Lynn Kyle, Nancy Cervetti, and Suzanne Young.

Works Cited

Addison, Joseph, and Richard Steele. *The Tatler*. 3 vols. Ed. Donald F. Bond. Oxford: The Clarendon Press, 1987.
Ansen, David. "The Many Guises of Love." *Newsweek* 121 (21 June 1993): 65.
Barrett, Eileen. "Response: Decamping Sally Potter's *Orlando*." In *Re:Reading, Re:Writing, Re:Teaching Virginia Woolf*, ed. Eileen Barrett and Patricia Cramer. New York: Pace University Press, 1995. 197-99.
Berger, John. *Ways of Seeing*. New York: Penguin Books, 1972.
Bruzzi, Stella. *Undressing Cinema: Clothing and Identity in the Movies*. New York: Routledge, 1997.
Burns, Christy L. "Re-Dressing Feminist Identities: Tensions Between Essential and Constructed Selves in Virginia Woolf's *Orlando*." *Twentieth-Century Literature* 40.3 (Fall 1994): 342-64.
Butler, Judith. *Gender Trouble: Feminism and the Subversion of Identity*. New York: Routledge, 1990.
Caughie, Pamela L. "Virginia Woolf's Double Discourse." In *Discontented Discourses*, ed. Marleen S. Barr and Richard Feldstein. Urbana: University of Illinois Press, 1989. 41-53.
Cervetti, Nancy. "In the Breeches, Petticoats, and Pleasures of *Orlando*." *Journal of Modern Literature* 20.2 (Winter 1996): 165-75.
Corliss, Richard. "A Film of One's Own." *Time* 141 (7 June 1993): 63.
Craft-Fairchild, Catherine. "Cross-Dressing and the Novel: Women Warriors and Domestic Femininity." *Eighteenth-Century Fiction* 10.2 (January 1998): 171-202.
———. "'Oh! Sappho, Sappho': Lesbianism and Literature in the Eighteenth Century." In *Lesbian Dames: Sapphism in the Eighteenth Century*, ed. John Beynon and Ashley Stockstill. Forthcoming.
Dargis, Manohla. "Sally Potter: A Director Not Afraid of Virginia Woolf." *Interview* 23 (June 1993): 42-3.
Degli-Esposti, Cristina. "Sally Potter's *Orlando* and the Neo-Baroque Scopic Regime." *Cinema Journal* 36.1 (Fall 1996): 75-93.
DiBattista, Maria. *Virginia Woolf's Major Novels: The Fables of Anon*. New Haven: Yale University Press, 1980.
Donohue, Walter. "Immortal Longing." *Sight and Sound* 3.3 (March 1993): 10-12.
Doty, Kathleen L. "Performing Gender: The Semiotics of the Body in Three Recent Films." In S*emiotics Around the World: Synthesis in Diversity*, Vol. 2, ed. Irmengard Rauch and Gerald F. Carr. New York: Mouton de Gruyter, 1997. 921-24.

Dowell, Pat. "Demystifying Traditional Notions of Gender: An Interview with Sally Potter." *Cineaste* 20.1 (Winter 1993): 16-17.

Dresner, Lisa M. "The Body and the Letter: the Fragmentation of the Male Subject in Woolf's *Orlando*." In *Re:Reading, Re:Writing, Re:Teaching Virginia Woolf*, ed. Eileen Barrett and Patricia Cramer. New York: Pace University Press, 1995. 53-8.

Ehrenstein, David. "Out of the Wilderness: An Interview with Sally Potter." *Film Quarterly* 47.1 (Fall 1993): 2-7.

Farwell, Marilyn R. "The Lesbian Narrative: 'The Pursuit of the Inedible by the Unspeakable.'" In *Professions of Desire: Lesbian and Gay Studies in Literature*, ed. George E. Haggerty and Bonnie Zimmerman. New York: MLA, 1995. 156-68.

Florence, Penny. "A Conversation with Sally Potter." *Screen* 34.3 (Autumn 1993): 275-84.

Garrett, Roberta. "Costume Drama and Counter Memory: Sally Potter's *Orlando*." In *Postmodern Subjects/Postmodern Texts*, ed. Jane Dowson and Steven Earnshaw. Atlanta: Rodopi, 1995. 89-99.

Gilbert, Sandra M. "Costumes of the Mind: Transvestism as Metaphor in Modern Literature." In *Writing and Sexual Difference*, ed. Elizabeth Abel. Chicago: University of Chicago Press, 1982. 193-219.

Glaessner, Verina. "Fire and Ice." *Sight and Sound* (August 1992): 13-15.

Haines-Wright, Lisa, and Traci Lynn Kyle. "From He and She to You and Me: Grounding Fluidity, Woolf's *Orlando* to Winterson's *Written on the Body*." In *Virginia Woolf: Texts and Contexts*, ed. Beth Rigel Daugherty and Eileen Barrett. New York: Pace University Press, 1996. 177-83.

Hankins, Leslie Kathleen. "*Orlando*: 'A Precipice Marked V' Between 'A Miracle of Discretion' and 'Lovemaking Unbelievable: Indiscretions Incredible.'" In *Virginia Woolf: Lesbian Readings*, ed. Eileen Barrett and Patricia Cramer. New York: New York University Press, 1997. 180-202.

———. "Redirections: Challenging the Class Axe and Lesbian Erasure in Potter's *Orlando*." In *Re:Reading, Re:Writing, Re:Teaching Virginia Woolf*, ed. Eileen Barrett and Patricia Cramer. New York: Pace University Press, 1995. 168-84.

Hoberman, J. "Woolf in Potter's Clothing." *Premiere* 6 (July 1993): 43-5.

Horner, Avril. "Virginia Woolf, History, and the Metaphors of *Orlando*." *Essays and Studies* 44 (1991): 70-87.

Hovey, Jaime. "'Kissing a Negress in the Dark': Englishness as a Masquerade in Woolf's *Orlando*." *PMLA* 112.3 (May 1997): 393-404.

Humm, Maggie. *Feminism and Film*. Edinburgh: Edinburgh University Press; Bloomington: Indiana University Press, 1997.

Jacobus, Mary. *Reading Woman: Essays in Feminist Criticism*. New York: Columbia University Press, 1986.
Kates, Gary. "D'Eon Returns to France: Gender and Power in 1777." In *Body Guards: The Cultural Politics of Gender Ambiguity*, ed. Julia Epstein and Kristina Straub. New York: Routledge, 1991. 167-94.
Kennard, Jean E. "Power and Sexual Ambiguity: The *Dreadnought* Hoax, *The Voyage Out*, *Mrs. Dalloway* and *Orlando*." *Journal of Modern Literature* 20.2 (Winter 1996): 149-64.
Klawans, Stuart. Review of *Orlando*. *The Nation* (12 July 1993): 77-9.
Knopp, Sherron E. "'If I Saw You Would You Kiss Me?': Sapphism and the Subversiveness of Virginia Woolf's *Orlando*." *PMLA* 103.1 (January 1988): 24-34.
Laqueur, Thomas. *Making Sex: Body and Gender from the Greeks to Freud*. Cambridge: Harvard University Press, 1990.
Levine, Michael L. "*Orlando* on Screen: Three Hundred Years of Nothing Happening." *Virginia Woolf Miscellany* 42 (Spring 1994): 3-4.
MacDonald, Scott. Interview with Sally Potter. *Camera Obscura* 35 (May 1995): 187-221.
Meese, Elizabeth. "When Virginia Looked at Vita, What Did She See; or, Lesbian:Feminist:Woman—What's the Differ(e/a)nce?" *Feminist Studies* 18.1 (Spring 1992): 99-117.
Parkes, Adam. "Lesbianism, History, and Censorship: *The Well of Loneliness* and the Suppressed Randiness of Virginia Woolf's *Orlando*." *Twentieth-Century Literature* 40.4 (Winter 1994): 434-60.
Parkin-Gounelas, Ruth. "The Other Side of the Looking Glass: Women's Fantasy Writing and Woolf's *Orlando*." *Gramma* 1 (1993): 137-53.
Phillips, Kathy J. *Virginia Woolf Against Empire*. Knoxville: University of Tennessee Press, 1994.
Pidduck, Julianne. "Travels with Sally Potter's *Orlando*: Gender, Narrative, Movement." *Screen* 38.2 (Summer 1997): 172-89.
Potter, Sally. *Orlando*. Adventure Pictures, 1992.
Rafferty, Terrence. "Born Under a Bad Sign." *The New Yorker* 69.17 (14 June 1993): 94-7.
Ribeiro, Aileen. *Dress in Eighteenth-Century Europe, 1715-1789*. New York: Holmes and Meier, 1984.
———. *Dress and Morality*. New York: Holmes and Meier, 1986.
Rich, B. Ruby. "Sexual Personae." *Mirabella* (1 May 1993): 40-5.
Schaffer, Talia. "Posing *Orlando*." In *Sexual Artifice: Persons, Images, Politics*, ed. Ann Kibbey, Kayann Short, and Abouali Farmanfarmaian. New York: New York University Press, 1994. 26-63.

Sheehan, Henry. "Beautiful 'Orlando' Can't Quite Handle Woolf's Bite." *Saint Paul Pioneer Press* (30 July 1993): 16B.
Silverman, Kaja. *The Subject of Semiotics*. New York: Oxford University Press, 1983.
——. "Fragments of a Fashionable Discourse." In *Studies in Entertainment: Critical Approaches to Mass Culture*, ed. Tania Modleski. Bloomington: Indiana University Press, 1986. 139-52.
Simon, John. "A Rheum in Bloomsbury." *National Review* (5 July 1993): 53-4.
Stout, Mira. "Raising Orlando." *Vogue* 183 (July 1993): 138-43.
Travers, P. "The Smart Choice: 'Orlando'" and "Introducing 'Orlando' Director Sally Potter." *Rolling Stone* (24 June 1993): 89-90.
Trumbach, Randolph. "London's Sapphists: From Three Sexes to Four Genders in the Making of Modern Culture." In *Body Guards: The Cultural Politics of Gender Ambiguity*, ed. Julia Epstein and Kristina Straub. New York: Routledge, 1991. 112-41.
Watkins, Susan. "Sex Change and Media Change: From Woolf's to Potter's *Orlando*." *Mosaic* 31.3 (Sept. 1998): 41-59.
West, Dennis, and Joan M. West. "Achieving a State of Limitlessness: An Interview with Tilda Swinton." *Cineaste* 20.1 (Winter 1993): 18-21.
Willis, Sharon. *High Contrast: Race and Gender in Contemporary Hollywood Film*. Durham: Duke University Press, 1997.
Wilmot, John, Earl of Rochester. *The Complete Poems of John Wilmot, Earl of Rochester*. Ed. David M. Vieth. New Haven: Yale University Press, 1968.
Woolf, Virginia. *Orlando: A Biography*. New York: Harcourt, 1928.
——. *A Room of One's Own*. New York: Harcourt, 1929.
Young, Suzanne. "The Unnatural Object of Modernist Aesthetics: Artifice in Woolf's *Orlando*." In *Unmanning Modernism: Gendered Re-Readings*, ed. Elizabeth Jane Harrison and Shirley Peterson. Knoxville: University of Tennessee Press, 1997. 168-87.

"When Ears are Deaf and the Heart is Dry": Traumatic Reverberations in *Between the Acts*

Judith Greenberg

> *Only when writing discloses an echo rather than an image, so that the sounding word has reverberations that transcend the economy of clarity and form do contradictions arise that shake the 'temples of wisdom and science'...."*
> —Geoffrey Hartman, xxiii

Resonant Fragments

When Louie Mayer, the "cook general" at Monks House, describes Woolf's daily routine, she provides a significant piece of information. Upon Mayer's arrival, an odd habit of her employer startles her: "There was one thing I found rather strange on my first day," Mayer recalls:

> The floors in Monks House were very thin, and the bathroom was directly above the kitchen and when Mrs. Woolf was having her bath before breakfast I could hear her talking to herself. On and on she went, talk, talk, talk: asking questions and giving herself the answers. I thought there must be two or three people up there with her. When Mr. Woolf saw that I looked startled he told me that Mrs. Woolf always said the sentences out loud that she had written during the night. She needed to know if they sounded right and the bath was a good, resonant place to try them out. He was so used to hearing her talk to herself in this way that he did not notice it at all. I became used to it too, but it startled me in the mornings for quite some time.(2)

This fastidiousness of Woolf toward the sounds, the audible resonances of her writing, I propose, not only illustrates her much-appreciated lyricism,[1] but speaks to her awareness of the power contained in the reverberations of words.

In *Between the Acts* Woolf employs voices and sounds with increased urgency. Her final novel foregrounds presentations of music and acts of listening that occur among a community assembled at Pointz Hall, the semi-ancestral home of the Oliver family, for the annual village pageant on a June day in 1939.[2]

---

[1]Certain lines exemplify the novel's attention to the palpability of words, such as when the maids at Pointz Hall "were talking—not shaping pellets of information or handling ideas from one to another, but rolling words, like sweets on their tongues, which, as they thinned to transparency, gave off pink, green, and sweetness." (10)

[2]As Woolf writes the novel in 1939, Hitler's Anschluss and the Munich Crisis in which Britain and France allow him to take Czechoslovakia have occurred. For a comprehensive discussion of the role of the war time context in the

The "safe" community lies in the shadows of violence both externally from Europe and internally from individual characters. Giles Oliver's well-known observation of a snake "choked with a toad in its mouth" illustrates the historical situation of a world on the verge of war through an allusion to *choked speech*. This "monstrous inversion" in which the "snake was unable to swallow; the toad unable to die," (99) refers to the paralysis of nations unable to stop warring and illustrates how situations of violence "choke." Woolf figures one form of resolution to the war-time situation in Giles's act of crushing both animals with his foot—continued violence, silencing and ultimate destruction, like that occurring under Hitler's metaphorical foot. Through repeating sounds that haunt both the characters within the novel and the reader *Between the Acts* investigates the ability to "voice" experiences of violence rather than stomp them out. Behind the novel's stammer of choked speech, repeated words, broken tunes, and disembodied voices lie fragmentary messages of past and present violence. Ultimately, the novel asks whether audiences (the members of the pageant and by extension the reader) listen to such messages. As an unidentified voice in the novel puts it, *Between the Acts* explores whether "ears are deaf and the heart is dry" (119).

In a contemporaneous essay, Theodor Adorno considers how the rise of fascism and violence is related to the repetition of fragments of music. His "On the fetish character in music and the regression of listening" argues that the commercial success of music in late-capitalism fosters regressive and fetishistic listening: "all contemporary musical life is dominated by the commodity form" (33). Adorno fears that the listeners of his age focus merely on a piece of music, played repeatedly by advertisers, radio shows and orchestras, and have abandoned a tradition in which the act of listening for a "unified whole" could tame sadistic impulses. The listeners of 1938 have a fetishistic relation to music based on a pleasure of recognition, much like the pleasure experienced at a football game. The familiar isolated moments, Adorno observes, "are not bad in themselves but in their diversionary function."(29) They permit a regressive listening that fosters a childish refusal of the difficult or oppositional. By absolving listeners of the need to hear the whole, the music creates "acquiescent purchasers"(29)[3] Adorno supports Woolf's fear that "ears are deaf" and warns that the outcome is serious. The "bad ears" of modern listeners give rise to powers that destroy individuality.

---

novel, see DiBattista's chapter on *Between the Acts*.

[3]While Adorno exempts Mahler—who is able to offer something new out of regressive listening—and Schoenberg and Webern—who give form to terror, anxiety and catastrophe in their music—other contemporary "light" music only participates in musical fetishism.

Between the Acts also examines how fragmentary music and sounds can affect violent impulses and the approach of fascism. Much as the day depicted in *Between the Acts* lies between the wars, between the lines of the novel peal repeated sounds that intimate violence. The fragmented acoustic refrains in Woolf's novel, however, do not enable the kind of regressive listening Adorno decries. Rather, they disrupt complacency regarding the violence both on the Continent and at home. The phonetics of Woolf's novel, specifically its echoes of fragmented sounds and music, create a call for an active form of listening. And what can be heard are hints of unspoken stories of trauma.[4]

What Did She Mean?

Isa Oliver wonders about Miss La Trobe's pageant: "The looking-glasses and the voices in the bushes, ... What did she mean?" (213) Much as Isa considers the pageant's techniques, Woolf's text invites its reader to wonder about its mirrors and voices. Does the abundance of fragmented music, disembodied voices and shattered reflections in *Between the Acts* mean something? While there are sufficient looking glasses of various sorts to comprise a separate study of visual reflections in the novel, I will focus on how the voices in the bushes and other echoing tropes stress the need for people to hear both the voices of others and voices within themselves. These repeating fragmented sounds are the "choked speech" of trauma.

In saying that *Between the Acts* uses a language of echoes to express traumatic themes I am not trying to name any particular trauma. Rather, I want to make apparent a method by which the novel points out the difficulty of representing trauma. I resist locating specific biographical traumatic events as "disguised" in literary fiction, but choose to read Woolf's ingenious ability to write trauma. I want to read the novel as a *literary* creation and not as a manifestation of Woolf's psyche. It is precisely through the unique powers of fiction that Woolf addresses issues of trauma: how it both lies beyond the boundaries of representation and yet insistently returns and demands representation. Ann Smock, in her introduction to Blanchot's *The Space of Literature*, expresses the unique position of literature to deal with otherwise inaccessible material: "Literature's 'space'... is the resurgence of the distance at which we must place anything we wish to understand or aim to grasp. Literature is this remove, coming back to us, returning like an echo" (12). I am struck by Smock's reference to

---

[4] DeSalvo's emphasis upon the very real suffering Woolf experienced has provided a vital contribution to discussions of Woolf's life and writing. Here, I want to use her insights as a launching point into more textually focused questions of the representation and reception of trauma.

literature's echo-like qualities for it is precisely an echoing "literary space" that Woolf creates to address trauma. Experiences return for characters as pieces of words that echo in their heads and as bits of a tune they cannot shake. But echoes have another function as well. The resonant fragment in the novel also figures acknowledgment by a listener, much as the phenomenon of an acoustical echo can seem to return a response or sense of audience to a speaker.[5] The echoing literary space of *Between the Acts* examines both the choked speech of trauma and its reception by an other.

A Language of Echoes

Between the Acts is full of echoes—repeated words and noises, fragmented music and phrases, and disembodied voices. Patricia Laurence identifies how the novel incorporates sounds of war:

> the daily sounds of war—the "zoom" of the planes; the voices of the newspaper reporter, Mr. Page; the presence of communal voices ("D'you believe what the papers say?"); the polyphony of the media—enter Woolf's writing for the first time. *The Waves*, written "according to a rhythm, not a plot," incorporates the harmonious sounds of nature; *Between the Acts* incorporates the dissonant music of war, the public voice of the media, and private speaking voices. (239)

While Woolf herself calls the novel "airy" (*D5*, 141), sound waves actually saturate that air: the "tick, tick, tick" and "chuff, chuff, chuff" of Miss La Trobe's machinery confronts the audience, trees hum and birds buzz, the "zoom" of twelve airplanes cut the Reverend Streatfield's words in two, and a nursery tune and letters of the alphabet, recited as scales, travel through the sky. A megaphone asserts strange and fragmented messages and a gramophone mixes records of various types of music. The pageant "ceases" with a gramophone that first repeats triumphantly but then eventually "gurgles" "Dispersed are we" (188-201). The profusion of sounds in the novel represents the repetitive "tune" of war hovering in the distance. It also reflects the importance of listening to sounds within.

---

[5]In this I share an understanding with Toni McNaron on the role of the echo. McNaron contends that echoes reflect Woolf's thoughts and allow them to develop; they "keep her alive and working" (505). For McNaron, the echo reaffirms or anchors identity. "In these passages, Virginia uses 'echo' as a synonym for resonance, context, or continuity. Unlike scientific echoes, which depend upon vast empty spaces and which give back a delayed version of what has been said, her echoes depend upon places and people. They furnish necessary questions, comments, additions, which allow Virginia to feel substantial and to develop her thought. Echoes serve as reflections of herself filtered through intelligences and feelings of others." (502) McNaron concentrates on

We can read the novel's fragmented form, full of broken dialogue, as its own "traumatized" condition as a literary work written during war. Examples of its fragmentation extend from the collapse of the megaphone and gramophone to the general discourse at Pointz Hall that hints at unspeakable violence through fragmented phrases. For instance, the exchange of unidentified voices from the audience at Miss La Trobe's pageant anticipate the war through incomplete sentences: "I've a friend who's just been to Russia. He says..." (121). The fragment implies unhappy stories and news of violence behind the piece of dialogue uttered. The fractured dialogue exposes both the speaker's inability to tell what is happening and the listener's/reader's inability to hear it. Another voice asks: "But what about the Jews? the refugees...the Jews. People like ourselves, beginning life again...," (121) alluding to Hitler's violence lurking outside the village. This appeal to the similarities among people, the need to consider the suffering of others rather than remain deaf to their concerns, appears as only a portion of a phrase. Between the lines and in the fragments of overheard phrases emerge such questions as "What about the Jews?" How much are people willing to be unsettled by the voices of others? Is this community willing to challenge a sense of harmony, complacency, and solipsism and listen instead to the cacophony of deeply unsettling messages? These "echoes" suggest the existence of material beyond the marks on the page.

One seemingly negligible passage exemplifies the potential significance of a sound heard at a distance, in fragmentary traces: "They were far from the sea. A hundred miles away, Mrs. Swithin said; no, perhaps a hundred and fifty. 'But they say,' she continued, 'one can hear the waves on a still night. After a storm, they say, you can hear a wave break...I like that story'" (28). The metaphorical storm breaking both in Europe and within the people living through the war (and within Woolf herself)[6] can be detected in sonorous fragments, such as the breaks of waves that travel across a great distance. Trouble is heard in reverberations. In another instance, Isa Oliver alludes to an unspeakable past event and its return

---

Woolf's need for the echoes of women who provide responses "like rings in a pool coming after a tossed pebble. This kind of echo is surely richer and more powerful for the sayer" (504). I do not define Woolf's echoes in contradiction to "scientific echoes," however. Rather, I find that the echoes "which depend upon vast empty spaces and which give back a delayed version of what has been said," can indicate the presence of otherwise unutterable traumatic material. That is, I argue that both the scientific and social echoes work together.

[6]McNaron argues that the crises preceding Woolf's suicide in 1941 can be understood as an accumulation of a loss of echoes (506).

through an acoustical refrain: "'that was the burden,' she mused, 'laid on me in the cradle, murmured by the waves; breathed by the restless elms; crooned by the singing women; what we must remember: what we would forget'" (155). Here, it is the *songs* of women and the *murmur* of waves that express some unforgettable burden. These acoustic reverberations require the reader to listen actively rather than simply consume the familiar. They speak to aspects of traumatic stories dormant but not fully silenced.[7] While we cannot—nor is it my aim to—name the actual traumas that exist for the characters, we can consider the echoes of the text to point to experiences of trauma lying in its sounds.

I have made the claim elsewhere that textual echoes—repeated phrases, broken songs and disembodied voices—often express traumatic themes.[8] I discuss the work of Cathy Caruth and others who argue that traumatic return in post-traumatic-stress-disorder involves a literal and belated return of pieces of the past. This symptom, I claim, can be thought of as a kind of echoing. Trauma overwhelms its subject at the time of its occurrence and thus cannot be known; an echo is not an original sound but its return. While trauma resists representation it is insistently re-presented in dreams, hallucinations, and inner voices Traumatic return occurs belatedly and in fragments, and an echo lingers as the fragmented after-effects of a sound. When Ovid attempts to create a narrative account for the origin of the acoustical phenomenon through the story of Echo, he presents her as a creature unable to originate her own phrases.[9] As a figure of choked speech, Echo can illustrate the impossibility of speaking or representing an original in testimonies of trauma. Caruth, Herman and others have discussed how survivors often cannot tell the story of a trauma in its entirety. I have made the case in greater detail that the parallels between Echo's story and the structure of traumatic return invite a reader to examine what traumatic messages may lie within the repeated fragmentary sounds or choked speech of a text. Much as the phenomenon of an acoustical echo returns actual versions of past sounds, textual echoes can act as traces of otherwise inaccessible traumatic material for characters or the narrative voice of the text as a whole. Thus I find that the "incompleteness" of *Between the Acts* does not merely reflect its posthumous

---

[7]In a discussion of the question of the power of language to signify in Woolf's work, Eisenberg writes that *Between the Acts* "exposes more than ever the limitations of language as such and the virtues of different communicative forms that might better pull life together" (255).

[8]See *American Imago*.

[9]Discussions of the significance of other mythological figures for Woolf's work can be found in Hussey, Haller, and Joplin. For discission of Echo's story see Brenkman and Nouvet.

publication but challenges the reader, like the audience at Miss La Trobe's pageant, to listen to its partial sounds. The novel's fragmented and belated form, tropes of repeated voices, and refrains and explicit usage of the word "echo" allow it to imply the layers of trauma that evade direct, full, and immediate representation. As Woolf writes in "Anon": "There is a barrier between the sayable and the unsayable. If he cannot speak, he must sing." If the "unsayable" is trauma, then the song and other acoustic tropes may "say" the trauma that cannot be spoken.

The act of investing sounds with reverberations of suffering emerges from the opening of the novel. The reader encounters a sound: "there was a sound outside and Isa, …came in" (4). That sound then develops into a character who fixes her attention to the aural dimension of words. She hears: "The words made two rings, perfect rings, that floated them, herself and Haines, like two swans down stream"(5). Isa transforms the acoustic "rings" of the words into a visual "ring" of a ripple upon water. Isa's poetic activity, creating a metaphor from a tonal phenomenon, demonstrates the layers of stories and frustrations unleashed upon hearing a sound. While at first Isa uses the sound to initiate a romantic fantasy of escape with a man she met at a bazaar, the frustrations of reality interrupt and unmask her entrapment in her marriage with Giles. The image of the swan falls from paradise: "but his snow-white breast was circled with a tangle of dirty *duck*weed; and she too, in her webbed feet was entangled, by her husband, the stockbroker" (5). The intrusion of duckweed that entangles Isa recalls the violation Woolf suffered at the hands of her half-brother George *Duck*worth. The "ring" of the words may reflect not only Isa's frustration but perhaps Woolf's submerged trauma as well.

In her diary entry on August 28, 1938, Woolf bemoans the cycle of war by way of the symbol of the *ringing of a bell*: "A single step—in Cheko Slovakia [sic]—like the Austrian Archduke in 1914 & again its 1914. Ding dong ding dong" (*D*5 164). Similarly, Isa listens to the ringing of church bells and wonders: "'Won't there be another note?' Isa, half-way across the lawn, listened…Ding, dong, ding…There was not going to be another note" (207). For Isa, the toll of the bells announces the monotony of her unhappy marriage to Giles and the absence of a "new tune" in her story. The sounds symbolize the repetitive nature of a warring world or marriage.

Another resonant sound, discussed in the critical literature, intimates violence against women and perhaps a hidden trauma in Isa's past as well. Early in the day, Isa reads a report in the *Times* of a British trooper raping a British girl: "And they dragged her up to the barrack room where she was thrown upon a bed. Then one of the troopers removed part of her clothing, and she screamed and hit him about the face…" (20). Soon after, the story returns to Isa's thoughts but this time as a ringing of a chime: "the same chime followed the same chime, only this year, beneath the chime she heard: 'The girl screamed and hit him about the face with a hammer'" (22). If the "ding dong ding" that Isa hears signals an empty future, then the repetition of a chime here acquires significance as an announcement of a painful past as well. Jane Marcus has described how this story of rape resonates during the day,[10] and indeed, its repetition underscores the violence performed by the very soldiers purported to "ensure" British safety. Notably, Woolf uses an acoustic trope, the chime, to testify to both the *lack* of protection the soldiers create and the *war against women* which exists as a consequence of the structure of the warring world. The story of this rape returns in Isa's thoughts at the end of the day: "The girl had gone skylarking with the troopers. She had screamed.... What then?" (216) articulating the need for a scream to protect oneself, yet uncertain of the effects of such a scream. The future echoes or reverberations of that "chime"—the after-effects of the story of rape—remain undetermined. Isa's question, "What then?" could mean: What is the consequence of these acts of violence? What emerges post-trauma? Or, What happened if the girl screamed—was anyone listening? Isa's question may also dare: What does the future hold if women *do* scream out?

The "chimes" that echo in Isa's head reveal further layers of meanings. The development from the first appearance of the story of rape ("she screamed and hit him about the face...") into a second version, an adapted and imagined chime Isa hears later in the day (the "girl screamed and hit him about the face with a hammer"), exemplifies how acoustic symbols reveal textual dynamics. Isa takes the story from the newspaper and changes it into a wished-for version in which the girl defends herself by hitting the soldier with a hammer. Isa's process of constructing this second "chime" resembles the process of dream-work that Freud describes in *The Interpretation of Dreams*.[11] Freud argues that the dreamer takes pieces of the day's residue and uses them to help construct the manifest (disguised) meaning of the dream. Analysis of the distortions and condensations in the dream, he argues, can help reveal the latent and true meaning of the dream:

---

[10] See Marcus 80. See also Patricia Laurence's reading of the parallels between the domestic rape and Hitler's political rape (241).

[11] Woolf knew Freud's work. Henke writes: "introduced by George Rylands to Freud's *Collected Works* in 1924, [Woolf] began to take an active interest in the new science of pyschoanalysis. Hermione Lee tells us that once the Hogarth Press had agreed to publish Freud's papers, his theories 'became one of the dominant topics of Bloomsbury... In her letters to Jacques Raverat, psychoanalysis featured as something Virginia was holding at bay, though the language of her confessions to him was influenced by what she was hearing of Freud'" (148).

a wish. Isa performs just this kind of synthesis when she creates the "chime" of hitting the soldier in the face with a hammer. The hammer that she introduces into the scene comes from the seemingly innocuous conversation between Bart and Lucy that occurs on the page between the two versions of the story of the rape. Isa listens to the brother and sister discuss the need to nail a placard on the Barn for the pageant and their exchange sounds to her like chiming bells: the words were like the first peal of a chime of bells.

> As the first peals, you hear the second; as the second peals, you hear the third. So when Isa heard Mrs. Swithin say "I've been nailing the placard on the Barn," she knew she would say next: "For the pageant" (21-22).

Isa takes this "background music" or daily residue to supply the necessary hammer in her wish for the girl's self-defense. Her condensation or misreading presents a fantasy that contradicts her prediction that "there was not going to be another note." In the wish expressed in this chime, Isa succeeds in introducing a "new note" of self-defense, a possible answer to her question, "What then?"

Moreover, the use of the trope of a chime to fuse these thoughts emphasizes the need for Woolf's reader to interpret actively acoustic tropes. The fact that Isa selects a hammer from the discourse between Bart and Lucy suggests that the conversation between brother and sister may not be irrelevant but may belie another message. If one "chime" signals a regular pattern, the predictability and repetitiveness of dialogue, then the other "chime" may also indicate a kind of regularity: the fact that the occurrence of rape may occur as frequently as the domestic banter.[12] Stories lie hidden in fragmented articulations.[13]

---

[12]DeSalvo discusses the frequency of abuse in Victorian homes, supporting such a line of analysis: "The Stephen family warrants our close and careful attention, not only because Virginia Woolf...grew up within it, but also because the record that she kept of her existence within it serves to illuminate a very shadowy area in history, the life that went on within the private enclave of the middle-class Victorian family. What happened to Woolf is far more common than had ever been imagined" (8). And: "At the very end of her life, Woolf devoted a considerable amount of her writing energy to describing the common experience of assault in women's lives. She was interested in recording her own exploitation, but at the same time she was also interested in recounting the fact that it happened to the other young women in her household, to her sister Vanessa and half-sister, Stella Duckworth" (15).

[13]If one reads the portion of text that exists between these "chiming" passages, one finds another reference to a hammer and thus perhaps another allusion to a sexual violation. In this piece of text, as Lucy Swithin confronts a hammer, she associates it with some hidden memory of her relationship with her brother: "Once, she remembered, he had made her take the fish off the hook herself. The blood had shocked her—"Oh!" she

The vexed symbol of the hammer reappears to tap out other silent stories. Bart Oliver strikes upon the halls of the kitchen with a hammer to elicit hidden memories that lie dormant in the house. Bart stirs up the imaginations of the servant girls by banging on an archway and listening to its *echo*: "If you tapped—one gentleman had a hammer—there was a hollow sound, a reverberation; undoubtedly, he said, a concealed passage where someone hid" (32). Bart uses the echo, the hollow and reverberating sound, to feed the girls' fantasies of ghosts hidden in the recesses of the house. But if he intends for his tapping to be playful, in effect it indicates the possible presence of repressed mysteries, an unspoken past. Most probably, these echoes suggest that the alcoves of the house hold untold stories of women's suffering, much like the rumor that Pointz Hall possesses the ghost of a woman who "drowned herself for love" in a pool of water (44). The possible allusion to Narcissus and his drowning in a pool of water here exemplifies a current at work in the novel as a whole: the ghost who has died in Woolf's rendition is not a Narcissus figure but a suicidal *woman* whose almost-forgotten story echoes faintly and indirectly in rumors that resound in cavernous hidden spaces. Finally, the image of a hammer returns at the end of the pageant, when an "inner voice" thinks "'When we wake' (some were thinking) 'the day breaks us with its hard mallet blows,'" (119) again reiterating, although through silent inner voices, the pervasiveness of suffering. The hammer, a symbol of retaliation and violence in Isa's fantasy, symbolizes both the noises of past acts of violence (the echoes or ghosts heard within Pointz Hall) and the persistence of suffering (the hard mallet blows of a new day).

Other echoing noises, such as those heard in the pageant, stir up unspeakable memories. When Eliza Clark, playing the Queen of England, forgets her lines after the wind pulls up her dress, the members of the audience turn their attention to the tune of the gramophone. Giles hears the music and fears "I am not in my perfect mind." Giles's thoughts resemble those of the shell-shocked Septimus Smith in *Mrs. Dalloway* and thus suggest that Giles has his own relation to trauma:

> Words came to the surface—he remembered "a stricken deer in whose lean flank the world's harsh scorn has struck its thorn. . .Exiled from its festival, the

---

had cried—for the gills were full of blood. And he had growled: 'Cindy!' The ghost of that morning in the meadow was on her mind as she replaced the hammer where it belonged on the shelf" (21). The blood that once disturbed Lucy now returns as a "ghost of that morning," a memory from the past. Could it be an indirect reference to a trauma (but never named) that transpired between a brother and sister, like the incest in Woolf's own history?

music turned ironical. . .A churchyard haunter at whom the owl hoots and the ivy mocks tap-tap-tapping on the pane. . .For they are dead, and I. . .I. . .I," he repeated, forgetting the words. (85)

The music Miss La Trobe creates invites Giles to contemplate his role as a survivor. His forgetting of the word "alive" or "survive" that should follow ("for they are dead and I. . .I. . .I") intimates a confusion between life and death common to survivors of trauma, like that felt by Septimus who also stumbles upon "I. . .I. . .I":

> "I—I—" he stammered. But what was his crime? He could not remember it.
> "Yes?" Sir William encouraged him. (But it was growing late.)
> Love, trees, there is no crime—what was his message? He could not remember it.
> "I—I—" Septimus stammered.
> "Try to think as little about yourself as possible," said Sir William kindly.
> (*MD* 148-149)

If these returning sounds, these "words that come to the surface," allude to the possible residue of trauma (and indeed Giles is the character most focused upon the news of war), then the "tap-tap-tapping on the pane" that he does successfully remember recalls the repeated sound of the butterfly tapping on the pane earlier in the novel, "beat, beat, beat; repeating that if no human being ever came, never, never, never, the books would be mouldy, the fire out and the tortoise-shell butterfly dead on the pane," (17) and intimates a familiarity with death. The instances of acoustic resurfacing convey layers of Giles's thoughts and feelings.

The acoustic fragments are not the only echoing aspects of the text to belie stories of trauma. Resembling Echo's final disembodied state in *The Metamorphoses*, the novel's disembodied voices display a "splitting" from the body like the splitting that can occur after trauma. Lucy Swithin's question: "Was it that she had no body?" (116) implies a sense of alienation from her body, like that felt by Rhoda in *The Waves*. Survivors of trauma often experience a disjunction of their voices from their bodies. Furthermore, when trying to narrate the "event," it may seem to the survivor that the voice of *another* may seem to tell of the experience.[14] The act of detaching voices from bodies and presenting them as literary entities in their own right troubles the relation between the voice who speaks and the story told. The opening of a gap between voices and bodies can reveal both the "splitting" that occurs for the teller and the potential for the disappearance of experience in that gap—all that may not reach the listener.

---

[14] I put event in quotation marks because trauma complicates temporal boundaries.

References to the potential existence of unfamiliar and divergent voices within appear in other "little twists of sound" and invisible voices in the novel. For instance, an unidentified voice utters a rhyme during the pageant that unmasks Isa's unhappiness. The narrator explains:

> But now that the shower had fallen, it was the other voice speaking. The voice that was no one's voice. And the voice that wept for human pain unending said:
> *The King is in his counting house.*
> *Counting out his money,*
> *The Queen is in her parlour...* (181)

The creation of a voice "that was no one's voice" in this refrain (which itself repeats a previous recitation (115)) underscores the profound effects of traditionally defined gender roles. There is a "voice that wept for unending pain," a disembodied voice that articulates the persistence of suffering, perhaps the uncontrollable return of trauma. Following this passage are more overt examples of Isa's death wish: "'Oh that my life could here have ending,' Isa murmured. Readily she would endow this voice with all her treasure if so be tears could be ended. The *little twist of sound* could have the whole of her" (181, italics mine). The "twist of sound" hints at the effects of divided gender roles upon Isa (the assigned places of the King and Queen) and Isa's desire to end her pain.

The "unidentified voice" which Isa would endow with her whole being belongs to a bevy of disembodied voices that populate the novel and reflects a trend toward disembodiment that gains prominence as the pageant concludes: "Over the tops of bushes came stray voices, voices without bodies, symbolical voices they seemed to hear, half hearing, seeing nothing, but still, over the bushes, feeling invisible threads connecting bodiless voices" (151). The audience at the pageant, like Woolf's reader, half-hears symbolical stray voices that convey an unspeakable truth. The voices culminate in an Echo-like figure, disconnected from any body, crying for the suffering that keeps returning: "the other voice... the voice that was no one's voice,...the voice that wept for human pain unending" (181).

From "I" to "We": Passing Out of Isolation

Woolf's act of imagining a voice that wept for human pain unending suggests a listener who hears and speaks for the various isolated and often silent suffering of many individual characters. Indeed, the fragment "I...I" uttered by both Giles and Septimus accentuates a state of isolation shared by many characters in the novel, a condition that becomes all the more resonant when read alongside Woolf's vision of this novel as one in which "'I' rejected: 'We' substituted" (*D5* 135). The substitution can be read as a wish to confront post-traumatic isolation and communicate the surrounding violence. If echoes belie hidden stories of trauma, they also disclose how isolated "I"s need to be exchanged in dialogue with others. The novel's echoes can connote sharing or exchanging sounds in order to move from solipsism into dialogue and mutual recognition. Miss La Trobe's music that stimulates Giles to stutter "For they are dead and I. . .I. . .I" stirs his thoughts out of hiding and may force some "passing out" of the isolation of trauma. While many characters, like Giles, live in a state of isolation, the echoes they share enable a recognition that each "I" belongs to a "we," a community.

Other textual uses of echoing imply a wish for dialogue, for the "we" of community. After the pageant, the "character" of the audience thinks: "O let us, the audience echoed (stooping, peering, fumbling), keep together" (196). The verb *to echo* here characterizes the wish not to fall into isolation. The predilection for exchanging thoughts and phrases among characters—such as the "tinker, tailor, soldier, sailor" refrain exchanged by Mrs. Manresa (50-51) and Bart, "'tinker, tailor, soldier, sailor' Bartholomew *echoed*" (217, emphasis mine)—reveals a current of communication that travels outside of speech acts and connects isolated characters. Other thoughts of suffering that resist articulation also find expression through echoes. Giles wishes to communicate with William Dodge, but cannot. However the two characters do echo one another's thoughts: "He [Giles] said (without words),'I'm damnably unhappy.' 'So am I,' Dodge echoed" (176). Giles and William share an echo, a mutual understanding of suffering, the fact that "they were all caught and caged" (176).[15] Here, echoing takes place between the silent and the narratable, between the sayable and the unsayable. Echoes successfully connect disparate characters within the house as well. Mrs. Sands, the cook, differs from her real-life counterpart, Louie Mayer, who *hears* echoes in Woolf's house, in that she actually *transmits* such echoes:

> she made those quick movements at the oven, cinder raking, stoking, damping, which sent strange echoes through the house, so that in the library, the sitting-room, the dining-room, and the nursery, whatever they were doing, thinking, saying, they knew, they all knew, it was getting on for breakfast, lunch, or dinner. (33)

---

[15]William Dodge's speech dissolves into fragments or traces of past pain that evade narration when trying to communicate with Lucy Swithin as well. "And he wished to kneel before her, to kiss her hand, and to say: 'At school they held me under a bucket of dirty water, Mrs. Swithin; when I looked up, the world was dirty, Mrs. Swithin; so I married, but my child's not my child, Mrs. Swithin. I'm a half-man, Mrs. Swithin; a flickering, mind-divided little snake in the grass, Mrs. Swithin; as Giles saw; but you've healed me. . .' So he wished to say; but said nothing; and the breeze went lolloping

The "strange echoes through the house" unite disparate listeners—from those within the house, to the audience at the pageant, to ourselves as readers. Through fiction Woolf is able to imagine a community of shared echoes.

If Woolf applies the word echo to mean communication, then it is interesting to note that Ovid's story of Echo, intertwined with that of Narcissus, can allegorize the need for the exchange of dialogue.[16] Claire Nouvet reads Ovid's stories as a way of rethinking "the duty of responding to the call of the other."[17] I have argued that the stories also illustrate the need to pass out of the isolation of *trauma* through communication.[18] Echo's repetitions of Narcissus's words serve to acknowledge his calls. He, on the other hand, refuses to grant her a response. When Echo rushes to embrace Narcissus, he shuns her and eventually she withers away. Echo's tragic fate can offer a warning of the dangers of failing to respond to others—the isolation and disembodiment it causes. Since Echo has nobody, she becomes no body. Ironically, although Echo never receives acknowledgment, she metamorphoses into continuous voice for others. She lives forever in rocky caves or woods and, by eternally returning the calls of others, she provides responses. To allude to Echo, then, can make use of a figure poised between a *failure* to be acknowledged or find an audience, the impossibility of speaking a story, and a condition of *generating* echoes—acknowledging voices—for others. Woolf's text, too, may be poised between a failure of acknowledgment, traumas that remain silent, and the generation of continual responses for others, echoes of the text for future readers. Her desire to substitute "we" for "I" may recognize not only the isolation of trauma but the desire to pass out of isolation and to provide acknowledging echoes for her readers.

Miss La Trobe, like Woolf, creates a panoply of odd sounds, her own "language of echoing," that demands a new engagement with art. Her deconstructive critique of history not only omits mention of the British Army, but includes a difficult series of *voices and refrains* that mimic, unsettle, and disturb the familiar

---

along the corridors, blowing the blinds out" (73). William cannot speak, however, and even his silent thoughts of his suffering emerge only as fragments.

[16]My reading of Ovid's tale relies heavily upon John Brenkman's interpretation in his excellent essay, "Narcissus in the Text," *The Georgia Review* 30 (1976): 293 - 327. Brenkman concludes his essay: "In this sense the Ovidian text is *dialogical*: a process of writing that squanders the security of a stable meaning, not a dialogue between voices that can be tied to a consciousness" (327).

[17]Much of my reading of the multiple meanings heard in Narcissus's speech is indebted to Nouvet's analysis of Ovid's story and I refer the reader to that essay for a more thorough interpretation.

[18]See *American Imago*.

paradigms of war. Her "play within a play" performs Woolf's inquiry regarding the predicament of representation in 1939: Can art enable people to *listen* to and recognize violence and trauma, as unsettling as that may be, or will people remain deaf to the problems and perpetuate the same paradigms that silence and destroy, as seen in Giles's crushing of the snake and the toad? While Adorno retreats into academic dismissal of the masses, both Miss La Trobe and Woolf try to affect an audience by generating disturbing echoes. Neither is assured of the impact she will have upon the listeners embedded in a violent world.

The novel itself is a kind of echo: the disembodied voice of the writer's words heard in the reader's head. Woolf can be said to portray her own role as a creator of echoes through the character of Miss La Trobe who is "not merely a twitcher of individual strings" but "one who seethes wandering bodies and floating voices in a cauldron and makes from its amorphous mass a re-created world" (153). She represents the artist as a "twitcher of strings"—perhaps not only a puppeteer but a musician, creating art by manipulating sonorous strings. The explicit rendering of voices in such passages as: "Across the hall a door opened. One voice, another voice, a third voice came wimpling and warbling: gruff—Bart's voice; quavering—Lucy's voice; middle-toned—Isa's voice" (37), stresses the resonating sounds that constitute the text. The attention to disembodied voices can signify the text's own posthumous presence as it echoes in the minds or ears of future readers. Such echoes in the novel raise the question of reception. The act of detaching voices from bodies mirrors the project of writing in general, of creating bodies that are "inner voices" (119)—symbols on a page that assume life when they echo in the reader's head.[19] Eventually, will Woolf remain "alive" by way of those resonating sounds she recites in the tub? Her text recognizes that art depends upon its audience: "Miss La Trobe was invisible" (191). It is up to future readers to hear a text's messages. Without an echo, a repetition of its sounds in the mind of the reader, the disembodied voice of the text falls into silence. Indeed, both Miss La Trobe and Woolf fear that readers may not listen and the voices of their texts will fall into such isolation.

The layers of "stages" in the novel—Miss La Trobe's pageant, the title's allusion to theatricality, the "natural stage" created by the terrace and trees, and the curtain that rises on the last page—accentuate the importance of the audi-

---

[19]Hartman writes "that writing cannot be an antidote to anything except itself, that it questions its own representational claims by a repetition that phantomizes presence. For every voice with presence is already an inscription; already speaking from the realm of the dead, as if aware of the ancestral world, or having anticipated its own passing" (121).

ence.[20] Miss La Trobe "scribbles...in the margin of her manuscript: 'I am the slave to my audience'" (211) and she, like Woolf, remains uncertain as to the reception of her art. The audience watching the pageant and the conversations between characters all foreground the general question of listening to the wars on the political stage, wars between family members, and the wars within the self. Bart Oliver articulates the weight of the individual as a receiver of art's messages: "Our part ... is to be the audience. And a very important part too" (58).[21] Will art communicate to its audience or will difficult stories dissolve into silence? The various stages pose such questions to the audience in front of the curtain raised at the end of the novel as well—that is, ourselves, the readers, and our own ability to *listen* to the text. What kind of an audience are we? Will we provide an echo for the fragments we hear?

To a certain extent, the villagers' reception of the pageant as incoherent suggests the futility of art, its inability to find an audience and effect change. Auditory failures permeate the pageant sections of the novel. For one, the voices of the actors hardly extend beyond the stage: "The words petered away" (78). "They were singing but only a word or two was audible...the wind blew away connecting words of their chant" (80). "The wind blew the words away" (125). When the children in the pageant begin to cry, it becomes increasingly difficult to hear the production: "All together they bawled, and so loud that it was difficult to make out what they were saying" (90). The singers who play pilgrims cannot be understood: "The voices of the pilgrims singing, as they wound in and out between the trees, could be heard; but the words were inaudible" (163-4). The acoustic failures of one cast member's words are telling. Phyllis Jones, the small girl playing England, first forgets her lines (77) so that no one can *hear*. Later, when her voice again peters out, "No one was listening" (95). The transition from failures to hear to failures to listen can denote a shift from a somatic loss to a psychological resistance; as Barthes says, "*Hearing* is a physiological phenomenon, *listening* is a psychological act" (245). The audience, inured to the difficulty of hearing, demonstrates an intentional deafness. This condition of deafness engulfs Pointz Hall and compounds the despair of the historical

---

[20] See Sallie Sears, "Theatre of War" (Marcus 212-35).

[21] The hovering Woolfian narrator emphasizes the significance of Bart's message while simultaneously alluding to the narrative's own dependence upon the sounds of words: "'We are the audience.' Words this afternoon ceased to lie flat in the sentence. They rose, became menacing, and shook their fists at you" (59). These words come to life with violent force, possibly alluding to the fist of the victimized girl in the newspaper story.

moment, supporting a pessimistic interpretation of the novel.[22] Although Isa echoes a fragment of one line of the play ("there is little blood in my arm"), she displays a general inability to hear the words and follow the plot. Isa may articulate Woolf's fear of the failure of art to reach the ears of its audience: "There was such a medley of things going on, what with the beldame's deafness, the bawling of youths, and the confusion of the plot that she could make nothing of it."[23] Is the pageant only a formal experiment, a play of signifiers, or is there a message to be found amidst the fragments? And if uncomfortable messages are contained in these fragments, is the audience doomed to ignore them?

Between the Acts does not wholly condemn the modern listener. The sounds and music of Miss La Trobe's pageant create uncertainty within the audience that generates a new kind of listening. At first, her music appears to unite and connect the members of the community, to create a "we" out of disparate "I"s. The audience at the pageant responds: "I hear music" says one member of the audience; "Music wakes us. Music makes us see the hidden, join the broken. Look and listen," (120) says another. This fantasy, however, does not sustain itself. Music does not serve to "join the broken," to feign a sense of community or render the illusion of the familiar. Rather, the music Miss La Trobe presents diverges from a soothing and peaceful harmony. Fragmented, broken, and dependent upon modern technology, it evokes otherwise silent "pulses" or drives. Unsettling tunes awaken the audience, sounding much like the cacophonous rhythm of war, full of planes flying overhead and shots fired in the background. "The tune changed; snapped; broke; jagged. Fox-trot was it? Jazz? Anyhow the rhythm kicked, reared, stopped short. What a jangle and jingle!" (183).[24] The jazz-like and fragmentary character of the pageant's music resembles the kind of regressive listening, the "vulgarization" of "purity" and "unity" into "bits and pieces," that Adorno laments. When the members of the audience wish for some "inner harmony" and criticize this modern form of art saying that "the young... can't

---

[22]Marilyn Brownstein finds it, "the saddest book I have ever read" (86), and Roger Poole reads "the last two pages of the novel as entirely bereft of hope" (93).

[23]A number of critics explain that the plot does not matter, in fact. For instance, Makiko Minow-Pinkey argues that it is essential neither to the play nor the novel as a whole (191). Gillian Beer stresses that plot "insists on origins, sequence, discovery, exclusion and closure," gestures the novel works to upset (131).

[24]DiBattista writes: "The contemporary ennui and despair afflicting the British 'soul' is reflected in the audience" (196). Indeed, many members of the community express a death wish, suggesting the pervasiveness of suffering. We find a soul resembling a postmodern condition of dissonance and difference: "'The glass is falling' said a voice'" (152).

make, but only break; shiver into splinters the old vision, smash into atoms what was whole," (183) they certainly fulfill Adorno's characterization of the audience in late capitalism. The "looking glass" here, the microcosm of society depicted in art, "reflects the soul" and shatters like a Cubist painting.

Woolf seems to have more faith than Adorno in the power of these modern fragments upon the public. The "scraps, orts and fragments" of Miss La Trobe's pageant invite not regressive listening and a sense of consumption but defamiliarization and contemplation. Like Echo's unsettling of Narcissus's words in Ovid's story, the returning ironical sounds of the pageant unsettle both the sense of unity among members of the audience and general patriarchal order. They elicit unconscious forces. While this disturbance does intimate a violent undercurrent, it does so in order to force recognition of it and demand a change, perhaps the "new note" for which Isa yearns.

The repetitions of the broken gramophone and the jagged tunes haunt the audience and demand that they rethink the echoing in their heads. Each member of the isolated Oliver family (Bart, Lucy, Isa and Giles) hears the echo of "dispersed are we" and assimilates it into his or her thoughts (96). Isa cannot shake the echo of the pageant and says: "The play keeps running in my head" (105) and later "I wish the play didn't run in my head" (113). The susceptibility of the characters to music here resembles the view that the immediacy of a tune can address emotions otherwise inexpressible in words. The power of the song to voice otherwise silent experiences is discussed by Shoshana Felman in her discussion of the role of the song in Claude Lanzmann's *Shoah*.

> On the borderline between dreaming and memory, the song—as a concrete, material residue of history—is that small element of reality that is evidence that we are not dreaming... [the song] is asking us to listen to, and hear, not just the meaning of the words but the complex significance of their return, and the clashing echoes of their melody and of their context." (270-271)

Felman's description could well apply to the music of the pageant. It forces the audience out of complacency and insists upon the darker noises both in the horizon and within themselves—"not quite themselves, they felt" (149); it stimulates a return of the unwelcome, whether repressed or traumatic. "Did she mean, so to speak, something hidden, the unconscious as they call it?" members of the audience ask themselves (199).[25] The music forces the audience to reconsider themselves. A mysterious voice asserts itself from behind the bushes: "Let's

---

[25]Indeed, Woolf was familiar with Freud's ideas of the unconscious, She was reading *Group Psychology and the Analysis of the Ego* while writing *Between the Acts*, she met Freud in 1938, and the Hogarth Press published *Moses and Monotheism* in 1939.

break the rhythm and forget the rhyme. And calmly consider ourselves" (187). The concluding tune urges the individuals attending the pageant to rethink both who they are and the layers of conflict within:

> The tune began; the first note meant a second; the second a third...The whole population of the mind's immeasurable profundity came flocking; from the unprotected; the unskinned; and dawn rose; and azure; from chaos and cacophony measure; but not the melody of surface sound alone controlled it; but also the warring battle-plumed warriors straining asunder. To part? No. Compelled from the ends of the horizon; recalled from the edge of appalling canvases; they crashed; solved; united. And some relaxed their fingers; and others uncrossed their legs.
> Was that voice ourselves? Scraps, orts, and fragments, are we, also that? The voice died away. (187)

The repetitive or echoing nature of notes following upon notes here indicates a pattern similar to the one Isa hears in the ringing of bells. But in this case, the tune brings out the "mind's immeasurable profundity," the "we" or many voices within. The music stirs raw and warring layers within and challenges the members of the audience to work at interpretation. Its fragmentation, then, does not summon simple regressive listening, but forces a confrontation with the repressed or traumatic.

The stirring of a "we" or many interior voices also evokes Ovid's story of Echo. Since Echo cannot originate her own phrases, she depends upon the words of another to create her own subjectivity in discourse. Her "I," constructed by borrowing parts of Narcissus's "I," is actually a composite, a "we." If Echo is a "we," who borrows words in order to create her own "I," then Narcissus too learns that his own "I" actually contains a "we," as Nouvet has argued. That is, Narcissus believes Echo's words to be the words of another, rather than the repetition of his own phrases. In so doing, he hears the other (and quite different) messages contained within his speech. Ovid's story reveals that his "I" actually contains a "we;" that multiple meanings exist within his speech acts. Ovid's pair, then, enact the substitution of "we" for "I" that Woolf proposes in her diary. Echo can allegorize the interchangeability of the terms "I" and "we": Every "self" is both composed by a dialogue with others and comprised by multiple voices within. If Echo's story can depict the many meanings behind a fragment, then the echoes of *Between the Acts* can underscore the many meanings to be heard in its phrases. Layers of the past that resist narration reappear through echoes. The anonymous member of the audience who observes: "But none speaks with a single voice. None with a voice free from the old vibrations" (156), testifies to the richness of any utterance and the layers of acoustic reverberations and possible traces of trauma embedded in speech acts. Pointz Hall is indeed an "open-air cathedral, a place where swallows darting seemed,...to make a pattern, dancing, like the Russians, not only to the music, but to the unheard rhythm of their own wild hearts," (65) possessing unheard rhythms, submerged layers of stories, chimes, and tunes.

To return to the question of whether the audience hears these tunes, Woolf figures an ultimate listener who hears all of the messages contained in the fragments. While ears may be deaf and the heart dry in the village audience, certain voices speak with authority and insight: "the voice had seen, the voice had heard" (138). The voices that emerge from behind the bushes during the pageant see and hear the pain that eludes narration; they intimate divine awareness, a phenomenon expressed by an unidentified voice (itself a disembodied voice) that asks: "Then those voices from the bushes...oracles? You're referring to the Greeks?" (198). These disembodied voices highlight a tradition that considers echoes as omnipotent.[26] Woolf's disembodied voices *know* of a pain that hovers in the air; they act as traces of the past. This knowing comes with years of suffering, a history that returns through the acoustic fragment, the "primeval voice sounding loud in the ear of the present moment" (140).[27] A "giant ear" links the disparate "I"s into a collective listening "we": "sheep, cows, grass, trees, ourselves—all are one. If discordant, producing harmony—if not to us to a gigantic ear attached to a gigantic head" (175). This giant ear hears a cacophony of histories—personal histories, political history and literary history—resounding in the noises of a June day in 1939.[28] Perhaps the "giant ear" belongs to future readers who do not retreat into a narcissistic isolation or stomping out but listen to the pain of the other.

---

[26]Hartman traces the etymology of the word echo in Hebrew as a disembodied voice with divine properties: the rabbinical term bat kol means daughter of divine voice, and has become the modern Hebrew word for echo. See "Meaning, Error, Text." *Yale French Studies* 69 (1986): 147. Wayne Koestenbaum, writing about the power of the voice in the opera, observes a similar phenomenon: "opera queens...believe that voices entering through the ear are forms of the Holy Ghost. Freud's disciple and biographer Ernest Jones, in his provocative essay 'The Madonna's Conception Through the Ear,' speculates on the ear's erotic significance. To hear is metaphorically to be impregnated —with thought, sensation and tone." (16)

[27]Avrom Fleishman finds that the novel reduces history to its elements (*The English Historical Novel: Walter Scott to Virginia Woolf* [Baltimore: Johns Hopkins University Press, 1971] 146) and Alex Zwerdling finds it sees history as moving from civilization back to barbarism.

[28]This voice also shares qualities with the battered beggar woman outside the Regent's Park tube station in *Mrs. Dalloway*, a voice of "no age or sex," who mourns her lost lover (a Narcissus?) and speaks/sings in fragments.

In 1941, as she concludes *Between the Acts*, the question of how people listen to sounds of suffering haunts Woolf. Her essay from the same period, "Anon," also explores the question of how people listen. The mythic figure she creates in that essay may be read as an outgrowth or personification of the themes of Miss La Trobe's pageant: her final disembodied voice. That is to say that the essay takes the unsettling detachment of the voice from the body that permeates the end of *Between the Acts* and, by embodying the idea of an "Echo" who travels through history, investigates processes of listening.[29] "Anon" offers one last instance of Woolf's "language of echoing."

At the heart of "Anon" lies the consideration of the role of art and its relation to its audience.[30] "Anon" represents a voice of poetry, performance, and an echoing relationship between artist and audience. Brenda Silver contends that "Anon" expresses Woolf's desire for an interactive form of art that challenges the destruction of the historical moment by involving its audience:

> Woolf saw the preparation and the writing of her history as a way to counter the destruction occurring all around her. What she searches for, what she claims as common, is not the tradition associated with established institutions or authorities, but what she calls the "song making instinct" and identifies both with the desire to sing and the desire to listen. At the heart of this tradition lies a literature that enacts the mutual strivings of artist and audience rather than the word structures of the solipsistic male voice. (652)

Silver underscores the mutuality or the "we" created between those singing/creating art and those listening to it. Like Ovid's Echo, Anon relies upon verbal exchange. The exchanged song might counteract a Narcissus-like solipsism and ensuing violence. Unfortunately, the essay concludes with a dire forecast: "Anon is dead." The communal song and the need to share voices expires.

Echo and Anon share strange vocal properties that reflect some qualities of traumatic speech. Anon lifts "a song or story from other people's lips" (680) much as the mimicking Echo, punished by Juno and unable to originate her own speech, is forced to do.[31] Anon's lost song, like Echo's inability to originate speech, may then symbolize an original/lost traumatic "event." Both can illustrate the inaccessible aspect of trauma and yet the persistent return of that

---

[29]See Eisenberg and DiBattista as well on the relation between the final novel and essay.

[30]I have discussed this in my analysis of *Mrs. Dalloway* as well (145-146).

[31]Pagination from "Anon" taken from its reprinting in *The Gender of Modernism* (680). Originally printed in Brenda R. Silver's "'Anon' and 'The Reader': Virginia Woolf's Last Essays." *Twentieth Century Literature* 25 (1975) (382-424).

unassimilated event. Anon "has no house" and roams through fields and yet "used the outsider's privilege to mock the solemn, comment on the established." Ovid makes Echo immortal and omnipresent: "So she's hidden in the woods and never can be seen on mountain slopes, though everywhere she can be heard; the power of sound still lives in her" (Mandelbaum 93). Both voices of Echo and Anon hover in the outdoors like the disembodied voices of Miss La Trobe's pageant. However, these outsiders to speech use their voices to subvert the conditions that exile them. Echo borrows Narcissus's words but changes them to create her own meanings. Anon "comments upon the established." And the pageant's "voices" borrow traditions to reinterpret them. These subversive outsiders can represent the survivor's sense of alienation and the need to speak one's story to reclaim one's identity. Further, both voices also undermine traditionally gendered roles, the divisions that so disturb Isa. Anon problematizes gender, existing as "sometimes a man, sometimes woman" (680). Although Echo is a female character, her gender status is complicated, for she speaks (repeats) the words of Narcissus, a male character and continues to perform the same activities even after her body has disintegrated. What is Echo's gender as disembodied voice?[32] The figures not only blur traditionally defined gender roles, but cause a reconsideration of the role of gender when the body is traumatized and when the survivor may feel disembodied—"no body" as Lucy puts it.

Finally, both characters transcend the temporal boundaries of mortality: Anon lives for centuries until "he" is killed by the printing press, and Echo survives her death as pure voice.[33] Survivors of trauma often struggle with the boundary between life and death—do they walk with the living or with ghosts? This immortal aspect of both figures also conveys the authors' questions about a writer's impact upon the future. Echo and Anon literally depict the *metamorphoses* that occur in the repetition of the voices of others—the author's "voice" reemerges in a reader's body—and thus speak to the possibilities and limitations of writing, its place in history as disembodied voice. Echo, Anon, and the disembodied voices in *Between the Acts* ask whether certain songs and stories will disappear or find an echo in a reader.

If the parallels between Anon and Echo seem accidental, then it is interesting to note, as McNaron has, how Woolf deploys the word "echo" as she grapples with the problem of receptivity in her diaries. As she writes "Anon" and *Between the Acts*, she devotes her attention to questions of war, the possibility for art to "counter the destruction occurring all around her" as Silver puts it, and the role

---

[32] This is a question for the beggar woman in *Mrs. Dalloway* as well.

[33] I use the masculine pronoun in imitation of Woolf, but the figure is "sometimes a man, sometimes a woman."

of audiences in sharing art. In her entry of June 9, 1940, fearing the approach of the Germans and the absence of an audience to listen to her calls for change, she perceives:

> A kind of growl behind the cuckoos and t'other birds. A furnace behind the sky. It struck me that one curious feeling is, that the writing "I" has vanished. No audience. No echo. That's part of one's death…But it is a fact—this disparition of an echo. (*D5* 293)

The "kind of growl" precludes the emergence of any echo, any sound of response, dialogue, interaction. Woolf fears that the world is deaf to the suffering of others. The lack of a receptive audience in the world, the "disparition of an echo," indicates "one's death." Woolf returns to the image of an echo a couple of weeks later: "Further, the war—our waiting while knives sharpen for the operation—has taken away the outer wall of security. No echo comes back. I have no surroundings" (*D5* 299). When the echo fails to return there is no receptive audience but rather a violent and warring world. The echo reappears yet again in her diary on July 24, as both a condition that connotes safety and as the response of the reading public: "All the walls, the protecting and reflecting walls, wear so terribly thin in this war. There's no standard to write for: no public to echo back; even 'tradition' has become so transparent"(*D5* 304). As in the first entry, she laments the absence of an echoing audience.

Woolf's creation of echoes and yet her despair about their reverberations leaves us with a contradiction. Will people hear stories of trauma in the fragments that remain? The fractured sounds which dissolve into the air and, like distant music, settle in the ears of the audience at the end of the pageant, present two poles: "Unity—Dispersity," eventually emerging as the fragmented echoes "Un…Dis…" (201). Does the village share in the exchange of art or do they return, each to a separate cocoon? Do they hear stirrings of trauma within and without? And, if they do, what can they communicate to one another? Will the separate "I"s pass out of isolation and into the "we" of exchange? The novel cannot answer simply by choosing "unity" or dispersity," although a tendency towards humanism or postmodernism may favor one or the other. I have tried to show that the novel's "language of echoing"—noises, music, explicit references to echoing, and disembodied voices—unsettle and bring stories of trauma out of silence, but what develops from these unsettling fragments remains to be seen. It depends upon the involvement of the reader.

The novel leaves its reader with the desire for unity intertwined with the reality of dispersity, the attempts to communicate alongside the failures of communication. The state of being "between the sayable and the unsayable," between hearing and not hearing, and between sharing refrains and retreating in isolation, is the position in which testimonies of trauma find themselves as well—some pieces may find articulation and pass out of isolation while others may resist being voiced. These conflicting possibilities and limitations emerge as the fragmented *sounds* that reverberate in the text and fill the reader's ears. "Un... dis" can signify our condition as listeners to the text: joined together in the act of reading and then dispersed as we hear our own individual and belated echoes. *Between the Acts* insists upon the urgency of listening to such echoes, both without—in the sounds of war heard in the repetition of the bell's toll—and within—in memories of trauma—in order to change the tunes of private and public wars.

Works Cited

Adorno Theodor. "On the Fetish-Character in Music and the Regression of Listening" (1938) in *The Essential Frankfurt School Reader*. Edited by A. Arato and E. Gebhardt. New York: Urizen Books, 1978.

Barthes, Roland. "Listening" in *The Responsibility of Forms: Critical Essays on Music, Art, and Representation*. Trans. Richard Howard. New York: Farrar, Straus, Giroux, 1958.

Beer, Gillian "Beyond Determinism: George Eliot and Virginia Woolf." *Arguing with the Past: Essays in Narrative from Woolf to Sidney*. New York: Routledge, 1989.

Brownstein, Marilyn, "Postmodern Language and the Perpetuation of Desire." *Twentieth Century Literature* 31 (1985): 73-88.

DiBattista, Maria. *Virginia Woolf's Major Novels. The Fables of Anon.* New Haven: Yale U P, 1980.

DeSalvo, Louise. *Virginia Woolf: The Impact of Childhood Sexual Abuse on Her Life and Work*. New York: Ballantine, 1989.

Eisenberg, Nora. "Virginia Woolf's Last Words on Words: *Between the Acts* and 'Anon.'" in *New Feminist Essays on Virginia Woolf*. Ed. Jane Marcus. Lincoln: U Nebraska P, 1981.

Felman, Shoshana and Dori Laub, M.D. *Testimony: Crisis of Witnessing in Literature, Psychoanalysis and History*. New York: Routledge, 1992.

Greenberg, Judith. "The Echo of Trauma and the Trauma of Echo." *American Imago*. 55, 3 (1998): 319-347.

Haller, Evelyn. "Isis Unveiled: Virginia Woolf's Use of Egyptian Myth." In *Virginia Woolf: A Feminist Slant*. Ed. Jane Marcus. Lincoln: U Nebraska P, 1983. 109-131.
Hartman, Geoffrey. *Saving the Text: Literature/Derrida/Philosophy*. Baltimore: Johns Hopkins UP, 1981.
———. "Meaning, Error, Text." *Yale French Studies* 69 (1986).
Henke, Suzette. "Virginia Woolf and Post-Traumatic Subjectivity." *Virginia Woolf: Turning the Centuries. Selected Papers from the Ninth Annual Conference on Virginia Woolf*. Ed. Ann Ardis and Bonnie Kime Scott. New York: Pace U P, 2000. 147-152
Herman, Judith Lewis, M. D. *Trauma and Recovery*. New York: HarperCollins. 1992.
Hussey, Mark. "Reading and Ritual in *Between the Acts*." *Anima* 15, 2 (Spring, 1989): 89-99.
———. Ed. *Virginia Woolf and War. Fiction, Reality and Myth*. Syracuse: Syracuse U P, 1991.
Joplin, Patricia Klindienst. "The Voice of the Shuttle is Ours." In *Rape and Representation*, Ed. Lynn Higgins and Brenda Silver. New York: Columbia U P, 1991. 35-64.
Koestenbaum, Wayne. *The Queen's Throat: Opera, Homosexuality, and the Mystery of Desire*. New York: Vintage Books, 1994.
Laurence, Patricia. "The Facts and Fugue of War: From *Three Guineas* to *Between the Acts*." In *Virginia Woolf and War*. Ed. Mark Hussey. Syracuse U P, 1991. 225-245.
Marcus, Jane. "Liberty, Sorority, Misogyny." *Virginia Woolf and the Languages of Patriarchy*. Bloomington: Indiana U P, 1987.
Mayer, Louie. "Virginia Woolf: A Recollection." In *Virginia Woolf: A Collection of Criticism*, Ed. Thomas S. W. Lewis. New York: McGraw Hill, 1975.
Minow-Pinkey, Makiko, *Virginia Woolf and the Problem of the Subject: Feminine Writing in the Major Novels*. New Brunswick: Rutgers UP, 1987.
Nouvet, Claire. "An Impossible Response: The Disaster of Narcissus." *Yale French Studies* 79 (1991).
Ovid. *The Metamorphoses*. Trans. Allen Mandelbaum. New York: Harcourt, Brace and Company. 1993.
Poole, Roger. "'We all put up with you, Virginia': Irreceivable Wisdom about War," In Hussey, ed.: 79-100.
Silver, Brenda R. "Cultural Critique." In *The Gender of Modernism*. Ed. Bonnie Kime Scott. Bloomington: Indiana U P, 1990.

Smock, Ann. Introduction. *The Space of Literature* by Maurice Blanchot. Lincoln: U Nebraska P, 1982. 1-15.

Woolf, Virginia. *Between the Acts*. New York: HBJ, 1977.

———. *The Diary of Virginia Woolf*. Volume 5. Ed. Anne Olivier Bell. New York: HBJ, 1984.

Reflecting the Subject in History:
The Return of the Real in *Between the Acts*
Kristina Busse

> *Whatever may be their use in civilized societies, mirrors are essential to all violent and heroic action.*
> *—AROO*

   For Virginia Woolf, World War II increasingly came to bear on her intellectual labor as she wrote *Between the Acts* against a backdrop of the loss of her London flat, daily bomb threats and blackouts, food rationing and fear of invasion. While she still could claim in September 1939 that the war is "bosh & stuffing compared with the reality of reading" (*D5* 233) and that "any idea is more real than any amount of war misery" (*D5* 235), she soon thereafter changed her views and reevaluated the relation between external violence and her inner psychology. In December 1939 and January 1940 she rejected Dr. Octavia Wilberforce's offer of food with the following: "I never heard a more absurd 'business proposition' as you call it. A month's milk and cream in return for an unborn and as far as I can tell completely worthless book.... Nothing we both ever have to write can outweigh your milk and cream at this bitter and barren moment" (*L6* 454, 458). Woolf's comparison in which her unfinished book "Pointz Hall," later to become *Between the Acts*, would come up short against milk and cream poignantly raises the issue of the relationship between a literary text and its material circumstances. *Between the Acts* exhibits Woolf's increasing awareness of history at the same time as it continues to focus on the protagonists' inner lives by addressing the changing role of the individual against a tenuous political and historical backdrop. Woolf's external struggle to justify the writing of literature in the face of war's realities mirrors internal conflicts within the novel itself. As a result, *Between the Acts* has invited both psychologically sensitive critiques as well as historically conscious approaches.

   Psychological and historical literary criticism have traditionally been mutually exclusive and often openly hostile toward one another. Just as New Historicism relegates Freud to an intellectual past and regards his theories as obsolete, psychoanalytic critics dismiss historical approaches as too simplistic because they overlook the ultimate power and influence of the unconscious.[1] This separation, however, is artificial and limiting, since neither approach intrinsically requires its competitor's disavowal; in fact, only a synthesis of the two

---

[1] A representative of the former is Michel Foucault in his discussion of psychoanalysis

techniques can ultimately render a comprehensive and insightful reading.[2] Virginia Woolf's last novel, *Between the Acts*, affords us a text which not only allows for such a dual reading, but also pervasively thematizes the interaction of psychological subjects and their historical environs. Like *Three Guineas*, which connects the war abroad with the patriarchy at home, *Between the Acts* links the external violent intrusions of war to the internal violent eruptions within subjects, thus showing how the two do not yield contradictory results but are instead closely related.[3]

The connection between the two is most apparent in the final scene of the pageant, which signals the ultimate breakdown of both psychological and historic constructions. As the players carry onto the stage broken mirrors in which the audience members must face their fragmented selves, their psychological constructions fail; as the audience is incorporated into the play, the historical constructions developed within and outside the play break down. In deliberately choosing the mirror, Woolf demonstrates these attempts at constructing order and coherence while revealing their futility. After all, mirrors hold a particularly prominent place in Woolf's work[4] and provide a generally privileged symbol for self-realization, revision, and change. In fact, throughout *Between the Acts*, they function both as subject and world forming devices.

I begin with an analysis of two mirror encounters—Clarissa's in *Mrs. Dalloway* and Isabella's in Woolf's short story "The Lady in the Looking-Glass: A Reflection"—to establish the relationship between mirror scenes and the construction of subjectivity.[5] Not only does the mirror function as a site for the

---

in *The Order of Things*, especially 373-89. An example of the latter is Joan Copjec's *Read My Desire*, tellingly subtitled *Lacan against the Historicists*, in which she presents a historically sensitive account of psychoanalytic criticism, thereby refuting the common complaint of psychoanalysis as ahistorical.

[2]While it may seem strange to employ psychoanalysis as a historical tool, Lacanian psychoanalysis in particular lends itself to such use. For a reading of Lacan that emphasizes this historical component, see Slavoj Zizek's discussion of the real as the central element of disruption in ideological and political constructions.

[3]For readings that trace the connection from *Three Guineas* to *Between the Acts*, see Herbert Marder and Patricia Laurence.

[4]In "A Sketch of the Past" Virginia Woolf comments on her looking-glass shame and her sexual abuse by Gerald Duckworth in front of a mirror (68-69). In *A Room of One's Own* Woolf describes how women function as looking-glasses for men (35). For discussions of the significance of mirrors in Woolf's writing, see Barbara Babcock, Hermione Lee, Beth Rigel Daugherty, and Susan Squier.

[5]Although Jacques Lacan was writing his groundbreaking article "The Mirror Stage

creation of subjectivity, this very function also allows it to fulfill the opposite role. As these two scenes offer an insight into the characters' simultaneous construction and destruction in front of the mirror, they reveal the tenuousness of any such construction as well as the arbitrariness of a subject's identity. I will use this discussion of mirror encounters as sites of subject formation to focus on *Between the Acts* and the various alternative theories of the subject it offers. Woolf not only presents a variety of possibilities for the construction of the subject competing in contemporary theory but also adumbrates and dismantles some of the more prevalent options. In fact, in the figures of Isa Oliver and Mrs. Manresa, Woolf renounces the modern theory of subjectivity in which the subject strives towards moments of completion and union, insight and understanding, at the same time as she resists the easy answers of postmodern constructivist relativism.[6] Woolf thus presents and undermines modern *and* postmodern theories of the subject only to offer an alternative of her own. While her characters strenuously attempt to construct a reality—fictitious though it may be—they can never completely escape its failure, the point where meaning fails to cohere. Instead, they are ultimately faced with a model of subjectivity constructed by and around a central and constitutive lack.

This lack at the very center of the reality the subjects attempt to create bridges the psychological with the historical in *Between the Acts*. As the final mirror scene emblematizes the failure of subject formation, it also indicates the disintegration of a very different construction—that of history. After all, at the

---

as Formative of the Function of the I as Revealed in Psychoanalytic Experience" in the thirties, there is little possibility Virginia Woolf could have read his work. Even though she overcame her resistance to psychoanalysis towards the end of her life and was studying Freud while writing *Between the Acts*, it is pretty certain that she did not know of Lacan's theories. For a discussion of the relationship between Woolf's and Freud's writings, see Elizabeth Abel's *Virginia Woolf and the Fictions of Psychoanalysis*. Abel connects psychological and historical approaches as she reads *Between the Acts* against Freud's later cultural theories, especially *Moses and Monotheism*. Yet while there are good reasons to emphasize the similarities between Freud and Woolf, Woolf's preoccupation with mirrors parallels Lacan's. In fact, her fiction tends to support Lacan's thesis that the mirror stage is the formative aspect in every subject's life, a correspondence which certainly demands closer investigation.

[6]Critics have remarked upon this emphasis on the subject-in-process as Woolf's postmodern strain, some going as far as calling *Between the Acts* "the first historical postmodern novel" (McWirther 808) and a "postmodern ancestor of *Gravity's Rainbow* and *Lost in the Funhouse*" (Daugherty 76). This is especially apparent on a formal level, where the text is remarkable both in its discontinuous and fragmented form—thoughts and sentence fragments float through the text—as well as in the different interlaced

center of the novel is the pageant which attempts to narrativize history and endeavors to re-construct England's past. This construction fails, however, when the different fictional layers collapse with the intrusion of a historical present predicated on war and destruction. Whereas the psychological approach to the novel traces the internal collapse of the subject's constructions, the historical reading of the text pursues the external intrusions that disrupt the narrative constructions.

Central to both themes is the desire to construct and the inherent failure of any such constructions. Accordingly, a close analysis of the traumatic intrusions into the symbolic framework of the play (and of the novel itself) explores and exposes the gaps and fissures in both the subject and history, i.e. the splitting subject and war, in order to investigate the relationship between the two. More specifically, a focus on the failure of constructions illustrates how the psychological breakdown (of both Woolf and her characters) must be seen as a reflection of the historical chaos posed by the Second World War. As such, it offers us a glimpse of the non-symbolizable register of the real, the term Jacques Lacan introduced to describe the failure of both symbolic and imaginary constructions.[7] This analysis of the real allows us not only to trace the psychic disintegration of some of the characters, but also to investigate closely the constant intrusion of historical circumstances into the text. While *Between the Acts* strains to maintain a consistent symbolic, imaginary constructions cannot con-

---

layers and frames, beginning with the title and the text-within-the-text and moving to the paradoxical ending. For postmodern readings of Woolf, see Patricia Waugh, Pamela L. Caughie, Bonnie Kime Scott, and Marilyn Brownstein. See also the papers on postmodernism and Woolf collected in *Virginia Woolf Miscellanies*, eds. Mark Hussey and Vara Neverow-Turk.

[7]While many Woolfian critics use psychoanalysis in general and the mirror stage in particular, most tend to restrict themselves to binary oppositions as they acknowledge the Lacanian "split subject" without further investigation into its traumatic residues. Tony Jackson, for example, reads *Mrs. Dalloway* as focusing on the metaphor/metonymy dyad, which underlies Clarissa's "two theories about her self" (147). In her Kristevan reading of the Woolfian subject, Makiko Minow-Pinkney concentrates on the semiotic/symbolic split and thus reads the lack and emptiness around which Clarissa constitutes herself as "the maternal body which she must repress to become a subject in the symbolic" (70). Patricia Waugh points out the resemblance between Clarissa Dalloway's mirror encounter and Lacan's mirror stage, but does not use Lacan any further. Daniel Ferrer's study is a remarkable exception in his reading of the real as the phenomenon that disrupts both imaginary and symbolic constructions in the text.

ceal the gaps created by a repeatedly interrupting and invading real.[8] By forcing the reader to encounter the horror and the void of the real in place of safer alternatives, *Between the Acts* becomes a text that disrupts and interrogates various understandings of the subject at the same time as it questions our conceptions of history.

Casting historical and psychological interpretations as complementary rather than mutually exclusive, this essay examines the intricate connection between history and the subject, between their constructions and disruptions. Arguing that Woolf's inquiries into subjectivity reflect her search for a proper understanding of historical forces and the individual's role therein, this essay scrutinizes the traumatic intrusions into the symbolic framework of the novel, thus exposing the gaps and fissures present in both subject and history. Neither symbolic nor imaginary constructions succeed in resisting the real, the violent remainder and reminder of both the lack at the center of the subject and the oppressive momentum of history in general. As a result, *Between the Acts* can be viewed as a text that connects the real at the core of the subject with the real at the fringes of history and, in so doing, bridges the gap between historical and psychological interpretations.

Before concentrating on *Between the Acts* with its different theories of subject formation, I want to focus on two earlier mirror scenes in Woolf's work that establish the general relationship between mirror encounters and the construction of subjectivity. The first of these mirror scenes occurs in *Mrs. Dalloway* where Clarissa Dalloway demonstrates how the subject can create her identity vis-à-vis a mirror image. When Clarissa views herself in the looking glass to fix her hair, she does not perceive an inner self or truth in her reflection. Rather, the mirror supports her imaginary construction; it allows her to (re)create the image she and others have of her. "[C]ollecting the whole of her at one point," Clarissa faces her self in the looking-glass, "pointed; dartlike; definite" (*MD* 37). Clarissa is aware that the persona she portrays is not "real" but a role she must adopt to function in society. She purposefully employs the mirror to constitute herself as a coherent subject. When Clarissa Dalloway "dr[aws] her parts together," she creates an identity that is modeled on an idealized, supposedly perfect, mirror image.[9] Distinguishing between the self Clarissa is "for the world" and the "dif-

---

[8]It is important to understand that Woolf was not suddenly faced with the real at the end of her life but rather that she openly confronted a battle she had been fighting all her life. In fact, Woolf's texts throughout indicate how the real—both psychologically as well as historically— is already exposed in all its unsettling and disturbing force.

[9]Clarissa's construction of an ideal mirror image, of course, recalls Lacan's description of the mirror stage in which the child encounters its apparently coordinated and

ferent" one which "she alone kn[ows]," the novel suggests that a distinction may exist between Clarissa's own vision of herself and the one she creates in front of the mirror. At the same time, however, Clarissa recognizes the arbitrary nature of both, so that she never commits the fallacy of regarding one constructed self as superior to the other.

The opposition between these two identificatory selves is further supported by Clarissa's encounter with her former lover, Peter. Peter presumes that he can distinguish between a true Clarissa whom he remembers from their days in Bourton and the spurious one she has become for her surroundings. Accordingly, we should be able to find a more original Clarissa who would most likely be revealed when she confronts Peter and remembers their time together. Yet when Clarissa imagines herself with Peter rather than with her husband, Richard, her casualness is striking. Within seconds, Clarissa has created a different identity as Peter's adventurous lover, enjoyed their exciting life together, and dismissed it (*MD* 47). This dismissal attests to her understanding that her own ideal image of herself is no more authentic than the image she creates to please others. Clarissa does not feel any sense of betraying herself when collapsing the two versions, when making herself want to be what she imagines others would like her to be. Whereas Peter still mourns for a genuine Clarissa, attempting to find her under the parties and social events, the pretty dresses and the small talk, Clarissa is fully aware that the person she is for Peter is also completely constructed.

Thus, Clarissa exposes the arbitrariness of the supposedly highly personalized choice of identification. Rather than representing a pure core self, internal identification obeys rules similar to the external ideal. As Clarissa faces the mirror, she acknowledges how each image is arbitrarily constructed, an insight that allows her to control her own identity—though only within the framework of possibilities offered by her social context. Clarissa's acknowledgement may seem cynical and jaded as the arbitrariness of her choice forecloses any political or social opportunities or moments of resistance that may reside in the subject's personal investment in its identification. At the same time, however, the romantic fantasy of loving Peter, this idealized vision of herself, does not subvert the social structure embodied by Richard Dalloway either, but rather forms an acceptable escape from it. Unlike Clarissa's love for Sally, which would have

---

whole image in the mirror as opposed to its own experiences of an uncoordinated fragmented body. The mirror thus functions as a tool to construct an imaginary specular image far superior to the experienced actual body. In Lacan's theory, the incompatibility of these two selves will be experienced as a lack that can never be filled.

seriously disrupted the social network, her love for Peter remains within allowable limits. Consequently, viewing Clarissa's love for Peter as resistance ignores the fact that such resistance is accounted for within the very structure it is trying to resist.

Mirror encounters are not necessarily always as benign and constructive as Clarissa's. In fact, in her short story, "The Lady in the Looking Glass: A Reflection," Woolf presents us with Isabella Tyson, whose failure of identification results in the complete destruction of her identity.[10] Thus, an analysis of Isabella's mirror scene supplements Clarissa's by offering insight into how the construction of the subject is not really a positive but a negative construction. Rather than encountering a more natural, less constructed person, the character behind the construction, the only thing left, is "nothing." Standing in front of the looking-glass, Isabella is "naked in that pitiless light"; in fact, as the narrator points out, "there [is] nothing" underneath the façade (*CSF* 219). As the looking-glass "bite[s] off the unessential and superficial . . . to leave only the truth," it does not reveal some truer or purer self; instead, "Isabella [i]s perfectly empty. She ha[s] no thoughts. She ha[s] no friends. She care[s] for nobody" (*CSF* 219). It is this scene, then, that exposes the mirror's destructive qualities. Clarissa Dalloway reenacts the mirror stage and its identification in order to be "whole" and face the outside world with its various expectations. Isabella, on the contrary, reverses this mirror stage process as her very being reveals itself to be a construction and all that Clarissa adds and achieves in her mirror encounter fails in Isabella's. Juxtaposing these two scenes, we see a complete reversal, leading us to the very center of the subject, albeit a center of lack, or rather, lack *as* the center. Isabella is the woman for whom identification has ceased to function; her parts do not draw together but rather fall apart, drop off, to reveal—nothing. As the mirror strips Isabella of all her possessions and qualities, it demonstrates how the construction of the subject is predicated on its very negativity by creating subjectivity around a lack.

These two mirror encounters illustrate Woolf's use of mirrors to establish her character's identities. Not only does she expose the arbitrariness of any such construction (regardless of whether the subjects themselves are aware of this), she also reveals that underneath these carefully created personalities lies the

---

[10]In his interesting reading of the story, Dean R. Baldwin suggests that "the mirror provides a glimpse of reality that direct observation does not" (55). Though Baldwin distinguishes between the life the narrator imagines for Isabella and the transcendence of the mirror, he nevertheless suggests that the mirror's revelation may indeed be only *one* rather than *the* truth (56).

abyss of nothingness as the ultimate building block of a person's identity.[11] Whereas Clarissa displays the process of constructing a subject's identity with all its ambiguity, Isabella presents the subject in the absence of such comforting, fictitious constructions. Though this identity as lack may be "truer" than Clarissa's creations, the story emphasizes the subject's inability to exist in this state, thus disclosing the necessity of constructed identities.

Turning to *Between the Acts* now, I want to show how Woolf returns to the mirror as the site of subject formation when Isa, Mrs. Manresa, and the pageant audience must confront their mirror images. Moreover, in these three mirror encounters, Woolf presents and criticizes different theories of the subject. While Isa adheres to a modern understanding of the subject in which a true identity may be hidden by an artificial one, Mrs. Manresa offers a postmodern alternative of playful constructivism in which her entire identity is pure creation. Woolf, however, ultimately dismisses both alternatives in favor of the most disconcerting third one, anticipated in Isabella's mirror scene. When the pageant audience members confront themselves in the broken mirrors, they suddenly come face to face with the failure of their constructions and begin to realize that the lack that they encounter may be at the center of their identities, that their very beings cannot be divorced from it.

At the same time, this mirror scene also opens up a historical gap, producing a historical encounter with the real. During the final scene of the pageant, the broken mirrors not only collapse the identities of the subjects, requiring the audience to face themselves and their central lack, they also break down the historical distance the audience members have comfortably maintained. Whereas up to that point they could safely detach themselves from history as a construction of the past irrelevant to their own existences, the breakdown of temporal and spatial distance between viewers and actors enforces the audience's complete immersion into the play, collapses the play into their realities. Consequently, audience members are faced with their own historical situatedness and the constructed nature of historical concepts and teleologies. As the mirror's quality of constructing and freezing both subjects and history fails, the audience confronts the lack around which both are constructed, the lack at the center of both the subject and history.

The first of the mirror scenes in *Between the Acts* occurs early in the text and exhibits Isa Oliver as an exemplary modern subject. While she enacts different versions of herself, Isa never doubts that there exists a deeper, truer self, which

---

[11] In a 1920 diary entry, Woolf compares life to a tenuous construction covering nothingness: "Why is life so tragic; so like a little strip of pavement over an abyss" (*D2* 72).

the subject can attempt to approach, revealing her hidden truths. After having been attracted to one of her neighbors the night before, Isa begins to distinguish several versions of herself while looking at her mirror image in the morning (*BTA* 13-4). It is plausible to interpret this scene as expressing the gap between the facade Isa must put forward to accord with social norms, and the true, the actual Isa, in love with the "romantic gentleman farmer." Thus, Isa encounters two versions of herself that are required to create her reality. On the one hand, we are faced with Isa's imaginary identification, the person she would like to be, i.e. "in love." On the other hand, "outside, on the washstand on the dressing-table, among the silver boxes and tooth-brushes," we see the reflection of her surroundings; here, Isa is steeped in her symbolic identification, the way *she* wants to be because she believes that is the way *others* want her to be.[12] Here she considers herself worthy of love as she obeys external demands and expectations. Isa thus clearly distinguishes between these two versions and attempts to separate them: inside, she is in love; outside, she is wife and mother. Of course, Isa does not perceive this differentiation in any strict distinction. Rather, she believes she *is* both versions when, in fact, she is neither; both simply function as identification to cover Isa's empty core subject.

Therefore, we can recognize how Isa deceives herself when she clearly differentiates between the person she imagines herself to be and the one she believes others want her to be: realizing her life as wife and mother to be artificial, she still believes her love to be true. Woolf's language, however, raises some doubt as to the authenticity of Isa's love. After all, the reader has experienced Isa's remarkably unromantic encounter with Rupert Haines the night before (*BTA* 4-5). Taking into account that Isa recognizes her phrase "father of my children" as a cliché, it seems probable to argue the same for her final thought, "Inner love was in the eyes; outer love on the dressing-table" (*BTA* 14). Like the poetry she writes in secrecy and hides (*BTA* 15), she pretends to conceal a deep inner life and uses her "love" as an escape from reality. Assuming her appropriate place in the symbolic network with a persona she enacts for other people and knows to be wholly created, Isa continues to believe that an actual and truer self exists underneath the constructed one. Yet the irony of the text toward its protagonist, as well as its lack of compassion for Isa's inner self, suggest that this internal life is no less imagined than the outer one.

---

[12]In psychoanalytic terms these two separate visions correspond to Lacan who, following Freud, differentiates between imaginary and symbolic identification, between ideal ego and ego ideal. The most detailed description of the differences between ideal ego and ego ideal occurs in Lacan, *Seminar* I 129-42.

Moreover, reading Clarissa's and Isa's mirror encounters together makes the illusory quality of the core self which Isa believes she possesses even more apparent.[13] Clarissa questions the validity of Isa's understanding of the subject as she suggests that the relationship between the subject and her environment follow an intricate and complex dynamic. In fact, we have seen how Clarissa's identity is primarily indebted to external influences insofar as her self is a result of multiple interactions with or, one might say, interpellations by her physical, psychological, and social surroundings. Isa, however, only acknowledges such external constraints for her public self, her life as wife and mother, while her private life appears to be free of societal mandates. We thus witness the illusion of a true core self, an identity untainted by outward restrictions that may, at moments, be accessible to the subject. In this version of subjectivity, Isa represents a thoroughly modernist conception of the self in which the individual can never be represented fully but, nevertheless, claims to possess a true core, unalterable and incorruptible.

In a later mirror scene, we can see how the subject requires the mirror to construct subjectivity not only on an individual but also on a communal level. Using the mechanism of the gaze of the other, this final act of the pageant discloses to the audience the illusion of their identity construction. In this scene, which constitutes the middle portion of the novel, the actors bring onto the stage mirrors and other objects, such as "tin cans," "bedroom candlesticks," "old jars" and even "the cheval glass from the rectory," in short, "[a]nything that's bright enough to reflect, presumably, [the audience]" (*BTA* 183). The reaction to this attempt to expose the audience to the notion of themselves as part of the play and its historical occurrences is startling. As the audience members face their own reflections, they are struck by panic, claiming, "that's cruel. To snap us as we are before we've had time to assume . . . And only, too, in parts . . .. That's what's so distorting and upsetting and utterly unfair" (*BTA* 183-4, all ellipses in the text).

---

[13]This comparison between Clarissa and Isa also repudiates the claims of some critics that Woolf's depiction of subjectivity delineates a clear progression from an early vision of the unified self as represented by Mrs. Ramsay or Mrs. Dalloway to the more dispersed and split subjects of *Between the Acts*. Karen Schneider, for example, describes the recognition in *Between the Acts* that "achievement of such unity is but a dream that fades in the face of cold fact" (108) and Mark Hussey emphasizes the split subjects when he comments that "Woolf puts in question the notion of history and its concomitant, a unified self" ("'I' Rejected; 'We' Substituted" 247). In contrast, my reading proposes that several notions of the subject coexist in Woolf's literary corpus without any clear trajectory.

If, as I have established thus far, the mirror allows us to realize our own construction, the audience members react to the necessity of facing their own constructedness—communally and viewed by others. The spectators confront themselves watching themselves; moreover, as they watch others watching themselves, they realize that others are observing their own gaze. In this communal spectatorial gaze, the very private, the very narcissistic, gesture of watching oneself in the mirror is made public. The communal experiencing of the distorting and disrupting mirrors is more upsetting and unsettling than the solitary encounters. The audience members have ceased to be pure onlookers who can passively observe and now must experience being watched. The cruelty is as much in the intrusive recreation of a narcissistic moment, the feeling of being "caught unprotected" (*BTA* 199), as in the invocation of the imagined gaze of an other returning their own gaze.[14] At any time, the gaze can be re-turned; the private mirror encounter with its performative constitution of identity can be observed. In short, when Miss La Trobe forces the audience to face the mirrors on stage, she enacts the gaze of the other which in the mirror encounter is only imagined. Thus, the imagined (and imaginary) other is implemented by an actual person observing the gaze, and the audience members are struck by panic when they realize the illusory character of their identities.

Woolf, however, does not limit the audience to one reaction to the broken mirrors, but instead, offers two distinct responses and, with it, two diverse theories of the subject. In fact, she uses this mirror scene to juxtapose Isa's earlier, distinctly modern version of subjectivity with a postmodern one in the figure of Mrs. Manresa, only to offer a third alternative to both of them, exemplified by the general panic and dismay of the pageant audience. Throughout the novel, Mrs. Manresa is a character completely in control of her actions, her appearances, and her impact on others. By manipulating and controlling her physical appearance as well as the facts she reveals about herself, she carefully fabricates an image for others. Accordingly, she maintains control of the mirror encounter, since she cannot be surprised by the knowledge of constructed subjectivity. Most consciously aware of her misrecognition, Mrs. Manresa *has* to be the only member of the audience who can face and embrace herself in the mirror.

As the audience members are confronted with their fractured selves in the reflection of the cracked mirrors, she is the one character who refuses to participate in the collective panic and, instead, calmly faces herself in the mirror. While

---

[14]In his theory of the scopic drive, Lacan elaborates on the concept of *I see myself seeing myself* as he describes how "[t]he gaze I encounter . . . is, not a seen gaze, but a gaze imagined by me in the field of the Other" (*Four Fundamental Concepts* 84).

"[a]ll shifted, preened, minced; hands were raised, legs shifted," while "[a]ll evaded or shaded themselves," Mrs. Manresa "facing herself in the glass, used it as a glass; had out her mirror; powdered her nose; and moved one curl, disturbed by the breeze, to its place" (*BTA* 186). Thus, Mrs. Manresa is the only character not to be distressed when perceiving her own reflection in the cracked and fragmented mirrors. She seems to be at ease with her own reflection when she takes out her own mirror in order to powder her nose and redden her lips so that "[a]lone she preserved unashamed her identity, and faced without blinking herself" (*BTA* 186). In fact, all an observer can grasp about Mrs. Manresa are exterior things, artificial and interchangeable, such as clothes and jewelry. Even her body parts are described through their cosmetic enhancements, such as her red lips and fingernails. Moreover, the information she reveals about herself is as carefully controlled as her appearance. We know little about her personal life, "nothing private; no strict biographical facts" (*BTA* 39), except for what she freely reveals as anecdotes and gossip about herself. It is not surprising, then, that Mrs. Manresa can best handle the illusion of the mirror encounter. Since her entire life is already presented in "scraps and fragments" (*BTA* 39), the "scraps, orts and fragments" (*BTA* 189) of the cracked mirrors cannot disturb her. Mrs. Manresa is the one character in *Between the Acts* who presumes herself to be completely aware of her actions, to be in complete control of her identity.

Mrs. Manresa's ability to face her own construction challenges Isa's understanding of the subject, but her philosophy of self-fashioning does not go without criticism either. Instead, Mrs. Manresa's acceptance of her own constructed identity is revealed to be as comforting an illusion as Isa's, since she constructs her own—fundamentally different but nevertheless equally consistent—symbolic universe. Throughout, the novel goes to great lengths to criticize Mrs. Manresa's superficial, even offensive, behavior. Likewise, the text clearly does not endorse her alternative theory of the self, a fact that becomes particularly obvious in the final act of the play. As she deliberately takes out her own mirror, Mrs. Manresa short-circuits the mirror encounter controlled by Miss La Trobe; refusing the insight of the fragmented mirrors, she substitutes for them her own construction. In so doing, she rescues herself from the devastating intelligence that the rest of the audience must face. Her ability to cover the gaps in the symbolic that the others experience simply displays a more sophisticated version of an imaginary symbolic, a construction less likely to be disrupted. In other words, by acknowledging her own constructedness, she anticipates and dissipates the uncertainties and anxieties the other audience members experience when confronted with their own constructions. Mrs. Manresa's alternative construction conceals its own inconsistencies, i.e. it constructs an imaginary symbolic that presents itself as consistent, in which all fissures and gaps appear as unreadable, as "outside" of any symbolic production of meaning. Accordingly, when she substitutes reality with her own, apparently consistent symbolic, she avoids the insight that all symbolic constructions are imaginary and inconsistent.

What she refuses is the fact that the fragmentation of the mirrors enhances their disturbing effects; it is, after all, the particularly unsettling vision of viewing themselves *in parts* that brings about the audience members' realization of their constructedness. The mirror-in-pieces simulates and thus evokes a body-in-pieces as the viewers confront fragmented body parts and disjointed limbs: "Here a nose . . . There a skirt . . . Then trousers only . . . Now perhaps a face . . ." (*BTA* 184, all ellipses in the text).[15] Not only does the scene describe dispersed parts, but this fragmentation is further suggested in sentence structure. Unlike Clarissa Dalloway's synthesizing mirror encounter, which was described in long and complex sentences, the short and fragmented character of the phrases in *this* mirror scene suggest a disintegration of subjectivity.[16] Thus, we can see how the audience's confrontation with the body-in-pieces in the mirror reveals the imaginary construction of both the subject's self-perception and its idealized image as lacking, a terrifying insight from which Mrs. Manresa rescues herself. As the fragments destroy the mirror's unifying function, they collapse the necessary opposition at the center of the creation of the subject and required to sustain it.

This terrifying insight—the subject is constructed around and maintained by a lack at the center—helps explain the pageant audience's reaction to the mirror fragments. While the discovery that one's self is constructed can account for some of the discomfort the mirror encounter produces, the excess of panic requires additional explanation. Focusing on the gaps and fissures in the symbolic offers such an explanation. The lack, i.e. the gap between the *imago* and the self-understanding of the subject as a body-in-pieces, can be understood within the third Lacanian register, the real.[17] The real, which resists both the mirror fantasy of the imaginary as well as any attempts at formalization in the symbolic, must be understood as the place where meaning fails to cohere, the gaps in the construction of the symbolic. Consequently, we only experience the real indirectly in terms of "left-overs"; as the symbolic construction fails or ceases to

---

[15]In his mirror stage article Lacan describes how the "fragmented body . . . appears in the form of disjointed limbs" ("Mirror Stage" 4), an account that is uncannily close to the pageant scene discussed here.

[16]Tony Jackson provides an in-depth discussion on the relation between subjectivity and narrativity as he discusses the dissolution of self and form in both *Mrs. Dalloway* and *The Waves*.

[17]See Lacan, *Four Fundamental Concepts*. For a discussion of the Lacanian real, see Zizek, especially 153-199.

function, the real becomes detectable in its interstices. It therefore must be understood as a horrible intrusion, an impasse, a failure in symbolization, rather than as an actual ontological entity. When Miss La Trobe faces the audience with itself "in parts," the reaction can only be terror and panic as they confront their own disintegrated bodies and with it a glimpse of the real.

The intrusions of the real into the pageant are particularly unsettling since theater with its illusory force traditionally functions within the imaginary realm and serves as a protective guard against confrontations with the real. After the illusion fails, the previously covered and repressed real returns in all its disturbing force and exerts a violence indicated by the imagery of blood throughout the novel. The repeated imagery of pouring blood and death is intensified by the curious fact that it is *life*, in the form of nature, which exerts this unbearable presence of the real. This relationship of the real to both life and death force is further explored in the most disturbing scene of the novel. During an intermission in the pageant, Giles encounters a freakish accident of nature, a snake, "choked with a toad in its mouth" (*BTA* 99). Overcome with repulsion at this "birth the wrong way," he kills both animals.[18] This "monstrous inversion" exemplifies the real's violent eruptions into reality as this impasse interrupts natural processes and magnifies the savagery barely hidden under the surface. Moreover, Giles' violent intervention illustrates his (and also the reader's) need to aggressively confront these intrusions; only by annihilating the monstrosity of both animals is Giles able to reinstate the symbolic. If we understand the Lacanian real as the moment where the symbolic breaks down and ceases to function, this scene eloquently captures the subject's inability to endure this situation, to exist in a place where the imaginary has failed to cover the inconsistencies in the symbolic universe. It is important to note, however, that the violence of the real is never absent, only hidden and repressed. Whereas Zwerdling, for example, reads this scene as indicating "the *return* of predatory forces into the garden world of the Olivers' country house" (*BTA* 225, my italics), the repeated imagery of violence throughout the text suggests that even the idea of a pure and undisturbed garden world is illusory.

The pageant audience's final confrontation with the fragmented mirrors recalls Isabella's dreadful mirror encounter and thus offers a third model of subjectivity. This version is not predicated on the belief in an original kernel of truth and integrity underneath a constructed facade as in Isa's understanding of the

---

[18] Clearly, the two animals intertwined in their death struggle function as a metaphor for contemporary politics and its perverse corruption of the natural order as they symbolize the inability of the new to take over the old.

subject. Nor does it subscribe to Mrs. Manresa's disenchanted notion of being in control by believing in a subject that is completely constructed (and thus wholly construct-able). Indeed, Woolf's mirror encounters offer the reader two alternative versions, only to dismantle them both in the final mirror scene by introducing an intrinsic, traumatic inconsistency into their subjectivity. These traumatic inconsistencies at the center of the subject can be understood as the gaps and fissures produced within the very process of subject formation. As cracks in the symbolic construction—usually concealed and covered by the imaginary—they reveal the irreducible element of the real within the subject. In the audience's encounter with the cracked and broken mirror fragments, this moment of the real where the symbolic fails and the imaginary cannot suture the gaps, Woolf's text exposes the subject in all its vulnerability and shows how it is constituted through the lack and absence at the center of its being.

At the same time as the pieces of reflecting glass expose the characters' fragmented selves and the lack at the center of their identities, they also shatter the carefully maintained and cautiously safeguarded constructions of history. Throughout the text, the reader confronts a world desperately trying to hold onto an order long lost. Ritually reenacting (or even newly instituting) traditions that offer a semblance of structure and coherence, the characters shelter themselves from a world that seems to produce only chaos and disarray. While stylistically implementing the disorder that threatens the rural community, Woolf also thematically questions whether the memories of a coherent past are simply illusory and as easily shattered as the mirror images of the self. In her pageant, she suggests that both present and past must be understood and read as narrative fictions that rhetorically create an order desperately needed. Accordingly, the fragmented mirrors of the last act disrupt the characters' ambitious historical constructions at the same time as they expose their personal ones.

Not surprisingly, this scene concludes a play that questions a historical understanding of factuality and certainty by portraying history as a narrative construction. This emphasis on historical construction, especially within the context of the pageant, calls for a historicized approach to the novel. Many recent critics have foregrounded such a historical interpretation and convincingly argue that the novel is politically conscious and historically contextualized through its definite sense of time and place.[19] Some even claim *Between the Acts* is a historical

---

[19]Critics remarking on Woolf's preoccupation with war in *Between the Acts* include Alex Zwerdling, Werner Deiman, Patricia Laurence, Karen Schneider, Sallie Sears, Judith Johnston, Gillian Beer, and Patricia Klindienst Joplin. See especially Mark Hussey's collection, *Virginia Woolf and War*.

novel, describing how "the novel refers constantly to events in the external world" (Zwerdling 221) and commenting that there is "an almost obsessive preoccupation with history on virtually every page" (Deiman 56).

Of course, the text's historical situatedness and its repeated reminders of current events establish *Between the Acts* as socially self-conscious and invite historicized readings. Still, the overall pastoral setting, the constant repression of history, and the emphasis on subjectivity and linguistic concerns demand a more nuanced approach to the novel's treatment of the past. After all, it is this very repression of political and social contexts—both within and without the text— which indicates Woolf's relationship to history. Neither a traditional historical novel, nor a text completely divorced from history, *Between the Acts* problematizes historiography and our ability to (re)construct historical events. In fact, the novel offers a variety of different approaches to history. Throughout, a highly personalized and anecdotal narrative history vies for attention with a more positivist factual interpretation.[20] These different alternatives are disrupted, however, when the audience members come face to face with their own historicity. Neither a factual description nor a narrative construction of the past, history suddenly becomes a reality suffusing the audience members' everyday lives. As the play metaphorically short-circuits historical past and present time reality, it collapses the constant allusion to violence and the impending war into the calm and peaceful pastoral setting of *Between the Acts*.

On first sight, the text actually invites the reader to overlook its historical context as it focuses on a group of insignificant characters, their trivial details, small problems, and petty quarrels. More than with the approaching war, most of the characters are preoccupied with themselves, their own identities, and, at most, each other. Instead of a direct engagement with the historical circumstances and the impact of a Europe awaiting war, the reader is confronted with a pageant displaying a literary history and its audience's thoughts and feelings throughout the day. Much of the historical context is confined to the margins of the text, fleeting thoughts of newspaper clippings, imperialist memories, and

---

[20]See Sabine Hotho-Jackson for an in-depth discussion on Woolf and historiography. She convincingly argues that "Woolf's approach to history displays a combination of a modern view of history [i.e., a history in which the present not only reconstructs but also reinterprets the past] and a traditional concept of history as story" (296). Even though she clearly views the latter approach as pre-modern, its narrative aspect can also be explained through postmodern theories of history. For examples of postmodern historiography, see Hayden White's *The Content of the Form* and *Tropics of Discourse*, Michel DeCerteau's *The Writing of History*, and Dominick LaCapra's *History and Form* and *History and Criticism*.

unaccountable fears. Still, the impending war is on everyone's mind, thus clearly situating the text historically. Like the cesspool discussed at the beginning of the novel, fascism and the coming war linger at the edges of the text, threatening the characters' tenuous hold on a seemingly calm and peaceful reality. Furthermore, the reader's knowledge of the war's imminence transforms the supposedly peaceful summer day and lends new meaning to the eruptions of violence. In fact, the text itself alludes to the approaching cataclysm as all the protagonists make an effort—though in vain—to evade the historical circumstances overshadowing this summer day on the eve of World War II (*BTA* 46, 53, 193). The pageant, the focus of everyone's thoughts and actions and the center of the novel itself, revolves around questions of historicity, historical change, and, most importantly, historiography. The play's contemplation of how to genuinely write and truthfully represent history culminates in its last scene as history and its literary representation collapses into present time and place, a present marked by the warplanes crossing over the scenes of the novel, disrupting the pretense of peace and order. As the airplanes disrupt the pageant, they fittingly form the last scene of a play recreating a history suffused with brutality and murder.

While the most obvious manifestation of the upcoming war, the planes are only the last in a series of allusions that implicate a repressed but nevertheless ever-present backdrop of violence, chauvinism, and war. In fact, *Between the Acts* is suffused with historical suggestions at the same time as its characters desperately attempt to confine war and violence beyond their field of visibility. Throughout, the protagonists encounter and then dismiss references to the world beyond Pointz Hall. Giles, who travels between the pastoral and seemingly timeless setting of the novel and the reality of a world on the brink of war, is most obvious in his preoccupation with history. He repeatedly returns to the political climate in Europe and is furious at the complacency and insularity of his family while he recalls the dead on the continent and the imminent threat to his home (*BTA* 46, 53). But while the others may not address the war as directly, it still occupies their minds. During intermission, for example, the snippets of discussion invoke dictators and Jewish refugees (*BTA* 121). Bart, of course, remembers his own days of imperial conquest when he daydreams about "his" India (*BTA* 18), and Isa remains obsessed throughout the day with a newspaper clipping that she read in the morning (*BTA* 20). In its description of the sexual assault of a young woman by a group of soldiers, the newspaper article connects male aggression and sexual violence in the forms of war and rape.[21] Linking the vio-

---

[21] As Stuart Clarke has shown, Woolf relies on an actual rape described in *The Times*.

lence of war and chauvinism, Woolf clearly connects the two by exposing the inner logic motivating both fascism and patriarchy. This association is similar to the argument explored in *Three Guineas*, in which Woolf most explicitly relates male violence against women with the violence exhibited in wars by demonstrating how the fight against fascism cannot be divorced from the one against patriarchy.[22]

Between the Acts' most important confrontation with history, of course, is the pageant, which forms the focal point of the novel, not only structurally but also thematically. Its theatrical form lends itself particularly well to questions of performativity as most of the village inhabitants enact historical characters (both fictional and nonfictional) while everyone else performs his or her role as audience member. Yet the play's historical situatedness is as repressed and evasive as that of the novel itself; in fact, the pageant mimics the novel as a whole in its strenuous attempt to leave out patriarchy, violence, imperialism, and war, all of which are at the very center and thus constitutive of the British Empire. It also parallels the novel, however, in its failure to create such a consistently ahistorical text. Instead, Woolf presents her audience—both within and outside of the novel—with a complicated and contradictory account of history. Similar to the novel as a whole, the play strives to present a coherent account of life that focuses on the natural and cultural achievements of England; nevertheless, prejudices, hatred, and war constantly intrude, thus exposing the attempted coherent constructions as faulty and contradictory. Unlike Woolf, though, the author inside the novel fails: Miss La Trobe's vision remains misunderstood as the players and the audience fail to understand the ironic undercurrents as they watch the play. Rather than acknowledging the competing versions of history, they view the pageant simply as a literary version of England, depicting the mother country at its most positive. Accordingly, by representing English history through a presentation of English literary history, the pageant emphasizes the cultural and intellectual heritage as opposed to the realities of life. By trying to divorce the cultural achievements of England from its warfare and more violent conquests and thereby concealing the way every English subject is implicated in a bloody and gruesome history, the text projects the threats onto Nazism, patriarchy, and the colonial enterprise in an attempt to preserve the civilized aspects of English imperialism while divorcing it from its (necessarily interdependent) other.

Still, the repeated intrusions of these historical realities into the safe literary world of the pageant as well as the violence experienced and perpetrated by the

---

[22]David McWirther, following Maria DiBattista, points out that Whitehall, the site of the rape, was also the place where the British war council assembled (McWirther 795, DiBattista 197).

characters themselves suggest an inherent inability to distinguish clearly between alternative histories. Accordingly, the constant and ominous intrusions of the war reveal the failure of any such clear distinction. After all, the pageant itself carries traditional historical overtones with it since, as Gillian Beer has pointed out, such village pageants were "often held on Empire Day" (283). Also, as Sears and McWirther have pointed out, a further association between the historical play and the actual historical circumstances is suggested by the often-used term "theater of war" (Sears 212, McWirther 799). And it may not be completely coincidental that this pageant, which takes place under the shadows of WWII, is in its seventh year, which puts the first performance in 1933, the year Hitler rose to power. The repressed yet conspicuous world of violence and war forms the backdrop for the more civilized version offered in the literary history of the pageant play. Thus, it becomes apparent throughout the novel that the dark aspects of history are part of—if not the principal condition of—the subjects' subjectivity.

This relationship of histories within and without the play is dramatized in the final scenes of the play. Whereas most of the pageant still strives to keep up the dramatic illusion by maintaining a safe distance for the spectators through both temporal and artistic displacement, the final act provokes a direct confrontation with the audience. Entitled "Present Time. Ourselves" (*BTA* 177), it attempts to extend the historical dimension of the play into the present, forcing the audience to perform within the play. Obviously, the breakdown between drama and reality unsettles the audience members as they encounter their own lives as part of history. While they easily accept these past protagonists as constructed subjects, they refuse to see the same in themselves. In an early scene of the text, for example, we are reminded by Lucy Swithin, who reads an Outline of History, that history is always an "imaginative reconstruction of the past" (*BTA* 9). Similarly, later in the play, the audience is asked to "imagine" a skipped chapter, thus suggesting the spectators' power to influence and even fabricate the play and, through it, history (*BTA* 141). Yet whereas it seems natural to the audience members to imagine and construct the history of previous times and *other* people, they vehemently refuse their own incorporation within historical processes as they strive to maintain their individuality: "'Ourselves . . .' [. . .] But what could she know about ourselves? The Elizabethans, yes; the Victorians, perhaps; but ourselves; sitting here on a June day in 1939—it was ridiculous" *(BTA* 178-9). This anonymous interior monologue displays the audience members' resistance to considering themselves on a par with the historical characters they encounter on stage. Denying their own historical specificity and refusing the comparison with the characters of the play as "ridiculous," they reject all similarities in an attempt to maintain the illusion of their own particularity and individuality. Drawn into the play as (unwilling) participants, the audience members must extend their insights about the nature of history and historical characters into the present time and, consequently, must recognize themselves as subjects-in-history, performing a historical role.

When the first line of defense falls and the audience members realize that they too might be implicated within larger historical processes, their refusal to see "ourselves" on stage proceeds to a personal protective stance: "'Myself'—it was impossible. Other people, perhaps" (*BTA* 179). The attempt to differentiate their own selves from others around them is exemplified by the speakers' defenses: as the communal distancing from a former past fails, the protection of "ourselves" shifts into a preservation of "myself." Once the speaker has realized that the audience may possibly be like the Elizabethans or the Victorians, she resorts to singling out herself against "the Major; old Bartholomew; Mrs. Swithin" (*BTA* 179). Yet even this separation must fail as the audience fidgets in their understanding that they too can be encompassed in Miss La Trobe's play. Accordingly, Miss La Trobe's desire to expose the audience to "present time reality" (*BTA* 179) and force them to experience themselves, results in sudden apprehension of the "reconstruction of the past" and, by extension, the construction of their selves.

As is to be expected, the audience members react negatively to Miss La Trobe's confrontation, and she begins to panic. Rather than realizing that the audience members' distraught response is the only logical one when confronted with their implementation into history, she misjudges the situation and fears that "something [is] going wrong with the experiment" (*BTA* 179). She believes that "illusion fails" (*BTA* 180) as reality intrudes and overpowers her painfully created performance, a failure that she believes could be remedied by shutting out reality. The previous act, however, has caused no problems for the audience, even though the players were clearly identifiable, forgot their lines, and improvised many of the stage props. Moreover, when nature intervenes and the rain shower falls, it relieves the problem rather than exacerbating it. If nature had been an intrusion that needed to be "shut out" (*BTA* 180), the rain shower could not have stabilized the desired atmosphere but would have disrupted it even more. Instead, the rain offers a necessary divergence so that the illusion works through its very failure, suggesting that the problem is rather *too much* illusion. In a sense, one could say, the illusion has become so overpowering as to expose itself and reveal its constructed nature. Consequently, the audience's fidgeting, which Miss La Trobe reads as the defeat of her experiment, in fact constitutes the audience's beginning awareness of its own involvement in history, its own insignificance in the face of historical progression. She fails only insofar as she anticipated her viewers to appreciate these insights when, in fact, the opposite occurs: the audience members are horrified when asked to face themselves. Thus, if her illusions were meant to expose the audience to its own complicity in present day history, she actually more than succeeds since panic and death must be the expected results.

Even the disturbed and confused audience's final attempts to recover any sense of coherence and meaning from the play are destroyed. As the Reverend G. W. Streatfield volunteers to reunite the "scraps, orts and fragments" (*BTA* 192) by trying to interpret the play, a formation of military aircraft disrupts his attempt to recreate a sense of unity and stability.[23] The audience's "representative spokesman; their symbol" (*BTA* 190) is silenced by the symbols of the war to come and, with it, the ultimate destruction of any semblance of order the audience might want to hold onto. Woolf carefully juxtaposes the order of the military planes flying "in perfect formation" (*BTA* 193) to the disoriented, unorganized, lost villagers who anticipate and fear a change they have not (and cannot yet) completely comprehend. Their complete loss of control becomes all the more obvious when contrasted with the other acts of the pageant in which history has become past and can therefore be neatly categorized, conveniently recreated, and scrupulously contained. The final act shatters these clear-cut boundaries as it disrupts the dichotomies of past and present, actors and audience, play and reality.[24]

The audience's panic is a logical reaction to the shattering of the boundaries essential for its self-understanding as historical subjects. Moreover, these transgressions call into question the necessary fictions the viewers have of themselves and their role in history. As their carefully maintained constructions of history

---

[23]See Gillian Beer's "The Island and the Aeroplane: The Case of Virginia Woolf" for a discussion of the central importance of the airplane for England's self-understanding in general and for Woolf in particular.

[24]By extension, this moment not only questions the audience members' perceptions of themselves and their role in history, but the readers' as well. Just as the shattered mirrors disrupt the villagers' perception of themselves as subjects in history, they expose the problems of construction and its failure in general. After all, the novel not only collapses boundaries within the play and between the play and the reality of the text, but also between the inside and outside of the novel. Beth Rigel Daugherty, for example, points out how "[u]sing her Chinese box structure as a mirror, Woolf confronts *us*, her readers, with our similarity to the audience on the lawn" (77). As a result, the novel as a whole performs the same function as the play does within the text: it disrupts the reader's attempt to construct the text and its characters as past and other as it short-circuits the safely maintained distance between text and self. Both thematically as well as structurally, *Between the Acts* exposes the reader to the real at the center and to our repeated attempts at constructing an imaginary that can contain it.

and the subject fail, they face the lack at the center of both. The novel thus suggests that psychological and historical approaches are intimately connected not only through their desire to construct themselves but more so by the very failure of these constructions.[25] In fact, the characters' sensation of uncertainty and loss is caused by an inner feeling of fragmentation and lack as well as by the anticipation of the chaos and confusion of the impending war. The repeated internal intrusions of the real into the narrative correspond to the external intrusions of the war into the peaceful pastoral scene of Pointz Hall.[26] The real cannot simply be seen as something outside ourselves (both as subjects or as nations), but resides at the heart, non-separable from the very center. Accordingly, the real must not only be understood as a psychic phenomenon that describes the lack at the center of the subject but also as a tool to explicate the fissures and inconsistencies within historical constructions on a larger historical plane. In the novel, the glimpses we catch of the real include the traumatic intrusions that threaten the subjects' certainties and consistencies as well as the incessant haunting of war and fascism that pervade the novel. *Between the Acts* thus parallels the external threats of war and all its social and political, personal, and existential consequences with an internal horror that is at the very center of the subject. The novel connects the real at the core of the subject with the real at the fringes of history and thus becomes a text concerned with both history *and* psychology. In it, neither symbolic nor imaginary constructions succeed in holding the real at bay, the violent remainder and reminder of both the lack at the center of the constructions of the subject and the uncontrollability of any construction of history.[27]

[25]Historical and psychological approaches coexist simultaneously in the characters' relationship to their experiences and environment, which, in turn, legitimates the critics' various methods of interpreting the novel.

[26]Since the mirror scene occurs *before* the intrusion of the airplanes, we cannot simply regard the audience's sense of lack as a *result* of the historical context. Instead, the two seem to occur simultaneously; they are interdependent but not in a one-directional causal way.

[27]One incident that invites opposing psychological and historical interpretations is the relationship of Woolf's suicide to her final novel. Most essays discussing the suicide see it either as a reaction to the political situation or regard it as result of her many bouts with depression. Accordingly, critics who tend to employ a historical interpretation understand *Between the Acts* as thematizing the impact of fascism and World War II on Woolf so that her suicide is read as a reaction to nightly bombings and the constant threats of a German invasion which signifies the external threat of fascism, complementary to the inner threats from chauvinist and misogynist politics. Scholars who privilege the personal, psychic reading that situates *Between the Acts* within Woolf's works on the artist figure and the questions of a coherent subject tend to read Woolf's suicide as the

Woolf's changing opinions on the relationship between literature and reality, between her final work of fiction and the life-sustaining provisions offered by Octavia Wilberforce, testify to the importance of remembering the crucial difference between fiction and reality, a distinction emphasized in the novel's proto-postmodern style. Similarly, this paper does not advocate a collapse of the competing theoretical methods: even though psychology and history may evoke

final step in a long progression of depressions and melancholia. Recent representatives of the two approaches can be found in Mark Hussey's collection *Virginia Woolf and War*, on the one hand, and Susan M. Kenney and Daniel Ferrer, on the other. My reading of *Between the Acts* offers an interpretation which bridges the gap between these mutually exclusive biographical approaches to her suicide; the real becomes the link between Woolf's final novel and her suicide.

In "A Sketch of the Past" Virginia Woolf confesses how she wrote *To the Lighthouse* as an endeavor to work through the trauma of her mother's death, to organize her thoughts and feelings and exorcise the ghost of her mother, the "angel in the house" (cf. *MOB* 81). If we consider writing as an attempt to order and construct life, then the constant intrusion of the real in her last work seems to imply the failure of this construction. The war that encroaches upon the pageant play and the pastoral scene in the English countryside also intrudes upon Woolf's life, an intrusion she may have warded off for a short time by recalling the time before the war as coherent and organized. Ultimately, however, her project fails as the text cannot hold and most certainly cannot organize the world and allow its author to exert control over her environment or even her own destiny. Her suicide at the conclusion of her novel may indicate both frustration with this loss of control and a final endeavor to maintain such control. In either case, the timing of her suicide suggests an intimate connection between her last attempt to create and control a fictional world and her final act of taking her own life.

What complicates the issue even further is the fact that Woolf left *Between the Acts* unrevised upon her death. Even though she considered the novel's publication, she planned further revisions (*L6* 482, 486), raising the question of whether her refusal to regard the novel as finished served to conceal the insight that the text itself was incompletable. By seeing it as unfinished, she could ignore the much more unsettling understanding that *Between the Acts* was in fact complete in its very failure of completion. If the gaps and fissures in the text are not read as idiosyncrasies of a yet to be finished draft, *Between the Acts* becomes Woolf's final—and failed—attempt to control the real via symbolic and imaginary creations. We cannot decide whether she left the text unfinished and to be revised as she claims in her letter or whether she realized the unfinishability of the text. We can say, however, that her last novel is not important *in spite* of the gaps, fissures, and inconsistencies but rather *because* of them. Whether it was the real of History or the distress of her recurring melancholia that overshadowed her novel, *Between the Acts* suggests that Virginia Woolf no longer admitted the easy comfort of pure constructedness but, instead, was finally faced with the horror of the real.

similar issues and display parallel structures, their particular implementations are different and crucial.[28] At the same time, Woolf's last novel does testify to the significance of not only maintaining both the psychological and historical approach, but also realizing that the two are not independent of one another. As Woolf confronts the audience—and thereby the reader—with the image of the cracked mirrors, she momentarily conflates past and present, outside and inside, fictions and reality in both psychological and historical constructions. What is more, she short circuits carefully maintained theoretical distinctions between psychological and historical approaches to literature by showing how both mirror as well as complement one another. Both historiography and the psychological development of the subject are similar in their quest for ontological and epistemological certainties; their stories resemble one another insofar as both are predicated on the trauma at their centers. Consequently, *Between the Acts* itself faults any critical reading of the novel that restrictively focuses on the psychological or the historical and demands the use of both theoretical frameworks as different yet equally valid and important modes of interpretation.

---

[28]For a thoughtful discussion that acknowledges the similarities while safeguarding the differences between psychological and historical models, see Dominick LaCapra's definition of structural and historical trauma (*History and Memory* 47-8). Whereas the first denotes a psychological caesura fundamental to any subject's development, the second refers to actual traumatic events. Criticizing thinkers who either conflate the two or subsume one under the other (i.e., reading any historical trauma as an instantiation of the subject's psychological development or completely ignoring psychology in favor of historical facts), LaCapra attempts to carefully maintain a balance that does justice both to the intricate workings of the psyche and the often unspeakable experiences endured by victims of trauma.

Works Cited

Abel, Elizabeth. *Virginia Woolf and the Fictions of Psychoanalysis.* U of Chicago P, 1989.

Babcock, Barbara A. "Mud, Mirrors, and Making Up: Liminality and Reflexivity in *Between the Acts.*" *Victor Turner and the Construction of Cultural Criticism.* Ed. Kathleen M. Ashley. Bloomington: Indiana U P, 1990. 86-116.

Baldwin, Dean R. *Virginia Woolf: A Study of the Short Fiction.* Boston: Twayne, 1989.

Beer, Gillian. "*Between the Acts*: Resisting the End." *Virginia Woolf: The Common Ground.* Ann Arbor: U of Michigan P, 1996. 125-148.

——. "The Island and the Aeroplane: the Case of Virginia Woolf." *Nation and Narration.* Ed. Homi Bhabha. London: Routledge, 1990. 265-90. Rpt. *Virginia Woolf: The Common Ground.* Ann Arbor: U of Michigan P, 1996. 149-178.

Brownstein, Marilyn. "Postmodern Language and the Perpetuation of Desire." *Twentieth Century Literature* 31.1 (Spring 1985): 73-88.

Caughie, Pamela L. *Virginia Woolf and Postmodernism: Literature in Quest and Question of Itself.* Urbana: U of Illinois P, 1991.

Clarke, Stuart N. "The Horse with a Green Tail." *Virginia Woolf Miscellany* 34 (Spring 1990): 3-4.

Copjec, Joan. *Read My Desire: Lacan against the Historicists.* Cambridge: MIT Press, 1994.

De Certeau, Michel. *The Writing of History.* New York: Columbia U P, 1988.

Daugherty, Beth Rigel. "Face to Face with 'Ourselves'" in Virginia Woolf's *Between the Acts.*" Eds. Mark Hussey and Vara Neverow-Turk. *Virginia Woolf: Themes and Variations: Selected Papers from the Second Annual Conference on Virginia Woolf.* New York: Pace U P, 1993. 76-82.

Deiman, Werner J. "History, Pattern, and Continuity in Virginia Woolf." *Contemporary Literature* 15 (1974): 49-66.

DiBattista, Maria. *Virginia Woolf's Major Novels: The Fables of Anon.* New Haven: Yale U P, 1980.

Ferrer, Daniel. *Virginia Woolf and the Madness of Language.* London: Routledge, 1990.

Foucault, Michel. *The Order of Things: An Archaeology of the Human Sciences.* New York: Vintage, 1973.

Hotho-Jackson, Sabine. "Virginia Woolf on History: Between Tradition and Modernity." *Forum for Modern Language Studies* 27.4 (1991): 293-313.

Hussey, Mark. "'"I" Rejected; "We" Substituted': Self and Society in *Between the Acts*." *Reading and Writing Women's Lives: A Study of the Novel of Manners*. Eds. Bege K. Bowers and Barbara Brothers, Ann Arbor: U of Michigan P, 1990: 141-52. Rpt. *Virginia Woolf: Critical Assessments*. Vol. 4. Ed. Eleanor McNees. Mountfield: Helm, 1994. 242-53.

——. Ed. *Virginia Woolf and War: Fiction, Reality, and Myth*. Syracuse: Syracuse U P, 1991. 225-45.

——. and Vara Neverow-Turk. Eds. *Virginia Woolf Miscellanies: Proceedings of the First Annual Conference on Virginia Woolf*. New York: Pace U P, 1992.

Jackson, Tony E. *The Subject of Modernism: Narrative Alterations in the Fiction of Eliot, Conrad, Woolf, and Joyce*. Ann Arbor: U of Michigan P, 1994.

Johnston, Judith L. "The Remediable Flaw: Revisioning Cultural History in *Between the Acts*." *Virginia Woolf and Bloomsbury: A Centenary Celebration*. Ed. Jane Marcus. Bloomington: Indiana U P, 1987. 253-77.

Joplin, Patricia Klindienst. "The Authority of Illusion: Feminism and Fascism in Virginia Woolf's *Between the Acts*." *South Central Review* 6.2 (Summer 1989): 88-104.

Kenney, Susan. "Two Endings: Virginia Woolf's Suicide and *Between the Acts*." *University of Toronto Quarterly* 44 (Summer 1975): 265-89. Rpt. *Virginia Woolf: Critical Assessments*. Vol. 4. Ed. Eleanor McNees. Mountfield: Helm, 1994. 203-25.

LaCapra, Dominick. *History and Criticism*. Ithaca: Cornell U P, 1985.

——. *History, Politics, and the Novel*. Ithaca: Cornell U P, 1987.

——. *History and Memory after Auschwitz*. Ithaca: Cornell U P, 1998.

Lacan, Jacques. "The Mirror Stage as Formative of the Function of the I as Revealed in Psychoanalytic Experience." *Écrits: A Selection*. Trans. Alan Sheridan. New York: Norton, 1977. 1-7.

——. *The Seminar of Jacques Lacan: Book I, Freud's Papers on Technique 1953-54*. Ed. Jacques-Alain Miller. Trans. John Forrester. New York: Norton, 1988.

——. *The Four Fundamental Concepts of Psycho-Analysis*. Ed. Jacques-Alain Miller. Trans. Alan Sheridan. New York: Norton, 1977.

Laurence, Patricia. "The Facts and Fugue of War: From *Three Guineas* to *Between the Acts*." *Virginia Woolf and War: Fiction, Reality, and Myth*. Ed. Mark Hussey. Syracuse: Syracuse U P, 1991. 225-45.

Lee, Hermione. "A Burning Glass: Reflection in Virginia Woolf." *Virginia Woolf: A Centenary Perspective*. Ed. Eric Warner. New York: St. Martin's P, 1984. 12-27.

Marder, Herbert. "Virginia Woolf's 'Conversion': *Three Guineas*, 'Pointz Hall' and *Between the Acts*." *Journal of Modern Literature* 14.4 (Spring 1988): 465-80.

McWirther, David. "The Novel, the Play, and the Book: *Between the Acts* and the Tragicomedy of History." *ELH* 60.3 (Fall 1993): 782-812.

Minow-Pinkney, Makiko. *Virginia Woolf and the Problem of the Subject*. New Brunswick: Rutgers UP, 1987.

Schneider, Karen. "Of Two Minds: Woolf, the War and *Between the Acts*." *Journal of Modern Literature* 16.1 (Summer 1989): 93-112.

Scott, Bonnie Kime. *Refiguring Modernism: Postmodern Feminist Readings of Woolf, West, and Barnes*. Bloomington: Indiana U P, 1995.

Sears, Sallie. "Theater of War: Virginia Woolf's *Between the Acts*." *Virginia Woolf: A Feminist Slant*. Ed. Jane Marcus. Lincoln: U of Nebraska P, 1983. 212-34.

Squier, Susan. "Mirroring and Mothering: Reflections on the Mirror Encounter Metaphor in Virginia Woolf's Works." *Twentieth Century Studies* 27.3 (1981): 272-88.

Waugh, Patricia. *Feminine Fictions: Revisiting the Postmodern*. London: Routledge, 1989.

White, Hayden. *The Content of the Form: Narrative Discourse and Historical Representation*. Baltimore: Johns Hopkins U P, 1987.

———. *Tropics of Discourse: Essays in Cultural Criticism*. Baltimore: Johns Hopkins U P, 1978.

Woolf, Virginia. *A Room of One's Own*. London: Grafton, 1977.

———. *Between the Acts*. New York: Harcourt Brace, 1941.

———. *The Diary of Virginia Woolf*. Vol. 5: 1936-1941. Ed. Anne Olivier Bell. London: Hogarth, 1984.

———. "The Lady in the Looking-Glass: A Reflection." *The Complete Shorter Fiction of Virginia Woolf*. Ed. Susan Dick. London: Hogarth, 1985. 215-19.

———. *The Letters of Virginia Woolf*. Vol. VI: 1936-1941. Ed. Nigel Nicolson and Joanne Trautmann. New York: Harcourt Brace, 1980.

———. *Mrs. Dalloway*. New York: Harcourt Brace, 1925.

———. "A Sketch of the Past." *Moments of Being*. Ed. Jeanne Schulkind. New York: Harcourt Brace, 1976. 61-137.

———. *Three Guineas*. New York: Harcourt Brace, 1938.

Zwerdling, Alex. "*Between the Acts* and the Coming of War." *Novel* 10 (Spring 1977): 220-36.

Zizek, Slavoj. *The Sublime Object of Ideology*. London: Verso, 1989.

Orlando on her Mind?
An Unpublished Letter from Virginia Woolf to Lady Sackville*

David Porter

Although as early as March 1927 Virginia Woolf was thinking ahead to the work that would become *Orlando*,[1] it is not until September 20 of that year that she suggests a more specific vision of where these preliminary musings will in fact lead:

> One of these days... I shall sketch here, like a grand historical picture, the outlines of all my friends... There may be something in this idea. It might be a way of writing the memoirs of one's own times during peoples lifetimes. It might be a most amusing book. The question is how to do it. Vita should be Orlando, a young nobleman... & it should be truthful; but fantastic. (*D*3 156-57)

Within just over two weeks, she has fleshed out the idea considerably, so much so that her diary entry of October 5 describes "a biography beginning in the year 1500 & continuing to the present day, called Orlando: Vita; only with a change about from one sex to another." Four days later, on October 9, Woolf writes a long letter to Vita, toward the end of which she for the first time broaches the idea to her hero/ine-to-be:

> [I] dipped my pen in the ink, and wrote these words, as if automatically, on a clean sheet: Orlando: A Biography... But listen; suppose Orlando turns out to be Vita; and its all about you and the lusts of your flesh and the lure of your mind...

---

*This article has benefited from the wise counsel and assistance of Tom Lewis, Louise DeSalvo, and Mark Hussey, and it is a pleasure to record my gratitude to them here. My warm thanks also to my wife, Helen Porter, whose gift of the Woolf letter almost made it worth turning 60. And like all students of Virginia Woolf, I am deeply indebted to *The Diary of Virginia Woolf*, ed. Anne Olivier Bell (New York 1977-84); and *The Letters of Virginia Woolf*, ed. Nigel Nicolson and Joanne Trautmann, (New York 1975-80).

[1] See especially her diary entry of March 14: "It struck me, vaguely, that I might write a Defoe narrative for fun. Suddenly between twelve & one I conceived a whole fantasy to be called "The Jessamy Brides"... Everything is to be tumbled in pell mell... No attempt is to be made to realise the character. Sapphism is to be suggested. Satire is to be the main note—satire & wildness... For the truth is I feel the need of an escapade

Within another two weeks—about a month after the first diary entry—she is totally immersed: "I have done nothing, nothing, nothing else for a fortnight; & am launched somewhat furtively but with all the more passion upon Orlando: A Biography" (*D*3 161).

On September 20, the same day that Virginia first mentions "Orlando" in her diary, she also wrote the following letter to Vita's mother, Lady Sackville. The letter, now in my possession, is published here with the permission of the Woolf estate:

Monks House, Rodmell, Lewes, Sussex.
20th Sept. 1927

My dear Lady Sackville,

I hope you don't mind my typing, as my hand writing is getting illegible. I was very glad to hear from you, as I enjoy your letters very much, and can make up a picture of you writing them which is I am sure exactly like you and extremely charming. About Vitas new book—I will certainly do my best to make her choose the title you want—it is a very good idea, I think; but as far as I know she has not yet begun to write it. She has only just finished Mrs Aphra Behn.[2] But her her energy is such that I have no doubt that she will start another instantly; and I shall remember your wishes and drop them tactfully into her ears.

I do hope you are better. It sounds very amusing, living at the Metropole. May I suggest that you should occupy your leisure, if you have any, in writing your Memoirs—not for Heinemann, but for the Hogarth Press? Nothing could be more interesting. But no doubt you will think me impertinent; so I will instantly stop with many thanks and best wishes. We would publish it with lots of pictures.

Your affectionate
Virginia Woolf

---

after these serious poetic experimental books whose form is always so closely considered. I want to kick up my heels & be off." For a useful survey of even earlier experiences that found their way into *Orlando*, see Quentin Bell, *Virginia Woolf. A Biography* (New York 1972), vol. 2, 132.

[2]In an August 16 letter, Vita told Woolf that she had just finished her biography of Aphra Behn (*The Letters of Vita Sackville-West to Virginia Woolf*, ed. Louise DeSalvo and Mitchell A. Leaska [New York 1985] 222); the "new book" to which Woolf refers is probably *Twelve Days*, on which Vita began working soon thereafter.

Monks House, Rodmell, Lewes, Sussex.
20th Sept. 1927

My dear Lady Sackville,

I hope you dont mind my typing, as my hand writing is getting illegible. I was very glad to hear from you, as I enjoy your letters very much, and can make up a picture of you writing them which is I am sure exactly like you and extremely charming.
About Vitas new book-- I will certainly do my best to make her choose the title you want--it is a very good idea, I think; but as far as I know she has not yet begun to write it. She has only just finished Mrs Aphra Behn. But her her energy is such that I have no doubt that she will start another instantly; and I shall remember your wishes and drop them tactfully into her ears.

    I do hope you are better. It sounds very amusing, living at the Metropole. May I suggest that you should occupy your leisure, if you have any, in writing your Memoirs--not for Heinemann, but for the Hogarth Press? Nothing could be more interesting. But no doubt you will think me impertinent; so I will instantly stop with many thanks and best wishes. We would publish it with lots of pictures.

                      Your affectionate
                             Virginia Woolf.

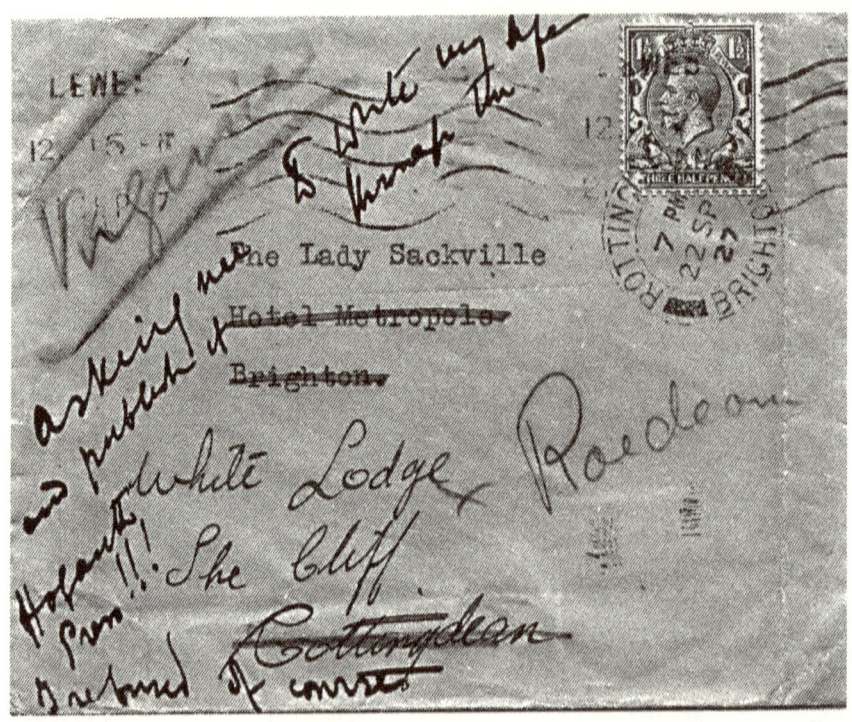

Accompanying the letter when it came to me was a brief note, dated 3 October 1982, from Nigel Nicolson to a previous owner of the letter. It reads in part as follows:

> Here is a small house-guest present. It is a letter from Virginia Woolf to my grandmother... It is not of any great interest, except to show that Virginia, in her pursuit of copy for the Hogarth Press, would make the rashest suggestions. If the illiterate, crazy old lady which Lady S. had become in 1927 had accepted Virginia's offer, what would the Press have done with the nonsense she produced?

Mr. Nicolson was certainly in a better position than I to assess the significance of this letter, and he is certainly right in noting with some amusement Woolf's obsession with finding material for the Hogarth Press. But the precise conjunction of this September 20, 1927 letter with the diary entry in which she first mentions *Orlando* leads me to wonder whether the letter, and Woolf's motive in writing it, are not in fact more interesting than Nicolson suggests.

By September of 1927 Woolf knew Lady Sackville well from her several years of interaction with Vita and her family. She and Lady Sackville had occasionally exchanged letters, and at one point, probably early in 1927, Lady Sackville had sent Woolf "about 20 pages in pencil about her miseries and loves and houses and servants and heart and daughter and secretary and Ethel Smyth and so on."[3] Woolf had also experienced, albeit indirectly, Lady Sackville's occasional irrational fits of temper. In July 1927, for instance, she wrote Vita that she was "outraged by your mother's habits," referring to a recent occasion on which Lady Sackville had kept Vita "up until 6 a.m. abusing everybody and pretending to be desperately ill."[4] And a March 1927 letter to Vita suggests Woolf's own interest in keeping on the right side of this emotionally unpredictable woman:

> Your mother writes me long letters on slips of paper with holes through the corners about love and death and you and Ebury Street and money. I answer suitably—rather more 19th than 18th Century now: profuse, romantic. Imagine us prancing and caracolling together; but like a pair of courting butterflies, never coming very close together.[5]

Given this background, it seems entirely likely that when on September 20, 1927, Woolf first committed to paper her inspiration that "Vita should be Orlando" she also imagined the reaction such a casting would elicit from Lady Sackville. As a gesture toward maintaining her cordial, if uneasy, "courting dance" with Vita's mother, and toward enlisting Lady Sackville as collaborator, not adversary, she wrote on the same day the warm letter we have here transcribed, with its chatty comments about Vita and her mother, and its concluding suggestion that Lady Sackville consider writing her memoirs for the Hogarth Press. One even wonders if Woolf's specific proposal may not owe something to the 20-page miscellany she had received from Lady Sackville earlier that year, as well as to the highly personal tenor of other more recent letters from her.

Woolf's subsequent letters and diary entries contain no indication that Lady Sackville answered the September 20 letter, nor does Woolf again mention the possibility of Lady Sackville writing her memoirs for the Hogarth Press. One suspects that this suggestion was a one-time effort on Woolf's part—and that when it elicited no response, she did not repeat it. We do know that her attempt

---

[3]Letter, January? 1927, to Edward Sackville-West (*L*3 316).

[4]Letter, 8? July 1927, to V. Sackville-West, and editors' note on this letter (*L*3 396). Her letter of 1 December 1926, to V. Sackville-West, alludes to an even earlier outburst. For the background, see Mitchell Leaska, *Granite and Rainbow. The Hidden Life of Virginia Woolf* (New York 1998) 277.

[5]Letter, 27 March 1927 (*L*3 353). A letter to Violet Dickinson, probably written on the

to forestall Lady Sackville's anticipated negative response to *Orlando* was not successful. While Vita and other members of her family loved and praised the book, Lady Sackville abhorred it. On October 14, 1928, she wrote Woolf, "You have written some beautiful phrases in Orlando, but probably you do not realise how *cruel* you have been. And the person who inspired the Book, has been crueller still." There is also the familiar story of how Lady Sackville pasted a photograph of Woolf into her copy of *Orlando* and wrote alongside it, "The awful face of a mad woman whose successful mad desire is to separate people who care for each other. I loathe this woman for having changed my Vita and taken her away from me."[6]

Though we know of no response from Lady Sackville to Woolf's letter, there is one piece of evidence which suggests her reaction—the small blue envelope in which it was originally mailed to her, and which still accompanies the letter. On this envelope, in a large and determined scrawl, Lady Sackville has written, "Virginia Asking me to write my life and publish it through the Hogarth Press!!! I refused of course." There is no way of determining when Lady Sackville wrote these words: when the letter arrived, perhaps suspecting Woolf of ulterior motives and wishing to maintain her distance? or at a later date, when the breach over *Orlando* was fully in the open? Either way, Woolf's hope to win her over in advance clearly failed, as Woolf herself realized well before the event. By October of 1928, just days before the publication of *Orlando*, she could write Vita about "that damned old witch" without even bothering to name Lady Sackville (*L*3 541). How far this is from the "courting butterflies" she described in March 1927, or the honeyed phrases of her letter of September 1927!

---

same day, describes Lady Sackville's letters in similar terms: "Lady S. writes me pages and pages—about secretaries, Ebury Street, Vita, death, life, food, money—in pencil on narrow pages with a hole through them. . ."(*L*3 355). Woolf's efforts to please Lady Sackville were ongoing. Five weeks earlier, on 16 February 1927, she had written Vita that she and Leonard had just received one of Lady Sackville's "most gracious letters...to which I have answered, suitably, I hope, in deep humility"(*L*3 329). It was a mode that Woolf had long since practiced in her letters to Lady Sackville: see, e.g., her letter of 7 March 1926 (*L*3 246).

[6]Both passages are cited in *L*3 548 n2. Harold Nicolson's reaction was hightly favorable (see loc. cit., n. 1), as was Vita's (see her October 11, 1928 letter to Virginia, quoted in the Appendix to the same volume, 573-575).

We could leave matters here, but it seems worth speculating in a bit more depth as to why *Orlando* so offended Lady Sackville.[7] On one level she had no right to blame Woolf and *Orlando* for the breach between herself and Vita, for it was a breach to which she herself had contributed significantly, especially in the spring and summer preceding the publication of *Orlando* in October 1928. Here is Woolf's account of one episode from this period:

> ...Vita has had a terrific culminating and final scene with Lady Sackville in a solicitor's office, with witnesses to take down all insults—The woman seems utterly mad, called her liar thief and harlot, cut her pearl necklace in half, and pocketed the twelve best stones, and then announced that she would consider her dead henceforward and stop every penny of her allowance. Vita swears she is going to earn her own living by her pen. (*L*3 487 to Clive Bell)[8]

At a deeper level, though, there is some truth to Lady's Sackville's claim that *Orlando* had taken Vita from her, even that *Orlando* contained a measure of cruelty on Woolf's part.[9] Especially perceptive is her comment that Woolf probably did not realize how cruel she had been, for in fact the "cruelty" grew intrinsically from the book itself: given Woolf's goals for *Orlando*, and her success in achieving them, the book could only be "cruel," could only open gulfs among Woolf, Vita, and Lady Sackville.

To understand how this was so we must return briefly to Woolf's activities in the months immediately before her September 20, 1927 diary entry and letter, a detour in which Vita's husband, Harold Nicolson, plays a major—if largely unintentional—role in helping Woolf see what *Orlando* might become. In a June 15, 1927 letter to Nicolson, Woolf commented warmly on his recently published book, *Some People*:

> ...I must scribble a line in haste to say how absolutely delightful I think it—how I laughed out loud to myself again and again. Yet at the same time it is rather serious—I can't make out how you combine the advantages of fact and

---

[7]This final section builds on conversations with Professor Tom Lewis of the Skidmore College English Department, who suggested the relevance of Nicolson's *Some People* to *Orlando* and encouraged me to probe more deeply into the reasons behind the breach between Woolf and Lady Sackville. Needless to say, I take full responsibility for any errors of fact or interpretation that remain.

[8]Woolf's letter of May 9 to Vanessa Bell adds further details. Earlier letters also suggest the deteriorating relationship between Vita and her mother—31 January 1928, to Clive Bell; 11 February 1928 to Vanessa Bell; 12 February [1928] to Edward Sackville-West; 31 March 1928 to V. Sackville-West.

[9]On Virginia's "cruelty," see Hermione Lee, *Virginia Woolf* (New York 1997) 515ff.

fiction as you do. I am also jealous—I cant help it—that all these things should have happened to you, not to me.

Some People remained very much on Woolf's mind in the months immediately following this letter, since, as she mentions to Nicolson in a September 13 letter, she had agreed to review it for the *New York Herald Tribune*. Her review, entitled "The New Biography," appeared there on October 30 and commented on the very qualities she had praised in her letter—the book's blend of humor and seriousness, of fact and fiction:

> For here he has devised a method of writing about people and about himself as though they were at once real and imaginary. . . *Some People* is not fiction because it has the substance, the reality of truth. It is not biography because it has the freedom, the artistry of fiction. . .Mr. Nicolson laughs. He laughs at Lord Curzon; he laughs at the Foreign Office; he laughs at himself. And since his laughter is the laughter of the intelligence it has the effect of making us take the people he laughs at seriously.[10] (*CE4* 232)

Woolf recognized that Nicolson's deft mingling of fiction with fact in *Some People*, and his lightness of touch, had been essential in enabling him to probe beneath surface appearances, beyond mere fact, and to attain an impact that was deeply serious. In turn, her thinking about *Some People* contributed directly to the evolution of *Orlando*. Her June 13, 1927 letter to Nicolson came in the middle of that period when she was moving from her March musings about "The Jessamy Brides" to her sudden realization in September that "Vita should be Orlando." In addition, her admiring description of what Nicolson had achieved in *Some People* foreshadows the mixture of humor and seriousness, of fact and fiction, that she herself would strive for in *Orlando*, the "new biography" to which Nicolson's book had helped point the way.[11]

---

[10]Nigel Nicolson calls *Some People* his father's "most original book" and refers to its "series of confrontations, some real, some imaginary" and its "amused, detached analysis of the nudging and jostling of people in their relations with one another" (*Portrait of a Marriage* [Chicago 1973] 212-213). Woolf's positive assessment of *Some People* contrasts with her negative response to Nicolson's earlier biographies of Tennyson (Letter, 3 August 1923, to Pernel Strachey) and Byron (Letter, 21 March 1924, to Lytton Strachey).

[11]Woolf's essay on *Some People* is but one of several from this period in which she discusses biography. She and Leonard were also about to publish Nicolson's *The Development of English Biography*, of which Woolf wrote to Nicolson on 19 February 1928, "...directly I am allowed a copy, I'm going to read Nicolson's Biography."

That she admired *Some People* is not surprising. Nicolson's down-to-earth honesty, and his ability to probe beneath the surface,[12] were qualities Woolf sought in her own writing, whether in her creation of a new fictional style in *Jacob's Room, Mrs. Dalloway*, and *To the Lighthouse*, or in the brief phrase she wrote in her diary on September 20, as *Orlando* first began to take shape in her mind: "It should be truthful; but fantastic." But this very goal returns us immediately to the gulfs *Orlando* was to create, for such honesty, such probing, not only reveals the truth but can also cause pain.

Vita had already recognized this implicit danger in her comments on *To the Lighthouse*: "Darling," she wrote Woolf, "it makes me afraid of you. Afraid of your penetration and loveliness and genius" (Letter, 12 May 1927). And Woolf herself, just days after she first revealed to Vita her plans for *Orlando*, and Vita's place in those plans, openly (if humorously) flaunted its potentially threatening revelations with reference to a flirtation in which Vita was currently engaged: "If you've given yourself to [Mary] Campbell, I'll have no more to do with you, and *so it shall be written, plainly, for all the world to read in Orlando*" (Letter, 13 October 1927; emphasis mine).

Mitchell Leaska has commented tellingly on the impact of *Orlando*'s naked truthfulness on Vita and her relationship with Virginia:

> If Virginia's penetration into the human heart in *To the Lighthouse* had made Vita "afraid" of her, we must try to imagine how unshielded she felt now, with *Orlando* staring at the world from the windows of bookshops. Virginia had been relentless in her search and brilliant in her exposition. Indeed the entire creation had about it a kind of ruthless virtuosity. Now there was nothing, Vita realized, either too private or too personal that she could withhold from Virginia, and with that realization, her feeling for her began once more to change. Toward Virginia the artist, Vita's adoration increased, but so did the distance that would now further separate them.[13]

---

[12] Cf. her review: "So it would seem as if one of the great advantages of the new school to which Mr. Nicolson belongs is the lack of pose, humbug, solemnity"; later she speaks of Nicolson's "freedom from pose, from sentimentality, from illusion" (*CE*4 232, 233). Woolf must have seen at least one chapter of *Some People* well before its publication: "Jeanne d'Hénaut," the essay that was to become its fifth chapter, was published by the Woolfs in November 1924 in a small, private edition, apparently for Nicolson's use as a holiday gift for family and friends. Only 55 copies were printed, and the small book remains one of the rarest publications of the Hogarth Press.

[13] DeSalvo/Leaska, *Letters of Sackville-West to Woolf* 36.

If *Orlando*'s penetrating truthfulness hurt even Vita, it is easy to imagine its impact on Lady Sackville. Not only did Woolf's book expose to the world, often with only transparent encoding, Vita's "lusts of [the] flesh"; it also brought the public even into Knole itself. That its tone, like that of *Some People*, was jesting and light-hearted must only have made it seem the more cruel. And Lady Sackville's claim that Woolf had "changed my Vita and taken her away from me" is true, even profound, to a degree that probably she herself did not recognize: *Orlando*'s mix of fact and fiction, of humor and seriousness, did indeed forever change Vita—not only for Lady Sackville, for Woolf, and for Vita herself, but for anyone who read *Orlando*; and once the book was published, its transformed Vita—and with her Knole and the Sackvilles—belonged not to Lady Sackville but to the world, and to the author of *Orlando*.

It is a lovely paradox that at the same time as *Orlando* was creating these painful separations it was also helping bridge a painful gulf between Vita and her ancestral home:

> With Lord Sackville's death in January of this year—1928, the year of the book's publication—Vita was made to face the one reality she dreaded most: the permanent loss of Knole... That monumental loss and all it represented to Vita was monstrous. With the birth of Orlando, however, its edge had been dulled. For in the deepest symbolic sense, Knole had been restored to her. Their pasts had been reunited. "You made me cry with your passages about Knole, you wretch," Vita wrote to its maker.[14]

The impact of this "restoration" is apparent in Vita's decision soon after the publication of *Orlando* to begin her own novel set in Knole, *The Edwardians*. It is even more telling that in 1958, seventeen years after Woolf's death, *Orlando* still remained a touchstone as Vita prepared a reissue of her 1922 book, *Knole and the Sackvilles*.[15] In an elegiac new appendix dealing with the passing of Knole from her family to the National Trust, Vita quotes from *Orlando*, commenting that Woolf "has put her fingers on the still living truth of this massive anachronism," and she concludes this appendix with yet another reference to the same *Orlando* passage.[16] Moreover, as Professor Tom Lewis has pointed out to

---

[14]DeSalvo/Leaska, *Letters of Sackville-West to Woolf* 35.

[15]Fourth Edition, published in 1958 by Ernest Benn Limited. In the Foreword to this new edition, Vita writes, "The resetting of the type in this new edition in 1958 gives me the opportunity of incorporating a few alterations, corrections, and additions, and also some material which has come to my notice over the course of years."

[16]Vita quotes Woolf on the people of the past who have made Knole what it is: "...the obscure 'Richards, Johns, Annes, Elizabeths, not one of whom has left a token of

me, Vita also adds to the book itself two pages dealing with the possibility that Shakespeare visited Knole, a topic missing from the original *Knole and the Sackvilles* but memorably handled in *Orlando*.[17] And just as *Orlando* opens with the hero indulging his fantasies in the attic of Knole, so at the start of her new section Vita casts herself in a similar role:

> I often entertained wild dreams that some light might be thrown on the Shakespearean problem by a discovery of letters or documents at Knole. What more fascinating or chimerical a speculation for a literary-minded child breathing and absorbing the atmosphere of that house? I used to tell myself stories of finding Shakespeare's manuscripts up in the attics...[18]

Orlando is powerful testimony to Aristotle's famous observation that fiction can sometimes be more truthful than history. For Vita, who had so feared Woolf's penetrating eye, the probing vision of Woolf's fictionalized history ironically was to provide a new and lasting hold on her ancestral home; for Lady Sackville, however, it brought only pain and separation. One wonders if even on September 20, 1927, when she wrote "Vita should be Orlando," Woolf, with a percipience informed by *Some People*, recognized that the truthfulness she sought in her

---

himself behind him, yet all, working together with their spades and their needles, their love-making and their child-bearing, have left this'" (1958 edition, 215, cf. *Orlando* [London 1928] 98). As Vita concludes the appendix, in effect transferring Knole to its new owners, she writes: "[L]et us suggest that some of the grace of another age may seep into the consciousness of the million wandering freely among these ancient courts, and that the new young Richards, Johns, Annes, and Elizabeths... may find enrichment in the gift of something so old, so courteous, and so lovely" (1958 edition, 217-218).

[17]The addition comes at the end of Chapter III, "Knole in the Reign of Queen Elizabeth." Vita even expands the index of the 1958 edition, including between the entries "Shadwell" and "Smith" of the 1922 edition a new entry, "Shakespeare."

[18]*Knole and the Sackvilles*, 1958 edition, 57-58.

"memoirs"[19] had the capacity not only to wound Vita's mother but even to "take" Vita and Knole from her. Is that why on that same day she wrote Lady Sackville, offering her the opportunity through her memoirs to create her own blend of fact and fiction—and thereby to keep Vita, Knole, and the Sackvilles for herself?

[19]Cf. Woolf's September 20 diary entry—just before her mention of Vita and "Orlando": "There may be something in this idea. It might be a way of writing the memoirs of one's own times during peoples lifetimes. It might be a most amusing book." Clearly "memoirs," whether her own or Lady Sackville's, were on Virginia's mind that day. It is tempting to see further links yet between Woolf's plans and her letter to Lady Sackville—e.g., between Woolf's comment about her "memoirs" (i.e., *Orlando*), "It might be a most amusing book," and her comment that same day to Lady Sackville about hers, "Nothing could be more interesting"; or between Woolf's concluding promise to Lady Sackville, "We would publish it with lots of pictures," and her realization soon thereafter that *Orlando* too would need illustrations (see her 13 October 1927 letter to Vita: "I must come down and see you, if only to choose some pictures").

Guide to Library Special Collections

This guide updates the information in volume 6.

Name of Collection: The Beinecke Rare Book and Manuscript Library

Contact: Vincent Giroud, Curator of Modern Books and Manuscripts
Patricia Willis, Curator of American Literature

Address: Yale University Library
P.O. Box 208240
New Haven, CT 06520-8240

Hours: Mon.-Fri. 8:30AM-5PM

Access Requirements: Register at the circulation desk on each visit.

Holdings Relevant To Woolf: General Collection includes autograph manuscript of "Notes on Oliver Goldsmith." Comments on Edward Gibbon, William Beckford Collection. Letters from Virginia Woolf in the Bryher Papers, the Louise Morgan and Otto Theis Papers, and the Rebecca West Papers. Related material: 41 letters from Vita Sackville-West to Violet Trefusis; files relating to Robert Manson Myers's *From Beowulf to Virginia Woolf* in the Edmond Pauker Papers.

Yale Collection of American Literature includes typewritten manuscripts of "The Art of Walter Sickert," "Augustine Birrell," "Aurora Leigh," "How Should One Read a Book?" "Letter to a Young Poet," "The Novels of Turgenev," "Street Haunting." Dial/Scofield Thayer Papers: manuscripts of "The Lives of the Obscure," "Miss Ormerod," and "Mrs. Dalloway in Bond Street." Letters from Virginia Woolf in the William Rose Benet Papers, the Benet Family Correspondence, the Henry Seidel Canby Papers, the Seward Collins Papers, the Dial/Scofield Thayer Papers, and the *Yale Review* archive. Material relating to translations of Woolf in the Thornton Wilder papers. Related material: Clive Bell, "Virginia Woolf" (Dial/Scofield Thayer Papers); 43 letters from

Leonard Woolf to Helen McAfee (*Yale Review*); 11 letters from Leonard Woolf to Gertrude Stein.

Name of Collection: The Henry W. and Albert A. Berg Collection of English and American Literature

Contact: Isaac Gewirtz, Curator

Address: New York Public Library, Room 320
Fifth Avenue & 42nd Street
New York, NY 10018

Telephone: 212-930-0802
Fax: 212-930-0079
E-mail: igewirtz@nypl.org

Hours: Tues./Wed. 11AM -5:45PM
Thurs.-Sat. 10AM-5:45PM
Closed Sun., Mon. and legal holidays

Access Requirements: Apply for card of admission at Office of Special Collections, Room 316. Traceable identification required. Undergraduates working on honors theses need letter from faculty advisor.

Restrictions: Virginia Woolf's MSS are now made available on microfilm. N.B. *All the Berg's Woolf MSS are on microfilm published by Research Publications and available at many research libraries.*

Holdings Relevant To Woolf: Manuscripts of *Between the Acts, Flush, Jacob's Room, Mrs. Dalloway* (notes and fragments), *Night and Day, To the Lighthouse, The Voyage Out, The Waves, The Years*; 12 notebooks of articles, essays, fiction and reviews, 1924-1940; 36 volumes of diaries; 26 volumes of reading notes; correspondence with Vanessa Bell, Ethel Smyth, Vita Sackville-West and others. Su Hua Ling Chen's Bloomsbury correspondence.

GUIDE TO SPECIAL COLLECTIONS 117

Name of Collection: The British Library Manuscript Collections

Contact: The Manuscripts Librarian

Address: 96 Euston Road
London NW1 2DB
England

Telephone: 0171-412-7513
Fax: 0171-412-7745
E-mail: mss@bl.uk

Hours: Please inquire

Access Requirements: Must be a graduate student and/or over 21. Letter of recommendation recquired from a person in a recognized position, along with proper identification.

Restrictions: Photocopies of selected items available upon receipt of written authorization for photo duplication from the copyright holder.

Holdings Relevant To Woolf: Diaries 1930-1931 (microfilm); Mrs. Dalloway and other writings (1923-1925) three volumes; letter from Leonard Woolf to H. G. Wells (1941); two letters from Virginia Woolf and three letters from Leonard Woolf to John Lehmann (1941); letter written on behalf of Leonard Woolf to S. S. Koteliansky (1946); notebook in Italian kept by Virginia Woolf; notebook of Virginia Stephen (1906-1909); A sketch of the past revised ts (1940); letters from Virginia Woolf in the correspondence files of Lytton and James Strachey; letter from Virginia Woolf to Mildred Massingberd; letter from Virginia Woolf to Harriet Shaw Weaver (1918); letters from Virginia Woolf to S. S. Koteliansky (1923-27); letter from Virginia Woolf to Frances Cornford (1929); letter from Virginia Woolf to Ernest Rhys (1930); correspondence of Virginia Woolf in the Society of

Authors archive (1934-37); letter and postcard from Virginia Woolf to Bernard Shaw (1940); three letters (suicide notes) from Virginia Woolf (1941); two letters from Virginia Woolf and three from Leonard Woolf to John Lehmann (1941).

Collection of RPs ("reserved photo copies"–copies of manuscrips exported, some subject to restrictions).

Recent Acquisitions: "Hyde Park Gate News" 1891-92, 1895 (add. MSS 70725, 70726). Letters of Virginia and Leonard Woolf to Lady Aberconway, 1927-1941. Letter from Virginia Woolf to Frances Cornford.

Name of Collection: Harry Ransom Humanities Research Center

Contact: Research Librarian

Address: The University of Texas at Austin
P.O. Box 7219
Austin, TX 78713-7219

Telephone: 512-471-9119
Fax: 512-471-2899
E-mail: reference@hrc.utexas.edu

Hours: Mon.-Fri. 9AM-5PM
Sat. 9AM-NOON
Closed holidays; intersession Saturdays; one week each in late May and late August.

Access Requirements: Completed manuscript reader's application; current photo identification.

Restrictions: Photocopies of selected items available upon receipt of written authorization for photoduplication from the copyright holder.

GUIDE TO SPECIAL COLLECTIONS 119

Holdings Relevant
To Woolf: The manuscript collection includes the typed manuscript with autograph revisions of *Kew Gardens,* and the typed manuscript and autograph revisions of "Thoughts on Peace in an Air Raid." The Center holds 571 of Woolf's letters, including correspondence to Elizabeth Bowen, Lady Ottoline Morrell, Mary Hutchinson, William Plomer, Hugh Walpole and others. Further mss. relating to Virginia Woolf include letters to her from T. S. Eliot and reviews of her work. A substantial collection of the first British and American editions of Woolf's published works, as well as 130 volumes from Leonard and Virginia Woolf's library and a collection of books published by the Hogarth Press, is also housed. An art collection holds a landscape painting of Virginia's garden and a series of Cockney cartoons in a sketch book, signed "V.W." The center also has extensive holdings of materials related to Leonard Woolf, Ottoline Morrell, Mary Hutchinson, Lytton Strachey, Dora Carrington, E. M. Forster, Clive Bell, Roger Fry, Vanessa Bell, Bertrand Russell, Elizabeth Bowen, William Plomer, Stephen Spender and Hugh Walpole.

Name of Collection: King's College Archive Centre

Contact: Rosalind Moad, Archivist

Address: King's College
Cambridge CB2 1ST

Telephone: 01223-331444
Fax: 01223-331891
E-mail: archivist@kings.cam.ac.uk

Hours: Mon.-Fri. 9:30AM-12:30PM and 1:30PM-5:15PM. *Closed during public holidays and the College's annual periods of closure.*

Access Requirements:	Proof of ID, letter of introduction, appointment in advance.
Holdings Relevant To Woolf:	Woolf MSS and letters: Minute book, written up by Clive Bell, of the meetings of a play-reading society, with cast lists and comments on performances by CB. Dec. 1907-Jan. 1909, Oct. 1914-Feb. 1915. Players included variously Clive & Vanessa Bell, Roger & Margery Fry, Duncan Grant, Walter Lamb, Molly MacCarthy, Adrian & Virginia Stephen, Saxon Sydney-Turner. *Freshwater, A Comedy*—photocopy of editorial typescript prepared from the MSS at Sussex University and Monk's House; photcopy of covering letter from the publisher to "Robert Silvers," 1.29.1976. Papers relating to the Virginia Woolf Centenary Conference held at Fitzwilliam College, Cambridge, 9.20-22.1982. TS with corrections of "Nurse Lugton's Curtain." Typed transcript of R. Fry's memoir of his schooldays. Correspondence with Clive Bell, Julian Bell, Vanessa Bell, Richard Braithwaite, Rupert Brooke, Mrs. Brooke, Katharine Cox, Julian Fry, Roger Fry, John Davy Hayward, J. M. Keynes, Lydia Keynes, Rosamond Lehmann, Charles Mauron, Raymond Mortimer, G. H. W. Rylands, J. T. Sheppard, W. J. H. Sprott, Thoby Stephen, Madge Vaughan. Woolf-related archival collections held: Charleston Papers; Rupert Brooke Papers; E. M. Forster Papers; Roger Fry Papers; J. M. Keynes Papers; J. T. Sheppard Papers; W. J. H. Sprott Papers. Various works of art by Vanessa Bell, Duncan Grant, and Roger Fry, held in various locations around King's College. Access via Domus Bursar's secretary.
Recent Acquisitions:	Roger Fry Papers: sketchbooks, 1880s-1920s. The papers of George Humphrey Wolferstan ('Dadie') Rylands (1902-99).

GUIDE TO SPECIAL COLLECTIONS   121

Name of Collection: Archives and Manuscripts, University of Maryland, College Park, Libraries

Contact: Belth Alvarez, Curator of Literary Manuscripts

Address: University of Maryland Libraries
College Park, MD 20742

Telephone: 310-405-9298
E-mail: ra60@umail.umd.edu
Hours: Mon.-Fri. 10AM-5PM

Access Requirements: Photo ID.

Holdings Relevant to Woolf: Papers of Hope Mirrlees contain five autograph letters and postcards (1919-28) from Virginia Woolf to Mirrlees. Also in the collection are 113 letters from T. S. Eliot to Mirrlees, and three letters from Lady Ottoline Morrell to Mirrlees.

Name of Collection: Monks House Papers/Leonard Woolf Papers/Charleston Papers/Nicolson Papers

Contact: Dorothy Sheridan, Head of Special Collections

Address: University of Sussex Library
Brighton
Sussex BN1 9QL
England

Telephone: 01273-678157
Fax: 01273-678441
E-Mail: Library.Specialcoll@sussex.ac.uk

Hours: By appointment

Access Requirements: Letter, to be received *before* visiting.

Restrictions:	Photocopying strictly controlled.
Holdings Relevant to Woolf:	The University of Sussex holds two large archives relating to Leonard and Virginia Woolf: The Monks House Papers, primarily correspondence and MSS of Virginia Woolf, including the three scrapbooks relating to *Three Guineas*; and The Leonard Woolf Papers, primarily correspondence and other papers of Leonard Woolf. (Monks House Papers are available on microfilm in many research libraries.) The Charleston Papers consist in the main of letters written to or by Clive and Vanessa Bell and Duncan Grant which had accumulated in their home; the library houses Quentin Bell's photocopied set. Also included are c. 900 letters from Maria Jackson to Julia and Leslie Stephen (Charleston Papers Ad. 1); letters from Roger Fry, Maynard Keynes, Lytton Stachey, Virginia Woolf, Vita Sackville-West, E. M. Forster, T. S. Eliot, Frances Partridge and others. The Nicolson Papers complement these three Sussex archives relating to the Bloomsbury Group, and consist of Nigel Nicolson's correspondence relating to his editorial work as principal editor of the six-volume *Letters of Virginia Woolf*, published between 1975 and 1980.
Recent Acquisitions:	The Bell Papers. A. O. Bell's correspondence relating to her editorial work on Virginia Woolf's Diaries. A parallel collection to Nicolson Papers.
Name of Collections:	Archives & Manuscripts
Contact:	Michael Bott, The Archivist
Address:	The University of Reading, The Library, Whiteknights P.O. Box 223 Reading RG6 6AE England

Telephone:	0118-931-8776
Fax:	0118-931-6636
E-mail:	g.m.c.bott@reading.ac.uk

Access Requirements: Appointment needed to consult material. Permission required to consult or copy material in the Hogarth Press and Chatto & Windus collections from Random House, 20 Vauxhall Bridge Road, London SW1V 2SA, UK.

Holdings Relevant to Woolf: Hogarth Press (MS2750): editorial and production correspondence relating to publications of the Press including Woolf's own titles. Production ledgers 1920s-1950s. Correspondence between Leonard Woolf and Stanley Unwin about progress with his collected edition of the works of Freud.
Chatto & Windus (MS2444): small number of letters 1915-25; 1929-31.
George Bell & Sons (MS1640): 5 letters from Leonard Woolf 1930-66.
Routledge (MS1489): Reader's report by Leonard Woolf on George Padmore's "Britannia rules the blacks" (1935); "How Britain rules Africa."
Megroz (MS1979/68): 2 letters from LW, 1926.
Allen & Unwin (MS3282): Correspondence with LW 1923-24; 1939-40; 1943; 1946; 1950-51, including letters concerning a reprint of *Empire and Commerce in Africa*, and concerning ill-founded rumors about the Hogarth press.

Name of Collection: Frances Hooper Collection of Virginia Woolf Books and Manuscripts/Elizabeth Power Richardson Bloomsbury Iconography Collection.

Contact: Karen V. Kukil, Associate Curator of Rare Books

Address:	Mortimer Rare Book Room William Allan Neilson Library Smith College Northampton, MA 01063
Telephone: Fax: E-mail:	413-585-2906 413-585-4486 kkukil@smith.edu
Hours:	Mon.-Fri. 9AM-5PM
Access Requirements:	Appointment to be made with the Curator.
Holdings Relevant to Woolf:	The Hooper Collection emphasizes Woolf as an essayist but also includes many Hogarth Press first editions, limited editions of Woolf's works, and translations. The collection includes page proofs of *Orlando*, *To the Lighthouse*, and *The Common Reader*, corrected by Woolf for the first American editions, a proof copy of *The Waves* that Woolf inscribed to Hugh Walpole, and the proof copies of *The Years* and of *Flush*. The Collection also has one of the deluxe editions of *Orlando* that was printed on green paper. Other items include twenty-two pages of reading notes from 1926, three pages of notes on D. H. Lawrence's *Sons and Lovers*, thirty-three pages of notes for *Roger Fry*, a six-page ms. "As to criticism," a five-page ms. of "The Searchlight," and a fourteen-page ms. of "The Patron and The Crocus." The Hooper Collection also owns 140 letters between Woolf and Lytton Strachey as well as other correspondence, including a 13 February [1921] letter to Katherine Mansfield and ten unpublished letters to Mela and Robert Spira. The Richardson Collection is a working collection of books and materials used by Richardson in preparing her *Bloomsbury Iconography*. It includes

Leslie Stephen's photograph album, ninety-eight original exhibition catalogs dating back to 1929, clippings and photcopies of such items as reviews of early Woolf works, and Bloomsbury material from British *Vogue* of the 1920s. The Collection also has three preliminary pencil drawings by Vanessa Bell for *Flush*.

The Mortimer Rare Book Room also owns Woolf's 1916 Italian ms. notebook and her corrected typescripts of "Reviewing" and "The Searchlight." In addition, there is a 1923 photograph of Woolf at Garsington. The Mortimer Rare Book Room also has a Sylvia Plath Collection that includes eight of Woolf's books from Plath's library, several of which are underlined and annotated, as well as Plath's notes from her undergraduate English 211 class at Smith (1951-2) in which she studied *To the Lighthouse*.

Name of Collection:	Woolf/Hogarth Press/Bloomsbury
Contact:	Robert C. Brandeis
Address:	Victoria University Library 71 Queens Park Crescent E. Toronto M5S 1K7 Ontario Canada
Hours:	Mon.-Fri. 9AM-5PM
Access Requirements:	Prior notification; identification.
Restrictions:	Limited photocopying.
Holdings Relevant to Woolf:	This collection, the most comprehensive of its kind in Canada, contains all the work of Virginia and

Leonard Woolf in various editions, issues, variants and translations; all the books hand printed by Leonard and Virginia Woolf at the Hogarth Press, including many variant issues and bindings, association copies and page proofs; a nearly comprehensive collection of Hogarth Press machine printed books to 1946 (the year Leonard Woolf and the Press joined Chatto & Windus) including presentation copies, signed limited editions, page proofs, variants as well as substantial amounts of ephemera. The collection is also very strong in Bloomsbury art, especially the decorative arts, and contains important examples of Omega Workshops publications and exhibition catalogues. Vanessa Bell correspondence/MSS; Leonard Woolf correspondence; Ritchie family materials and correspondence re: Anne Thackeray Ritchie/Stephen family.

Recent Acquisitions: Vanessa Bell dustwrapper designs for Woolf novels; Quentin Bell correspondence; S. P. Rosenbaum mss. 97 additional items: Ephemera Collection.

Name of Collection: Library of Leonard and Virginia Woolf (Washington S U)

Contact: Laila Miletic-Vejzovic, Head Manuscripts, Archives and Special Collections

Address: Washington State University Libraries
Pullman, WA 99164-5610

URL: www.wsulibs.wsu.edu/holland/masc/masc.htm

Hours: Mon.-Fri. 8:30AM-5PM

Access Requirements: Letter stating nature of research preferred; student or other identification.

Restrictions: Materials must be used in the MASC area under supervision. Photocopying or photographing is permitted only when it will not harm the materials and is permitted by copyright.

Holdings Relevant to Woolf: WSU has the Woolfs' basic working library including many works which belonged to Virginia's father, Sir Leslie Stephen, and other family members. Over 800 titles came from their Sussex home, Monks House, including some works bought at auction soon after Leonard Woolf died in 1969. Later additions include: 1,875 titles from his house in Victoria Square, London; 400 titles from his nephew Cecil Woolf; and over 60 titles from Quentin and Anne Olivier Bell. WSU has been actively collecting: all works in all editions by Virginia; all titles by Leonard; works published by the Woolfs at the Hogarth Press through 1946; books by their friends and associates, especcially those by Bloomsbury authors and about Bloomsbury artists; relevant correspondence and original works of art. Original artwork by Vanessa Bell; scattered letters by Vanessa Bell, E. M. Forster, Roger Fry, Leslie Stephen, Lytton Strachey, and Leonard Woolf. Original artwork by Richard Kennedy for illustrations in his book *A Boy at the Hogarth Press*; scattered letters by Roger Fry, Leslie Stephen, Ethel Smyth, and Leonard Woolf.

Recent Acquisitions: Virginia Woolf's initialed copy of *Cornishiana*; Leonard Woolf's annotated copy of *An Anatomy of Poetry* by A. William-Ellis; Leslie Stephen's copy of *Lapsus Calami and Other Verses*, inscribed by James Kenneth Stephen. Several letters from Virginia Woolf, including two written in 1939 to Ronald Heffer, and a letter to Edward McKnight Kauffer. New in the Hogarth Press Collection are a copy of E. M. Forster's *Anonymity, an Enquiry*, bound in cream paper boards, and what Woolmer calls the third label state of Forster's *The Story of the Siren*.

Name of Collection: Yale Center for British Art

Contact: Elisabeth Fairman, Associate Curator for Rare Books

Address: 1080 Chapel Street
P.O. Box 208280
New Haven, CT 06520-8280

Telephone: 203-432-2814
Fax: 203-432-9695
E-mail: elisabeth.fairman@yale.edu

Hours: Tues.-Fri. 10AM-4:30PM

Restrictions: Permission needed in order to reproduce.

Holdings Relevant
to Woolf: Rare Books Department: 94 letters from Vanessa Bell and Duncan Grant to Sir Kenneth Clark. Prints & Drawings Department: 2 designs by Vanessa Bell and 2 studies by Duncan Grant. Paintings Department: 1 painting by Vanessa Bell, 2 by Duncan Grant (including a portrait of Vanessa Bell).

Reviews

> Virginia Woolf: The Novels
> Nicholas Marsh (NY: St. Martin's P, 1998) 224pp.
> Virginia Woolf: To the Lighthouse, The Waves
> Jane Goldman, ed. (NY: Columbia UP, 1998) 191pp.

As critical attention to Virginia Woolf's work has increased, so have the resources available to assist in the study and teaching of Woolf. Mark Hussey's *Virginia Woolf A to Z* (1995) represents the best of this work to appear in recent years. With deft cross references, Hussey uses and transcends the alphabetical organization prescribed by the *A to Z* series to produce an accessible, readable, and informative work. Two recent additions to the supplementary resources designed to help readers appreciate Woolf's works are Nicholas Marsh's *Virginia Woolf: The Novels* and Jane Goldman's *Virginia Woolf: To the Lighthouse, The Waves*. All three books are available in reasonably priced paperback editions.

Part of the Analysing Texts series, whose emphasis is on providing the tools for "close, detailed analysis" (x), Marsh's *Virginia Woolf* promises to demystify the study of literature for the common reader. Comparing his "*empirical* approach" to that of the scientist, Marsh assures his reader that "literature is not a different, mysterious kind of study" (3). He devotes the first six of the volume's ten chapters to analysis of Woolf's three most frequently taught novels, *Mrs. Dalloway*, *To the Lighthouse*, and *The Waves*. Rather than organize a chapter around the explication of one novel, Marsh focuses on a different element in Woolf's writing that he illustrates through analysis of key passages from each novel. In chapter one, for example, he selects the scenes when Peter Walsh visits Clarissa Dalloway, Mrs. Ramsay assuages Cam's fear of the boar's head, and the young Rhoda prepares for bed in *The Waves*. He points out Woolf's characteristic features—direct speech, attention to narrative details, and long sentences— to convey how the novice reader can unravel and appreciate Woolf's style. "Virginia Woolf does not have a very odd style," he assures his audience. "She does not have a single, distinctive *style* at all, but rather a variety of narrative flavours and techniques which she switches and flows between at will . . . .There is no single *style*, but in a broader sense there are characteristic features which will be worth looking for in any part of Woolf's writing"(14).

In subsequent chapters, he concentrates in greater detail on sentence structure, distinctions between direct and indirect speech, diction, and repetition of imagery. His close readings of selected passages also explore how Woolf's narratives convey mental processes, critique gender, and provide social commentary. He concludes six of the seven chapters in part one with suggestions for how readers might analyze different sections of the novels on their own. In the three chapters that compose part two, Marsh turns to Woolf's context and her critics. He briefly covers Woolf's biography, discusses her other writings, and summarizes her psychological, narrative, and lyrical contributions to the development of the novel. In his final chapter, he provides excerpts from Erich Auerbach's "The Brown Stocking," Elizabeth Abel's "Narrative Structure and Female Development: the Case of *Mrs. Dalloway*," and Gillian Beer's "The Island and the Aeroplane: The Case of Virginia Woolf."

In general Marsh is no fan of Woolf criticism, which he describes as "often written in a confusing, over-complicated or pretentious style" (196), and his discussion of the critics he includes is a bit disingenuous. After presenting Auerbach's analysis, for example, Marsh notes "that we have been able to reach similar perceptions, and in some cases more thorough and advanced understanding, through our own unaided approach to these texts" (204). Although this might instill the confidence to read and understand Woolf's novels on one's own, it implies that Marsh's interpretations are uninformed by Auerbach's 1946 essay. Whereas Marsh notes Woolf's rich, varied style, with his empirical approach and his belief in the unifying meaning of Woolf's *oeuvre*, he aligns himself with the new critics. Throughout I longed for him to deconstruct his own readings and reveal the multiple, contradictory meanings rather than the singular interpretation in Woolf's work. Nonetheless, his thoughtful, detailed analysis of Woolf's language and imagery illustrates the pedagogical effectiveness of close reading.

For those who want to engage students in the critical dialogue, Jane Goldman's *Virginia Woolf* is part of the Columbia Critical Guides series whose purpose is to offer "balanced and nuanced approach to criticism" and "provide students with ready access to the most important secondary writings on a single text." Focusing on *To the Lighthouse* and *The Waves*, Goldman devotes each of the book's six chapters to different decades of Woolf criticism, beginning with the early reviews, and traces the criticism though its modernist, feminist, and postmodernist incarnations. Her introduction recognizes the obstacles to this selection process as she attempts to represent "the broad, shifting, critical demarcations by which *To the Lighthouse* and *The Waves* have been understood as well as sample some of the most influential and discerning critical essays" (6).

Goldman intersperses her selection of early reviews by Louis Kronenberger, Conrad Aiken, and Edwin Muir, among others, with relevant excerpts about the novels from Woolf's diaries. In her chapter on the criticism of the 30s and the 40s, she covers the vitriolic attacks on Woolf's work that appeared in *Scrutiny* and appropriately places Auerbach's celebrated article—"the most important, stimulating, and highly influential, point of reference for Woolf studies"—center stage (29). Chapter three addresses the mythical and philosophical approaches

Works Cited

DeSalvo, Louise. *Virginia Woolf: The Impact of Childhood Sexual Abuse on Her Life and Work.* Boston: Beacon Press, 1989.

Hussey, Mark. *Virginia Woolf A to Z: A Comprehensive Reference for Students, Teachers, and Common Readers to Her Life, Work, and Critical Reception.* New York: Facts on File, Inc. 1995.

Oxindine, Annette. "Sapphist Semiotics in Woolf's *The Waves*: Untelling and Retelling What Cannot Be Told." In *Virginia Woolf: Themes and Variations: Selected Papers from the Second Annual Conference on Virginia Woolf.* Eds. Vara Neverow-Turk and Mark Hussey. New York: Pace U P, 1993. 171-81.

that dominated the criticism of the 50s and 60s with well chosen selections. Joseph Blotner's key essay suggests the mythic patterns in *To the Lighthouse*, Shiv Kumar's book studies the influence of Henri Bergson, Jean Guiguet attends to the role of subjectivity in the novels, and Frank McConnell introduces a phenomenological approach to *The Waves*.

The two chapters that Goldman devotes to the 70s and 80s, however, are a disappointment. To represent the 70s, a period when feminist analyses explored Woolf's critique of patriarchal culture, the profound influences of other women upon her art, and the relevance of her work for contemporary feminism, Goldman chooses critical studies that emphasize male influences: Allen McLaurin's on Roger Fry, Perry Meisel on Walter Pater, and Gillian Beer on Hume and Leslie Stephen. The work of such major critics as Nancy Topping Bazin, Evelyn Haller, Jane Lilienfeld, and Madeline Moore is either summarized in brief passages or not mentioned at all. Although she titles chapter five "The 1980s: Sexual/Textual Readings" and includes excerpts from articles by Gayatri Chakravorty Spivak, Garrett Stewart, and Rachel Bowlby, Goldman notably neglects those interpretations that address the sexual abuse in *To the Lighthouse* and *The Waves*, such as Louise DeSalvo's *Virginia Woolf*, or that reflect the increasing importance of lesbian readings, such as Annette Oxindine's "Sapphist Semiotics in Woolf's *The Waves*." Instead Goldman derives her chapter heading as well as her bias in favor of deconstructive and psychoanalytic approaches from Toril Moi's *Sexual/Textual Politics: Feminist Literary Theory*. While Goldman calls Moi's book "one of the most influential works of literary criticism," it synthesizes theory, summarizes complex ideas, and diminishes creative insights. In these two chapters, then, Goldman misses the opportunity for a vibrant, inclusive, and representative critical dialogue.

Fortunately, to represent the 90s in her final chapter, Goldman selects excerpts from two of the most impressive essays to emerge from post-colonial debates of Woolf: Jane Marcus's "Britannia Rules *The Waves*" and Janet Winston's "'Something Out of Harmony': *To the Lighthouse* and the Subject(s) of Empire." Thus when supplemented with feminist readings from the 70s and 80s, Goldman's *Virginia Woolf* adequately introduces students to the ongoing critical conversation among Woolf scholars.

—Eileen Barrett, *California State University, Hayward*

Virginia Woolf Icon
Brenda R. Silver (Chicago: U of Chicago P, 1999) xvii + 353pp

Virginia Woolf Icon charts the curious and exemplary journey of a novelist, essayist, and feminist theorist named Virginia Woolf into the spectacular world of international media stardom. "She" is everywhere: on t-shirts, mugs, refrigerator magnets; in movies, TV sitcoms, and beer commercials; in songs, on postcards, and posters; she is at once icon of political correctness and avatar of the highest culture. As a human sound bite (the phrase is Holly Brubach's), Virginia Woolf is used by both popular culture and academic discourse to figure anxiety about gender and sexuality, about social class and cultural class ("in the American version," writes Silver, "cultural class and cultural power are inseparable from gender"). In her (for some) long-awaited book, Brenda Silver proves a witty, insightful, at times angry, and always thought-provoking tour guide to the peregrinations of multiple versions of "Virginia Woolf."

The consistency with which Woolf has been associated with fear provides the solid structure beneath the sometimes fluid and glittering litany of iterations of Virginia Woolf icon. Beginning with the consignment of Woolf to the "feminine" and "aesthetic" by the self styled "intellectuals" clustered around *Partisan Review* in the 1930s and '40s, Silver reads the meanings of "Virginia Woolf" through the present in a series of interpretations whose cumulative effect is to leave no doubt whatsoever that the cultural and political stakes in representations of Woolf, particularly in the United States, are extremely high. Silver demonstrates over and over that Woolf exists on the boundary between many binary oppositions: "the boundary disruptions and social struggles marked by [her] contested appearances can be located in historical periods characterized by major shifts in the status of women in society."

Many of these battles concern feminism, and Woolf has been claimed as emblem by many versions. As "poster girl" for the *New York Review of Books*—a "black hole" in which all scholarship on Woolf turns to antimatter and ceases to exist—Woolf has long played a role in a discourse of gender and cultural class anxieties that "demonizes academic feminism" even as it legitimates Virginia Woolf. (This version of Woolf was much in evidence at the PEN/*New Yorker*-sponsored event in March 2000, "Virginia Woolf Writing Life," at which the audience in New York's Town Hall was told that it was "ironic" that the women's movement was responsible for her current prominence as she was "not a feminist" and had "a wide range of interests.")

Silver notes that in the United States Woolf's "star image" was shaped from the beginning (the 1937 *Time* magazine cover) by her visual image. This specular woman, reflecting whatever commentators wished it to, later reinforced by Quentin Bell's announced intention *not* to consider her as a writer simultaneously with his launching the post-Albee Woolf at a crucial time for feminism (1972-73), has become a spectral figure haunting arguments about class and cultural hierarchies, women's roles, and who gets taught what.

Woolf was propelled into the 1960s "and its cultural frays with her hair flying" by Edward Albee's 1962 play, *Who's Afraid of Virginia Woolf?* and, more significantly for her public persona, by the 1966 film directed by Mike Nichols. It is through Albee that Woolf's name particularly becomes "synonymous with the power to elicit fear and wreak psychological death and destruction" in a "conjunction of Medusa, Sphinx, and Virginia Woolf." Appearing at a time of rising fear of women's sexual independence, Albee's image of a monstrous woman and his play's "queering of the heterosexual family" dispersed a complex of associations with Woolf's image and name that turn out to be at the heart of our most bitter cultural battles.

As the self-styled "intellectual" media attempted to contain Woolf's image "to keep it from becoming heroic," while at the same time exploiting its "star quality," feminist scholarship, in what seems in Silver's reading to be almost a parallel universe, was creating another version of Woolf, one rooted in her writings. Silver has exhaustively explained why the Woolf of the feminist academy—"our" Woolf—is so very different from "theirs": the "image of the etiolated, fragile, apolitical Virginia Woolf" that serves the ends of "high" (male) culture and its institutions. One telling example of the political consequences of the claiming of Virginia Woolf icon in this latter version is Silver's reference to Reagan NEH appointee Jeffrey Hart's hostile review of the *Norton Anthology of Literature by Women* in which he claims that if feminists had "let Woolf be Woolf" there would be no feminist criticism of the kind he deplores.

The note on Hart occurs in a discussion of adaptations of Woolf, most significantly Patrick Garland's cut and pasted *Room of One's Own*, performed by Eileen Atkins to great critical and public acclaim. The silencing of Woolf's feminist complexity in this version is but one example of the consistent effort to contain and resist Woolf that has been perpetrated for decades by the "intellectual" media, by some segments of the academy, and by Woolf's family, an effort anatomized in Silver's skillful readings of Virginia Woolf icon's myriad appearances. "There are," she notes, "as many Virginia Woolfs as there are Shakespeares, and the battles to assert which one is authentic are inseparable from battles over what constitutes a legitimate feminist critique or gender politics or literary canon: battles that have been fought through performances of her texts." Silver's reading of Sally Potter's *Orlando* through the lens of German avant-garde filmmaker Ulrike Ottinger's *Freak Orlando* in this section of the book throws into relief the heterosex-as-norm of the Potter film, providing yet another angle of vision on the iconic role Woolf has assumed.

From Albee's *Who's Afraid of Virginia Woolf?* to British playwright Alan Bennett's 1978 TV play *Me, I'm Afraid of Virginia Woolf*, from t-shirt caricatures to posters on the wall of sitcom bedrooms, Virginia Woolf icon circulates in popular and self-styled "intellectual" discourse as a frightening, asexual or devouring, *brainy* woman. In a "take" on the 1996 Bloomsbury/Bohemian fashion revival, Silver focuses on the refrain, "Virginia Woolf, like fashion, like postmodernism . . ." to illustrate the way Woolf invites us to "play with identities" in a distinctly postmodern way. The theoretical excursus of this part of the book leads away from Woolf to a wider consideration of the "necessity of exploring the historical and social contexts of each and every manifestation of Virginia Woolf, of charting the patterns." It is in charting the patterns of Virginia Woolf icon's reiterations in various cultural discourses that the book is most significant for it leads to the claim that Woolf "throws into question one of the central boundaries in the construction of cultural class: the boundary that divides modernism, high culture, and maleness—not to mention fear of feminism and feminization—on the one side, from women, the mob, mass culture, and consumption on the other."

Taking off from a consideration of the "Chapel Hill hybrid"—a figure composed of Woolf's head on Marilyn Monroe's body—into a brilliant riff on the Medusa, Silver develops her thesis that the contradictions of Virginia Woolf icon reveal "the contradictory nature of culture itself." In so brief a space it is hard to do justice to the mass of detail Silver has arranged in telling patterns in *Virginia Woolf Icon*. It is doubtful that the archons of the self-styled "intellectual" media will deign to read a book published by a university press, let alone one about Woolf (after all, it might distract them from their usual occupation of publishing diatribes about Bloomsbury "cults" and feminazis), but *Virginia Woolf Icon* is a vital resource for those who have been puzzled by the vast gap between the experience of reading her words and that of hearing her discussed in the popular discourse. It also, most valuably perhaps, emphatically resists freezing Woolf into any one of the frames in which she is seen, whether constructed by filmmakers, cartoonists, or feminist critics.

—Mark Hussey, *Pace University*

The Dialogic Self: Reconstructing Subjectivity in Woolf, Lessing, and Atwood
Roxanne J. Fand (Selinsgrove: Susquehanna U P, and London: Associated UPs, 1999)
241 pp. (Cloth.)

Heralds of the Postmodern: Madness and Fiction in Conrad, Woolf, and Lessing
Yuan-Jung Cheng (NY, Bern, Frankfurt am Main, Vienna, Paris: Peter Lang, 1999, "Studies in Literary Criticism and Theory" V.4) xii + 120pp. (Cloth.)

Both Roxanne J. Fand in *The Dialogic Self: Rconstructing Subjectivity* and Yuan-Jung Chen in *Heralds of the Postmodern: Madness and Fiction* read the three authors each considers in provocatively postmodern ways. Fand's book is eye-catching and timely in linking the dissolution of the outmoded cult of the individual and model of an isolated concept of self to a new interdependence, harmonious both with the interactivity of the internet and with Barbara Herrnstein Smith's concept of the "dialogic self" as a "marketplace where all subject-positions . . . as in the material economy, have an exchange rate of relative worth with respect to everything else" (21-2). Fand bases her reading of Woolf, Lessing and Atwood reconstructing subjectivity initially on Mikhail Bakhtin's theory of the dialogic self, but she branches out gratifyingly soon to explain ways in which Herrnstein Smith (*Contingencies of Value*, 1988), Gayatri Spivak (*The Post-Colonial Critic*, 1990), and Rita Felski (*Beyond Feminist Aesthetics*, 1989) theorize possibilities for reconstructing the feminine self. Yuan-Jung Chen provocatively focuses on postmodernism's identification of the "reality" portrayed in fiction with madness, harking back to Nietzsche. Citing Foucault, from *Mental Illness and Psychology*, "The experience of Unreason . . . still remains for us the mode of access to the natural truth of man" (5; Foucault 74), Chen acknowledges that although her work is "literary and rhetorical," not "philosophical nor socio-historical" like Foucault's, she is "greatly indebted" to him (10). Chen explores the transgression of the world of madness into the order of art, and vice versa: "While literature rescues pieces of madness from oblivion, . . . it resists the . . . pitfall of unintelligibility. While madness saves literature from . . . tyrannical rationality, . . . it refuses to be colonized and dominated" (14).

Before going any further, I must emphasize that both these books are immensely readable, in addition to being provocative primers of current applications of postmodern theory. Both would enrich libraries. Undergraduates as well as scholars would find these authors' discussions of individual novels immensely helpful. Roxanne Fand alternates chapters synthesizing theory of the concept of self with a particular author's life and work with chapters applying the dialogic concept to a particular novel of that author, to "The Dialogic Design" of *The Waves*, in the case of Virginia Woolf; to "Nay-Saying as Wall Building" in Doris Lessing's "Children of Violence" series, her Martha Quest tetralogy in Africa; and to "Herself A-mazed in a Funhouse Mirror" in Margaret Atwood's *Lady Oracle*. The brilliance of this method is that a reader can glean whatever level of theoretical content is possible for her from the general chapter, then use the application chapter as a handbook to interpreting the novel. Similarly, in prose of admirable clarity, Yuan-Jung Cheng explores aspects of madness-as-sanity in both the structure and content of Joseph Conrad's *Heart of Darkness*, of Virginia Woolf's *Mrs. Dalloway*, and of Doris Lessing's *The Golden Notebook*. Cheng uses emboldened subject headings throughout her discussion—for example, one-paragraph explanations of Lessing's ideas on *Capitalist Art* and on *Communist Art* as developed in *The Golden Notebook* are included. These headings would be helpful in pointing an undergraduate to historical and theoretical relevancies of what is being said. At the same time, they strike a scholar as a witty application of the fragmentation of postmodernism to the book itself.

It is impossible for a critic interpreting three authors to cover the scholarship on those authors exhaustively and still to maintain coherence in her discussion. Both authors list more than 150 sources in their works cited. In her introductory chapter, Roxanne Fand admirably explains the ways in which Derrida and Bakhtin are taken in new directions by theories of the disintegrating self, from Alasdair MacIntyre's *After Virtue* (2nd ed. 1984) to Kenneth Gergen's *The Saturated Self* (1991), as well as by Barbara Herrnstein Smith's, Rita Felski's, and Gayatri Spivak's ideas of limited possibilities for reinventing the female self. Still, with respect to Woolf scholarship, neither author consults Lucio Ruotolo's *The Interrupted Moment* (1986) or Mark Hussey's *The Singing of the Real World* (1986), both significant contributions to the sense of self in Woolf's novels. In addition, Fand omits reference to Patricia Ondek Laurence's *The Reading of Silence* (1991), although Cheng does consider Laurence's major contribution to the implications Woolf presents for postmodernism. Fand's omission of Harvena Richter's *Virginia Woolf: The Inward Voyage* (1970—Cheng includes it) is serious because the Woolf novel Fand chooses to explicate is *The Waves*, to which Richter's book is entirely devoted. Furthermore, with her intriguing emphasis upon the relationship between economic/political concerns and the self, it is hard to see how Fand could have overlooked not only Ruotolo, but also all of Jane Marcus' books and Michael Tratner's *Modernism and Mass Politics*. (To be fair, Fand cites several sources published as late as 1997—but I am not certain how long after its 1995 copyright Tratner's book actually became available.) In discussing Woolf, Fand does range satisfyingly through Pamela Caughie's 1997 *PMLA* article, Makiko Minow-Pinkney's *Virginia Woolf and the Problem of the Subject* (1987), Carolyn Heilbrun's *Towards a Recognition of Androgyny* (1973) and the critical debate that followed it, Elaine Showalter's *A Literature of Their Own* and other sources from the 1960s to the early 1980s, Kathy Phillips' *Virginia Woolf Against Empire* (1994), and Judy Little's *The Experimental Self* (1996).

Fand represents Lessing and Atwood scholarship somewhat better than Woolf scholarship, crediting the contributions to Lessing scholarship of Lorelei Cederstrom (*Fine-Tuning the Feminine Psyche*, 1990), Claire Sprague and Virginia Tiger (*Critical Essays on Doris Lessing*, 1986, and Sprague's *Rereading Doris Lessing*, 1987), Carey Kaplan and Ellen Cronan Rose's collection (*Doris Lessing: The Alchemy of Survival*, 1988), Gayle Greene (*Doris Lessing: The Poetics of Change*, 1994), Roberta Rubenstein (*The Novelistic Vision of Doris Lessing*, 1979, and *Boundaries of the Self*, 1987), and Molly Hite's writings on both Lessing and Atwood—on Atwood in *The Other Side of the Story* (1989). Notable omissions are Cora Agatucci's "Breaking from the Cage of Identity" (in *Redefining Autobiography in Twentieth-Century Women's Fiction*, ed. Janice Morgan and Colette T. Hall, 1991) and both Earl Ingersoll's *Doris Lessing: Conversations* (1994) and his *Margaret Atwood: Conversations* (1990). Fand's consideration of scholarship on Margaret Atwood admirably includes the two major books published in 1993—Sharon Wilson's *Margaret Atwood's Fairy-Tale Sexual Politics* and Shannon Hengen's Canadian book, *Margaret Atwood's Power*. Otherwise, Fand focuses her Atwood scholarship a bit more concentratedly in the 1980's than one would like, from Sherrill Grace's *Violent Duality* (1980) and Arnold E. and Cathy N. Davidson's collection, *The Art of Margaret Atwood* (1981), to Judith McComb's *Critical Essays on Margaret Atwood* (1988). Omitted are Kathryn VanSpanckeren and Jan Castro's collection, *Margaret Atwood: Vision and Forms* (1988), and J. Brooks Bouson's *Brutal Choreographies* (1993), with its psychoanalytic approach that seems central to Fand's focus on subjectivity. A refreshing aspect of Fand's scholarship, though, is her mention of articles from *College English*, such as Phyllis Van Slyck's "Repositioning Ourselves in the Contact Zone" (1997). The wide availability of such sources enhances the value of her book as a resource for undergraduate readers. For the non-theorist of postmodernism who nevertheless wishes to remain current in literary theory, Yuan-Jung Cheng's opening chapter is a gratifyingly lucid summation of philosophy of madness and the self, and the ways in which Nietzsche, Foucault, Blanchot, Derrida, de Saussure, and Kristeva interrelate on the subject. Cheng's bibliography includes recent works whose titles entice the general scholarly reader: James Bernauer and David Rasmussen's *The Final Foucault* (1988); Marianne deKoven's *Rich and Strange: Gender, History, and Modernism* (1991); Maggie Humm's *Border Traffic: Strategies of Contemporary Women Writers* (1991), and Daniel Ferrer's *Virginia Woolf and the Madness of Language* (1990). Nevertheless, *Heralds of the Postmodern* is less ambitious than Roxanne Fand's book and its scholarly omissions more glaring. For someone writing on madness in Woolf's fiction, to omit both Thomas Caramagno's *The Flight of the Mind: Virginia Woolf's Art and Manic-Depressive Illness* (1992) and Louise DeSalvo's *Virginia Woolf: The Impact of Childhood Sexual Abuse on her Life and Work* (1989) seems unthinkable. Cheng does refer, however, to theoretical books on postmodernism and its roots published as recently as 1994: John Gregg's *Maurice Blanchot and the Literature of Transgression*, Gary Gutting's *The Cambridge Companion to Foucault*, Gabriele Schwab's *Subjects without Selves*, and Cedric Watts's *The Deceptive Text*, and she is careful to include at least one recently-published scholarly book on each individual author: Andrea White's *Joseph Conrad and the Adventure Tradition: Constructing and Deconstructing the Imperial Subject* (1993), Mark Hussey and Vara Neverow's *Virginia Woolf: Emerging Perspectives* (1994), and Earl Ingersoll's *Doris Lessing: Conversations* (1994). Cheng overlooks Gayle Greene's *Doris Lessing: The Poetics of Change* (1994) but includes Greene's 1991 book, *Changing the Story*. Considering that Cheng teaches at National Sun Yat-sen University in Taiwan (her doctorate is from the University of Washington), she should probably be commended for coming within five years of her publication date in her scholarship. Fand is also operating under the handicap of distance, though, since she teaches at the University of Hawaii at Manoa, and she has done amazingly well to include 1997 scholarship in her book published in 1999.

Both authors present intriguing fresh interconnections among what has been said about each of the books interpreted. Fand extends Woolf's wish to "eschew the 'damned egotistical self'" from both her life and her writing to the idea "that Woolf sought to claim the male right of an impersonal gaze upon the objective world" (45-6). Fand further connects this "freedom to pursue an impersonal, more egoless state" with the peace sought by Mrs. Ramsay and Bernard alike: "One shrunk, with a sense of solemnity, to being oneself, a wedge-shaped core of darkness, something invisible to others" (Fand 48, *TTL* 95). In *The Waves*, at first Bernard cannot bear the "pressure of solitude," but later he can "tolerate the chaos": "I see far out a waste of water. A fin turns. This bare visual impression is unattached to any line of reason" (67; *TW* 307). Fand interprets this as follows: "Bernard turns to recreate himself as his own partner, thereby reinventing referentiality in the wake of the unreferential fin, which is Woolf's image for a blank signifier in a waste of infinitely deferred meanings" (67). Since Fand does not explicitly connect the "wedge-shaped core of darkness" with the "fin" far out, she does not harmonize the welcome peace connoted by the wedge-shaped darkness with the chaos portended by the fin—but Fand comes close to this consistency, insofar as she sees that the artist staves off chaos by reinventing meaning.

Fand believes that as far as the dialogic self is concerned, Doris Lessing takes up where Virginia Woolf leaves off. Fand admires Lessing's "commitment to self-discovery as process, not to any self-construct as product" (104). Lessing admits "that dialogue in the face of mystery is what art and life are all about" (106). "The process of becoming a personal-transpersonal-impersonal-and-comprehensive self is a dialogic, relational one" (107). Anna Wulf's "game of concentration is only a paradigm of the process of expanding consciousness, one that can be repeated with *new contents* that achieve new points of transcendence" (107). Yuan-Jung Cheng agrees. Devoting an entire chapter to *The Golden Notebook*, Cheng declares that although Anna's notebooks are the products of her efforts to "make patterns and create order, . . . they are false patterns and self-imposed order. . .. The constant revision of her perception and repeated self-reproach . . . make it hard for the reader to reach a fixed conclusion. . . .By attempting to 'break certain forms of consciousness,' Doris Lessing also makes her readers break their habitual ways of thinking" (90-1). By keeping the notebooks Anna Wulf satirizes and transcends both the simplistic capitalistic view of art and Communist views of art as ideology. It does seem paradoxical, though, that Cheng (a Chinese Nationalist professor) makes Lessing's "process" sound somewhat like a Communist re-education process.

Finally, Roxanne Fand's fifth chapter, "The Concept of Self in Margaret Atwood," is a comparison of Atwood's postmodern ideas of the dialogic self to Woolf's and Lessing's, in a magnificent reprise of all that has gone before. Fand dutifully acknowledges Atwood's overturning of sentimental ideas of "sisterhood" among childhood girlfriends in *Cat's Eye* and, in *The Robber Bride*, Atwood's creation of an antagonist, Zenia, who is the incarnation of the three protagonists' "own dark impulses" (172), but these acknowledgments do not go beyond earlier critics' interpretations. Fand does make an original contribution, though, in noting that "*The Robber Bride* illustrates the Nietzschean reversal of the good-evil discourse of the world's religions that gives homage to the meek" and "exposes the vulnerability of intellectual, spiritual, and materialistic pride that Zenia exploits in . . . the protagonists" (172). Fand recognizes that "what Atwood does with good and evil in *Robber Bride* is different from what Lessing does, . . . in that Lessing draws a sharper polarity. . . . Atwood's transcendence is a kind of cosmic laughter, a mockery of *all* positions, including the 'goody-

goody' and 'bleeding-heart' liberal ones" (175). Perhaps because of this marvelously complex comparison in Chapter 5, it is only in Chapter 6, "*Lady Oracle*: Herself A-mazed in a Funhouse Mirror," that Fand realizes the tremendous sense of fun with which Atwood regales the reader. Fand notes that *"Lady Oracle* focuses squarely on the postmodern problem of the decentered subject in the heroine, Joan Foster," whose "problem is a protean multiplicity gone wild"(176). Joan, a writer of romance novels, avoids "getting stuck" in the romantic plots she ceaselessly invents for herself (196). Joan even tries to imagine relationships among her fantasized selves. Fand identifies *Lady Oracle* as "a parody on the quest-for-self genres" but notes that the novel has "serious implications" about "the way we construct our self-images in response to social pressures that force us to deny our multiplicity" (196).

Fand concludes that "the integrity of the observer that transcends . . . any . . .et of polarized positions is, paradoxically, the most reliable and stable as well as fluid. . . .The dialogic model may be difficult, but in its apparent maze of choices there are ways out, not just dead ends" (197). In her brief conclusion, Fand moves beyond Bakhtin's dialogism to propose a "discourse of *sustainability*, which posits balancing diverse interests and recycling resources to address our ecological, economic, and cultural interdependence" in our "compressed world" (199). Thus, Fand displays inventiveness in relating the marketplace economy to dialogism in her introduction and—having moved from dialogism to reinventing the self—she also cleverly relates the communal awareness she has defined as part of the reinvented self to a new theoretical topic, "sustainability."

—Sally A. Jacobsen, *Northern Kentucky University*

Other Sexes: Rewriting Difference from Woolf to Winterson
Andrea L. Harris (Albany, NY: S U of New York P, 2000) xv + 187 pp.

Ten years after Robyn Warhol's *Gendered Interventions* was published, a new book by Andrea Harris shows the continuities and the changes in the field of gender studies. Warhol in 1989 placed herself among the "practitioners of gynocritics" when she looked for the differences between "strategies that dominate novels signed by men" versus those "signed by women" (17); Harris, in contrast, attacks the stereotypes gynocriticism unintentionally, perhaps, upheld. She criticizes gynocritics as "privileging . . . body, nature, passivity, matter, other" as "obligatory connotations of the feminine" (3). Warhol, while extolling gynocriticism, states that she "departs from gynocritics and moves toward gender theory" because she does not see exclusivity in strategies, because she realizes that writers, male or female, can write "as a woman" (18, original emphasis), and because she questions the sexism of extant critical models. Harris's study offers a more exacting, critical, and political version of gender studies than does Warhol's earlier criticism by trying to explode the defining categories used by earlier critics: Harris argues that, paradoxical to expected effects, "the sex/gender binary" itself "works to conceal rather than reveal difference" (xi). She contends that "only when the end result of privileging the feminine is the questioning of gender norms can such a strategy be considered a feminist one" (4).

I bring up Warhol's book in this review of Harris's because earlier books such as Warhol's have been the necessary critical foundation that make a book like Harris's possible, even though Harris must implicitly critique the earlier results of gynocriticism. I bring up Warhol's book because Harris does not bring it up, nor does she bring up many others of the critical books on gender of the last decade. And this is a good decision, in part because Harris must establish a way of thinking about gender that radically departs from conceptions represented by Warhol; she must foster a conception that does not come easily. Instead of confronting critics of gender who, thankful to have these theories, have used theories of gender without much critique of those theories, Harris contends with the theorists of gender themselves. She goes back to Jardine's *Gynesis*; she examines Derrida; and she uses Spivak and Schor in order to expose the opposing female and male binary as a "narrowly conceived static opposition" (xiii). It is a hard task, because, even with the innovative thinking on gender of Butler and Irigaray (work that Harris draws upon extensively) and of commentators like Schor and Spivak, both language and culture collude against an understanding of gender as something that is *not* limited to binary thinking.

Harris, however, aims to do just that. Using novels and theories of gender, she discusses gender in terms of boundary crossings. She thinks about identity and language, particularly the ways that, without the "border between masculine and feminine," binary definitions of identity and language preclude representation of "other sexes" (xii). She embraces "the place where these terms overlap and intersect, forming other sexes that cannot be described with the language at our disposal" (xii).

Harris shows how 20th-century novelists Virginia Woolf, Djuna Barnes, Marianne Hauser, and Jeanette Winterson cross boundaries in their novels to imagine gender as something other than masculine and feminine. Combining stereotypically gendered traits is one of the tactics used by these authors to imagine "other sexes." For instance, Bernard in Woolf's *The Waves* becomes other than masculine or feminine, when he uses both language that is stereotyped feminine ("fragmentary, feminine language of the body") and language that is stereotyped masculine ("masculine language of the mind"); "he learns to speak both ways" (25). Bernard, through his learning of other languages and his own fragmentation of identity, must be seen as concomitantly both male and female, Harris explains. Harris states that the identification with the binary seems to reinforce the binary, but that Woolf "opens a fertile ground of exchange" by creating in Bernard "a fluid reintegration of genders" through his displacement of and integration with the other characters (62).

Crossings like this rely not only on combinations of traits traditionally designated as masculine or feminine. Harris suggests that crossing the boundaries also takes place through "feminine figures": Harris gives examples of "Woolf's 'little language,' Barnes's Third sex, Hauser's secret second tongue, and Winterson's bodily writing" (23). These figures "stand for the integration of oppositions," Harris argues (23), and through them the novelists cross boundaries to discover other sexes.

Harris opens her discussion by considering 20th-century theories that can help readers conceptualize and find language for what these novelists represent. She begins by quoting Woolf: "we have too much likeness as it is, and if an explorer should come back and bring word of other sexes . . . nothing would be of greater service to humanity." The explorers Harris applauds, of course, are the novelists and the theorists of gender who "bring word of other sexes." Indeed, of great use in this critic's presentation are her discussions of the theorists of gender. For instance, she examines Luce Irigaray's ideas about mimesis and the sensible transcendental; she explains Judith Butler's theories about performance and drag. Monique Wittig's ideas about gender as a linguistic category further complicate theory and readings. The concepts about gender repeatedly inform Harris's readings of the novels, and her readings of the novels help her to question and assess the theories. Harris's introduction of these concepts is impressive, in that even readers who had not been exposed to them previously will understand Harris's explanations of them and because readers who have been exposed to the ideas will appreciate Harris's recontextualization.

Each chapter marks a successive level of conceptualizing gender. The chapter on Barnes and *Nightwood* is a center point of the book. In it, Harris turns from a primary focus on explaining how binary masculine/feminine can be used to explore "other sexes" to a fuller focus on "gender identity as an open-ended range of possibilities rather than as a strict choice between masculine or feminine" (63). The chapter on Hauser's novel *The Talking Room* discusses gender as performance. Harris argues that *The Talking Room* "destabilizes the simple binary schemes for gender by rewriting gender as performative" (113). The chapter on Winterson uses *Written on the Body* to discuss how assumptions about the universal are gendered and how language participates in these assumptions. Harris presents this novel as one about the ethics of love and the spiritual dimensions of love; Winterson, deliberately making readers uncomfortably aware of gender, uses a "meeting of mundane and spiritual" as "a means of restoring the repudiated feminine . . . to its central place in Western thought" (130).

Harris establishes that 20th-century novelists have created a tradition of exploring gender beyond the binary equation of male versus female. The usefulness of Harris's work comes not only for her readings produced through her focus on gender, but also for the extensions to other narratives that the discussion would illuminate. Other texts by Woolf, Hauser, Barnes, and Winterson besides the ones she discusses would be illuminated by applying the focus. And texts by other 20th-century writers, by writers such as Gertrude Stein or Jean Rhys, would show how such a tradition expands beyond those parameters necessarily imposed by Harris's study. Stein's story "Melanctha" for example, with Melanctha's wanderings so like those of *Nightwood*'s Robin Vote's wanderings and so like J's wanderings in *The Talking Room*, comes to mind, as does her *Lifting Belly*, whose mimesis—"'playful repetitions'" (12)—through an other's point of view and though experiments with language—parallel those Harris points out in *The Talking Room* and *Written on the Body*.

Harris's thought-provoking book owes debts both to those novelists who represent their imaginings of gender as other than masculine or feminine and to those scholars who theorize possibilities of gender beyond the binary oppositions brought to the forefront by gynocriticism. With these texts as its foundation, it will interest critics of gender, of Woolf, Barnes, Hauser, and Winterson, and of

20th-century narratologies. The ideas in the introduction extend and spiral with each successive chapter, presenting more complex ideas about narration and narrators, identity, language, bodies, and boundaries as they complicate gender.

—Georgia Johnston, *Saint Louis University*

No Room Of Their Own: Gender And Nation In Israeli Women's Fiction
Yael S. Feldman (NY: Columbia U P, 2000) 248pp

Virginia Woolf compiled her scrapbook about men's will to battle and wrote her protest *Three Guineas* in the encroaching shadow of what would turn out to be the single most destructive and necessary war of the century. As I write this review in November 2000, the violence unfolding daily in the Middle East only confirms the daring and cogent originality of Yael Feldman's study, which offers a dialogue between Woolf's polemic and the writing of Israeli women. For once again, the lives and imaginations of Israeli women writers are thrust into their nation's despairing state of siege. It is in this light that Feldman's canny use of Woolf's "leaning tower" is both an illuminating and prescient introduction to these compelling writers. Feldman sees Woolf's "metaphor for the crumbling of old demarcation lines at a time of political upheaval" as "useful for characterizing the changing climate in Israel of the seventies," but as the violence continues, we see how "the leaning tower" continues to resonate in the lives and consciousness of these Israeli women writers (141). While viewing her writing subjects through the complex prisms of Virginia Woolf's thought would thus seem to be a comfortable fit for Feldman's study, it was also risky, since the canonical superstar could easily have overwhelmed if not obscured the distinctive creativity of writers who are only beginning to be translated and available in English. But as it turns out, Woolf is also useful in reminding us that women's writing lives can rarely afford to be solely personal, especially in Israel, where there is no separation between individuality, history and politics.

A nation that is constructed whole cloth out of a vision of reconstructing and transforming an ancient homeland, out of a response to genocide, and in an ongoing struggle with its rejecting neighbors, is grist not only for historical and political debate, but for a literature that dramatizes women's personal struggles with policies engendered by the nation's foundational ideologies. Unlike the experience of Woolf's young men, who at one time found philosophy of "much more pressing interest" than politics, for Israeli women writers, the word "Nation" is never allowed to retreat into the Ivory Tower. By contrast, Israeli women constructed their relationship to the history of their nation as primary. For them, the imperative was how to situate narratives of their personal, individual struggle in the urgent, anxious, and yet utopian vision which had not, despite its rhetoric of equality, granted them equal status. In response to the challenges facing any critic who introduces a literature that grows out of a contested but not necessarily well-known historical and political experience, Feldman's study provides a multifaceted theoretical and textual analysis of Israeli women writers. Her analysis also serves as a necessary guide, especially if we consider the multiple difficulties of translating these experiences into a language that is still in formation. For Hebrew is a language that must keep pace with tumultuous change while retaining the integrity of the historical consciousness invested in it. After translating all of that into yet another language, it is no wonder, along with the historical marginalization of Israeli women writers, that we know so little about them and their work seven thousand miles to the west.

One of Yael Feldman's many achievements is to use her theoretical arguments and close readings to introduce Israeli women writers as a compelling read. Her theoretical frame is broad sweeping in its scope, including not only Woolf, but Simone de Beauvoir, and contemporary feminist theorists and their debates about social, psychological, and political constructions of gender. In turn, Feldman connects the tensions and anxieties that have shaped the experiences and responses of Israeli women to a history of feminist debates about women's subjectivity and agency in a world of male dominance. This connection does not, however, universalize women's political and psychological oppression, but rather offers a frame of reference that Israeli women acknowledge themselves in their fiction and non-fiction alike. This is a frame, moreover, which they also question and transform in the circumstances that shape their own identities and experiences. Along with Feldman's discovery that Israeli women writers have actually responded to Woolf are the conjunctions and disjunctions that shed critical light on these women of different national and cultural identities. We see this in the ways her writers transported, translated, and transformed themes from American feminism into the Hebrew language and into their own concerns. Feldman accomplishes the daunting task of tracing the semantic and etymologically related meanings of the original Hebrew not only to their biblical sources, but to medieval and modern Hebrew literary traditions. Readers who might be put off by such philology as being arcane and irrelevant to their concerns would be very mistaken, as the example of Feldman's reading of the Hebrew word, *rahamim* shows. Its semantic relation to womb and biblical reference to "the unloved one" leads to a feminist reading of associations with "the female womb in the Hebraic and Greek traditions" (211).

In her theoretical relationships, Feldman engages feminist critics in a rich analysis that coordinates with her construct of "psychopolitics." From her close reading of diary entries, Feldman rejects conclusions that take Woolf literally as having discovered Freud's writing very late in her career, and the result is illuminating. For Woolf's political analyses now emerge with even greater complexity as they can be seen to ascribe the vicissitudes of interpsychic, interpersonal relations to the socializing processes of men's education. It is this process that leads men to strut their stuff on the playing fields of Eton and on the battlefield. In the Israeli context, "psychopolitics" becomes a different kind of national and cultural hermeneutic. Consistent with the national foundational narrative where Biblical stories are often read as exegesis on the psychology of the Jewish people, Feldman locates an "Israeli psychopolitics" that allows Israeli women writers to see their personal and political and professional yearnings and experiences in the light of the nations psychology. As she says, "never had Zionist ideology been placed on the analysts couch as it has been in recent Israeli fiction" (162).

The relationships Feldman draws between Woolf's concerns about the "psychopolitics" of masculinist domination and the responses of Israeli women writers are further complicated by the discussion of Woolf's responses to fascist domination. Though Feldman is right to criticize Woolf for equating "male dominance over the fair sex with the would-be fascist dominance over the human race" as "disproportionate and tactless, especially from a post-World War II perspective," her defense of Woolf as not being able to "foresee the horrors that the future had in store must consider the following political and literary history" (147). By 1934, with the passage of the Nuremberg Laws, which in their implementation of Nazi anti-Semitic policies, ripped citizens and more fundamental rights away from the Jews, it was clear that anti-Semitism in any form was a dangerous rhetoric. And yet in 1937, Woolf published her story, "The Duchess and the Jeweller," which as I have analyzed elsewhere, is replete with age-old anti-Semitic stereotypes and derogations. In the light of Woolf's willful (she was asked by her American publisher to delete the anti-Semitic references), decision to barely mask her portrait of the venal Jew, any literary historical relationship between Woolf and Israeli women writers raises troubling questions that must be addressed. For whatever their religious or secular beliefs and however they perceive the success or failure of Zionism, the historical, political, and creative consciousness of Israeli women writers has been shaped by two millennia of Jewish persecution. As regards Woolf's lack of foresight about the Holocaust, the fact that she sold her manuscript to provide funds to rescue Hitler's victims shows that she could not have been ignorant of intensifying Jewish persecution. At the same time however, there were other British women writing in the early and mid-thirties who, on the basis of their taking Hitler at his word, predicted and warned against a Nazi disaster for the Jews. Katharine Burdekin's 1937 *Swastika Night* and Phyllis Bottome's 1937 *The Mortal Storm* are especially wise in their own close readings of the historical moment.

If the concept of "psychopolitics" is complicated by context, another concept that Feldman applies to her study, "feminist romance", casts critical light on the way Israeli women have had to resolve and leave unresolved, conflicts between their own personal, professional, and political desires and those dictated by national needs for achieving some kind of security and stability. Because of a relentless experience of siege and war, "the displacement of the feminist concerns of *contemporary* authors. . .tells us about the cultural status of Israeli feminism" (author's italics, 38). Within the urgency of these national needs, women's struggles between homemaking, caregiving and work exacerbated their already "minority position" and "conflict between gender and nation" (40, 193). For Feldman, "the New Hebrew Woman (that is, feminist emancipation)" must be negotiated between "the unresolved tensions between sexual difference and female otherness" (89).

If, on occasion, the interweaves of this study become tangled in their densely packed backwards and forward references to its theoretical themes and personages, this also clarifies the profound relevance of these unfamiliar writers to American, British, and European readers. In turn, as we continue to become more inclusive and complicate our understanding of what it means to build a multi-cultural canon, Yael Feldman's study is profoundly important in making it imperative that Israeli women writers are no longer marginalized.

—Phyllis Lassner, *Northwestern University*

Outsiders Together: Virginia and Leonard Woolf
Natania Rosenfeld (Princeton: Princeton U P, 2000) 215pp.

The fertile political and artistic borderlands that emerged from and were negotiated by the marriage of two differently disenfranchised outsiders, Virginia and Leonard Woolf, is the subject of Natania Rosenfeld's *Outsiders Together*. The day-to-day marriage of one of the more intriguing couples of the twentieth century is minimally evoked in this study, for personal biography is merely a backdrop for setting up Rosenfeld's overarching tropes of "marriage and annexation," which she deploys throughout the book in a number of significant new readings of Virginia Woolf's fiction, some brilliantly executed. Rosenfeld reads the Woolf marriage as one that "negotiated the dangers of inbuilt hierarchy through self-awareness on both sides, always leaning toward metaphor and away from traditionally conceived actuality" (3). One of Rosenfeld's primary objectives is to illuminate the ways in which Virginia's work was inspired by Leonard's political activism and especially how "her alliance to an impecunious Jew with the highest connections in British academe and politics multiplied and illuminated the contradictions in her own identity politics" (3). In addressing Virginia's own antisemitism (as well as Leonard's, which, of course, was much more complicated), Rosenfeld claims to do so in the spirit of "illuminat[ion]" rather than "excoriat[ion]" (15). It is one of the admirable qualities of this book that Rosenfeld maintains that spirit throughout.

Rosenfeld's prevailing ethos, though not evenly sustained, is to honor the modernist contributions of both Virginia Woolf and Leonard Woolf in a way that does not elevate one at the expense of the other, a fairly prevalent strategy of the past. However, while Rosenfeld claims that some critics "too readily claim [Woolf] for . . . feminism," there are moments in her study in which she may be accused of doing the same for Leonard. In arguing against Laura Moss Gottlieb's claim that the Woolfs "'wrote for different audiences,'" (178) Rosenfeld falls into the trap of elevating Leonard's political awareness at the expense of Virginia's. "While Leonard seldom likens international power politics to the oppression of women by men, it is not an equation he rejects," argues Rosenfeld rather weakly, as if Leonard's position could be called feminist by default. Her deflation of Virginia's political seriousness follows: "Virginia, on the other hand, is in some ways less 'radical' than . . . her own late writings superficially suggest" (179). But this sort of maneuvering is rare in a study that by and large rejects the idea of Leonard as a "self-sacrificing angel" (149). Instead,

Rosenfeld's book puts forth new readings which locate Virginia Woolf's evolving and complex ideas about subjectivity alongside the evolving and complex experiment of her marriage, which Rosenfeld views as a "remarkably successful negotiation of tension and breakdown" (10). That Rosenfeld is also a poet is evidenced in her original and evocative metaphor for describing the essence of the Woolfs' marriage. Both, she contends, wanted to move away from a "vertical," hence hierarchical, definition of their relationship. "To achieve a sense of balance, of mutual recognition across the lines of difference, and to construe those lines as horizontal—like a hyphen rather than a ladder—was their lifelong engagement" (81).

The first third of the book explores corresponding themes in the early work of both Virginia and Leonard. Read together, Rosenfeld contends, Virginia's *The Voyage Out* and Leonard's *The Village in the Jungle* "illuminate the ambivalent attitudes toward body and intellect, self and other, that writ so large in the ideologies of imperialism, also informed the two writers' initial conceptions of each other" (19). In moving beyond their initial impressions to their actual engagement, and using as thematic inspiration the exclamation of "Ha! Ha!" that heads the note announcing their engagement to Lytton Strachey, Rosenfeld contends that, read together, Leonard's *Wise Virgins* and Virginia's *Night and Day* "illuminate [their] conception of their engagement as a joke" that is finally "against the convention [of marriage] itself" (80). Five years after their marriage, with the establishment of Hogarth Press, Virginia's fiction begins to flourish while Leonard's reaches an impasse that would cause his turn to other genres. In her reading of Hogarth Press's joint publication of "Three Jews"and "The Mark on the Wall," Rosenfeld argues that Virginia Woolf was "not marked" by her outsider status as "her father's daughter" in the same way Leonard was marked and stigmatized by his "precarious station as English Jew" (83-84). Rosenfeld then uses this discrepancy in their outsider status to argue that fictional tropes of escape were possible inventions for Virginia but not for Leonard, though both stories share a "resentment toward reigning ideologies" (11). Leonard's story "nails home his entrapment" (84), signaling the "ultimate demise of Leonard's fictional enterprise" (90); whereas the structure of Virginia's story is "inclusive, inconclusive, and suggestive, open[ing] out into Virginia's further flights" (84), signaling, conversely, the "launching point of [her] bold literary experiments" (90). Later in her study, Rosenfeld notes the same tendency in Leonard's autobiographical works, contending that he never could free himself from the "carapace" he needed to protect himself as a young man, as a Jew among Gentiles and the only Jew to be an Apostle at Cambridge (148). While Rosenfeld does an excellent job throughout her work of bringing to light the double bind that informed Leonard's position as an English Jew, she can at times be rather dismissive about the identity issues that arise from what she continually casts as Virginia's more privileged status: "It [the 'carapace'] is a defense people like Virginia don't need, because of either their background or their genius, or some felicitious combination of both" (148).

Yet it is with Virginia Woolf's genius, manifested in her literary experiments, that the heart of the book concerns itself. In a number of close readings, Rosenfeld explores Woolf's evolving "politics of intersubjectivity" (9). Her reading of *Mrs. Dalloway* is illuminated by Woolf's growing awareness of class issues as a result of her work with the Womens' Co-Operative Guild and her introduction to *Life as We Have Known It*, stories of working women, collected by Margaret Llewelyn Davies. Rosenfeld makes the interesting suggestion that Woolf leaves Rezia Warren Smith's "plot open" so that Rezia "may still finish the hat" (110). Rezia's hats—which she will make for rich women who will appreciate the product but not Rezia's artwork of "found objects as metonymies of the disparate human race"(110)—parallels Woolf's web throughout the novel, for Woolf means her web to be a paradox, in which links are the very things that divide" (96). Other original moments in Rosenfeld's readings include her treatment of Mrs. Ramsay's knitting as a "cerebral . . . activitity of measurement" that undermines her charity (126); Mr. Ram-say as one whose speech "is ramming" (134); and the semicolon as used by Woolf in *Orlando* as reflective of her view of androgyny: "an ambivalent mark, which can signify opening or interdependence, or stand for a closed gate and mutual autonomy" (135).

In her final chapter, Rosenfeld returns again to reading the Woolf's works together as she engages the material world threatened by fascism in the 1930s. She explores the "metaphors of obscene coupling" (13) that emerge in both of their anti-fascist writings, and reads the infamous snake-toad scene in *Between the Acts* as being in part a response to Leonard's "ambivalent stance" toward pacifism in *The War for Peace*. Rosenfeld reads *Between Acts* as a "redemptive rewriting of the heterosexual ur-plot" (157), in which "Marriage is posited as a microcosm whose repair can be cosmically redemptive" (176). In her reading of La Trobe, she makes the compelling argument that "the continual collapse of unity into dispersal . . . is in fact a redemptive movement" (173). "In casting La Trobe as the rewriter of Genesis," contends Rosenfeld, "[Woolf] was propounding a reconception of human—and international—relations (165). That Rosenfeld does not appreciate the irony of the fact that Miss La Trobe, who will write the first words of the "new Adam and Eve" (157), is a lesbian character is an oversight that leads to my major complaint with Rosenfeld's otherwise savvy reading of borders and differences.

I find it truly astonishing that Rosenfeld has managed to write a book that addresses Virginia Woolf as an outsider without even *briefly* considering the ways in which her well-documented sexual attraction to women may have contributed to her understanding of and negotiations with her own outsider status, the evolution of her sexual politics, or to the rich complexities of her marriage. The "issues" Rosenfeld outlines as "central to Woolf's project and encapsulated in the phrase 'border cases'" are those of "gender, class, racial and national identity, and the hybridization of these categories that causes such confusion" (16). Conspicuously absent in Rosenfeld's list of issues is sexuality. Her most overt reference to Woolf's own sexuality as anything other than ambivalently heterosexual makes note of Woolf's "fascinat[ion]" with Vita Sackville-West's sexuality: "Fascinated (as well as, briefly, seduced) in the late '20s by her friend Vita's bisexuality, Virginia Woolf was trying to theorize the transcendence of gender" (120). That Woolf's erotically-charged relationships with women are parenthetical, even literally so, in a work primarily concerned with her relationship with Leonard is to be expected; what I take issue with is that in Rosenfeld's seemingly reactionary parentheses, same-sex love just barely dare speak its name. It is also curious that in a study which claims to embrace borders and which values Woolf's "evolving effort . . . to imagine the varied configurations formed by difference" in her own writing (5), Rosenfeld's sophisticated multi-layered close readings of individual novels consistently resist any *mention* of lesbian subtexts or characters, even those who have been read as lesbian—Miss La Trobe, for example— for over a decade by even some fairly resisting readers.

In discerning Rosenfeld's motive for distancing Woolf and her works from any association with lesbianism, one must be content with the rationale she seems to offer in a footnote in which she quotes Rachel Bowlby, whose commentary she finds "incisive" with regard to "Woolf's 'treatment' by critics and biographers":

> Childhood seduction, madness, confinement, frigidity, anorexia, lesbianism, suicide: in the very extremity of its outlines, the tale can become either a demonstration of common female oppression—the norm revealed at its outer edges—or proof of her exceptional status. In her oddness or in her representativeness, Virginia Woolf is always treated as a 'case'" (qtd. in Rosenfeld, 192n.4).

In the company of such maladies, lesbianism does seem a most unsavory condition. Ambivalent heterosexuality, which Rosenfeld repeatedly ascribes to Woolf, apparently makes Woolf seem less of a "'case.'" In a footnote Rosenfeld reports that "one or two" of Woolf's diary entries "allude to some sexual activity" in the Woolf marriage, "enough to suggest that Virginia Woolf's sexuality was not simply repressed or directed only toward women—common interpretations of the past." "I agree," continues Rosenfeld, "with recent writers . . . who see Virginia

Woolf's writing as saturated by a sensual relationship to the object-world that belies her supposed frigidity and suggest that such categorizations oversimplify sexuality." I applaud Rosenfeld's reluctance to oversimplify sexuality in general and Woolf's in particular; too bad she did not see fit to advance a more complicated reading other than to insinuate in several footnotes that Woolf was not lesbian.

It is difficult to imagine anyone interested in Woolf studies having an indifferent reaction to this thought-provoking study of the complexly complementary minds of Leonard and Virginia Woolf. It is also difficult to imagine a reader not being impressed by the sophisticated theoretical *and* metaphorical weaving of Rosenfeld's analyses. Simply put, it is always a pleasure to read the work of someone who writes well, whose love of language seems omnipresent throughout a text. I look forward to reading other works that will profit from Natania Rosenfeld's intellectually rigorous and metaphorically ripe analysis of the emotional, artistic, and ideological terrain of the Woolf marriage—hopefully, works which will engage the fertile trope of marriage yet divorce themselves from the facile trap of heterosexism. Utlimately, however, Rosenfeld's study echoes in its approach what she astutely regards as "Virginia and Leonard Woolf's vision of international as well as interpersonal politics": it "admits dialogue" (176).

—Annette Oxindine, *Wright State University*

Virginia Woolf's Essays: Sketching the Past
Elena Gualtieri (NY: St. Martin's P, 2000) 210 pp.

What is most striking about Elena Gualtieri's *Virginia Woolf's Essays: Sketching the Past* is its placement of Woolf's essays within the Continental tradition. Gualtieri's argument is that when the essay is viewed within the European concept of "Essayism," it is easier to understand how Woolf uses the essay to investigate the relationship between genre and gender. The book has a tripartite structure, beginning with a discussion of the form of the essay and moving into discussions of feminism and history. The focus is on Woolf's use of the modern essay, with its genre-bending qualities, to articulate the problems of gender representation as well as the nuances of writing literary and personal history.

The Introduction begins with an excellent critical survey of the reception of Woolf's essays. As Gualtieri points out, Woolf is "suspended between two different conceptions of the [essay]" (3), the English and the Continental. The notion of the essay as *belles lettres*, a form of writing which aims to pursue style and good form, is a very English conception of the essay and has guided the reception of Woolf's essays in the second part of the twentieth century. Another conception of Woolf's essays is more Continental, and this perspective finds Woolf thinking about history and modernity in a different way. It signals the emergence of a kind of literary history that questions the identification of modernity and history itself as a linear and teleological narrative.

Gualtieri places the Continental conception of the essay in line with Marxists such as Lukács and Adorno. This tradition of the essay addresses ontological questions about the relationship between cognition and aesthetic experience. Lukács' theory of this relationship is explained in the following manner:

> ... the essay as criticism does not stand in opposition to the essay as *belles lettres* but rather represents the realization of the essence of the genre. ... As form, the essay attempts to bridge the gulf between knowledge and experience by giving knowledge the form of aesthetic experience. Rather than producing knowledge the way that science does, the essay creates a form where knowledge can be experienced as art. (5)

The form of the essay lets experience itself shape the text, and it makes it difficult for the essay to make an appeal as an objective and scientific narrative.

Gualtieri chooses Robert Musil's concept of "Essayism," a concept in the Continental tradition of the essay that represents a form of writing that is dispersive and without an organizing center; it allows the essay to take its form from the experience it is trying to express. Gualtieri claims that the aim of *Virginia Woolf's Essays* is

> to investigate whether a modernist understanding of the genre as Essayism is compatible with Woolf's practice as one of the first feminist historians of literature. . . . [while] at the same time, using Woolf's own essayistic practice to question the boundaries that define the difference between "Continental Essayism" and the English essay. (17)

This is the crux of Gualtieri's argument, and it allows her to merge the discussion of form with issues of history and feminism—all three connect and separate in different configurations. We learn from *Virginia Woolf's Essays* that it is impossible to discuss genre, feminism, or history without addressing the other two subjects.

Chapter 1, "Eccentric Histories," is essentially a survey of Woolf's early forays into essay writing. In addition to being an excellent narrative of Woolf's development as a reviewer and essay writer, this chapter begins to reevaluate Woolf's unique position in the history of feminist criticism. It focuses on the fluidity of generic boundaries between Woolf's early journals, her essays, and her short stories. The chapter also stresses Woolf's developing sense of the *lacunae* that mark the smooth narrative of historiographic institutions such as the *Dictionary of National Biography*. Woolf identified these gaps with a series of marginal figures, first called "eccentrics," then the "obscure" and, ultimately, "Anon." We also see in this first chapter the way in which Gualtieri mixes her discussion of better known pieces, such as "Mr. Conrad: A Conversation" with essays that have until this point received little attention, such as "The Eccentrics" and "Julia Margaret Cameron." This mixture continues throughout the book.

The next chapter, "The Essay as Form," describes Woolf's outline of a tradition of essay-writing that runs from Montaigne to the Edwardians. The chapter leads us to a split or conflict that Woolf herself discovered. Woolf stresses the essay's affiliation "with a form of autobiography that offers a non-narrative alternative to traditional biography" (19). For Woolf, the essay becomes an ideal modern form. However, Woolf also becomes aware of the link between the modernity of the genre and the emergence of mass readership, consumer culture, and narcissism. For Woolf, "the essay functions both as a modernist form that might offer an alternative to the relentless drive forward of the dialectic and, at the same time, as one of the foremost participants in the process of commodification of thought . . ." (18). This conflict causes Woolf to consider the connection between writing for money and women's emancipation. As Woolf states in *A Room of One's Own*, in order for a woman to be a writer she must have money of her own. Writing for money, however, encourages mass readership and commercialism, causing the writer's patron and critic to be part of the economic culture.

Chapter 3, "Professing Literature," and Chapter 4, "Sketching the Past," both address the complicated configuration of essay writing, feminism, and history by looking at more traditional Woolfian works such as *A Room of One's Own*, *Three Guineas*, and *Orlando*. Chapter 3 describes how Woolf differentiates between women writers and working women, and Gualtieri shows how this distinction manifests itself in *A Room* and *Three Guineas*. *A Room* shows a synthesis between writing women and working women through the androgen metaphor. *Three Guineas* represents a permanent separation between them through a rhetoric of Spanish photographs and images.

Chapter 4 continues the analysis of the relationship between text and image by focusing on Woolf's memoir, "A Sketch of the Past," and her mock biography, *Orlando*. Gualtieri brings these works to her discussion because they demonstrate the extreme flexibility of the essay genre and are infused with the historiographic concerns of Woolf's critical writing. In "A Sketch" we find Woolf's real concern with the visual image, where her fear of writing autobiography forces her into a more spontaneous writing process, writing sketches of her memories. The sketch is a method of essay writing that both uses visual images for continuity and allows for gaps in narrative, one of the original preoccupations found in her discussions of history. Gualtieri's reading of *Orlando* illustrates how various genres can exist simultaneously. *Orlando* "plays against each other the conventions of different genres and discourses—biography, historical romance and fiction—and yet manages to retain as operative some of the constitutive features of those genres" (20).).

Chapter 5 deals with the debates about the possibility of writing a specifically "feminist type of literary history" (20). In the final parts of the chapter, Gualtieri is at her most radical. We find ourselves being asked to read Woolf through a Marxist lens. Gualtieri admits that Woolf is attempting to write a feminist history. Woolf's essays on painting and literature (such as "The Royal Academy," "Walter Sickert," and "Foreword to *Recent Paintings by Vanessa Bell*") demonstrate her "discomfort with a purely formalist understanding of art that is intrinsically linked to the intervention of class structures within English literature" (20). According to Gualtieri, Woolf develops a belief that imagination is a "hopelessly limited faculty whose arena of intervention is strictly defined by the artist's position within a class-system that Woolf describes as a cluster of 'glass boxes', invisible yet isolating" (21). Woolf's understanding of a female literary history reflects her knowledge that form is always imbued with issues of social class.

Gualtieri's four-page Postscript brings us back to the theory of the essay, "Essayism" and the Continental tradition. Essayism becomes "effectively indistinguishable from the Marxist critique of the dialectic of the Enlightenment and might therefore suggest a certain compatibility of intents between the critique and Woolf's historiographic project" (146). Gualtieri concludes that "essayism was used here as a critical angle capable of articulating and addressing the question of Woolf's relationship to literary history, both in terms of the history she wrote and in terms of the history that has been written about her" (146).

There are some flaws in *Virginia Woolf's Essays* that prevent the reader from following the larger argument of the book. Though a close reading of the Introduction and Postscript provides the reader with enough information to support the book's continuity, Gualtieri needs more accessible connections between the chapters so that one does not lose sight of the book's trajectory. Also, some of her readings, such as the reading of *A Room of One's Own*, seem to run over well worn and conventional trails; however, what redeems the book and surprises the reader are her conclusions, which turn out to be extraordinary in their originality and insight.

Complicated and carefully argued, *Virginia Woolf's Essays* is refreshing in its use and practice of theories of Marxism, genre, and history in the Continental context. It opens up discussions of Woolf's non-fiction prose as well as the rest of her *oeuvre*. It is time for Woolf scholars to more fully utilize a Continental methodology, a method that stresses the flexibility and openness of the essay and asks questions about the ontological status of truth and history. If we do not learn to consider these alternatives to traditional, linear conceptions of history, we will become trapped in our own "glass boxes."

—Beth Carole Rosenberg, *University of Nevada Las Vegas*

Virginia Woolf: Public and Private Negotiations
Anna Snaith (NY: St. Martin's P, 2000) xi + 194 pp.

Juxtaposing Virginia Woolf with the terms "public" and "private" calls up competing images of her: the frail, apolitical aesthete and snob cocooned in Bloomsbury vs. the radical feminist and socialist public intellectual; and competing interpretations of her literary style: elitist and obscure vs. experimental and deconstructive of liberal patriarchal ideology. Anna Snaith sets out to complicate our understanding of Woolf's use of the terms "public" and "private" and to destabilize various critical tendencies: to place Woolf on one side or the other of these terms, to link stylistic experimentation with feminist politics or to separate politics from style, and to see Woolf's writing through a teleological perspective in which "Woolf's *oeuvre* becomes a search for the final, perfect relationship between politics and art" (4). Snaith describes her approach in her book as follows: "To avoid attaching Woolf exclusively to one side or the other of a public/private division means, first, attention to contingency: the historical and biographical situatedness of Woolf's politics and of her investment in privacy, and second, awareness of the *changing* relations between the public and the private and the shifting meanings and contexts of the words themselves in her work. What is crucial is the variety of ways in which she used the terms and the variety of ways in which she can be seen as both a public and a private thinker" (5). Snaith suggests that "perhaps what is needed is a relinquishing of the need to generalize, to fix: to allow space for the indisputable complexities, ambivalences and contradictions in Woolf's life and writing. We need to allow her to be two things at once, particularly given her own revulsion at the thought of the fixing of her reputation or identity. "Two books on Virginia Woolf have just appeared—in France & Germany. This is a danger signal. I must not settle into a figure" (*D*4 85) (5-6). Throughout six chapters, Snaith manages to maintain her focus on placing Woolf's work in historical and biographical context and on tracing the changing meanings of public and private in Woolf's work over time. Thus, fittingly, Snaith leaves us with no definitive conclusion that "public" meant this for Woolf and "privacy" meant that, but with a heightened awareness of what she calls Woolf's flexibility of ideas and of style, a flexibility that Snaith links to Woolf's feminism and anti-fascist pacifism.

Snaith begins, in her introduction, with an analysis of "public" and "private" in the political theory of Habermas, Arendt, and Richard Sennett, in recent feminist theory and social science, and in Woolf's own work. She argues that the work of feminist historians and sociologists is more relevant to Woolf than the theories of Habermas, et al., because they have explored the historical exclusion of women from the public sphere, the ideology of separate spheres, and the debates about the public/private split both within and caused by the women's movement from the nineteenth century to the present. It was in the context of the tradition of nineteenth-century liberalism, the turn-of-the century women's movement, and the breakdown of separate spheres that Woolf came of age as a person and a writer. Snaith's first chapter traces these biographical and historical influences on Woolf's changing and ambivalent attitudes to the public spaces of the city and to the women's movement. Of particular interest in this chapter, I think, is Snaith's illumination of the significance of Bloomsbury, the place, in women's political history, Woolf's life, and in literature. Snaith gives a brief history of Bloomsbury and its role in the first decades of the 20th century as a locale where single, independent women could find flats or rooms and where various political societies and clubs found offices and meeting rooms, in particular women's suffrage organizations. Thus Woolf's sense of liberation upon the Stephens' move to Bloomsbury has political as well as personal resonances. And her "use of a flat in Bloomsbury to symbolize a single woman's chance of independence" (in for example, "Phyllis and Rosamond" and later, by inference, *A Room of One's Own*) was culturally au courant, not singular; novels by Olive Birrell, Violet Hunt, C. F. Keary, and Radclyffe Hall, published in 1900, 1906, 1905, and 1924 respectively, use apartments in Bloomsbury the same way.

This is one of the strengths of Snaith's book: her use of a wide range of primary sources to set Woolf's work in specific historical context. For example, in the fifth chapter, "The Reading Public: Respondents to *Three Guineas*," Snaith uses the 82 letters to Woolf from readers preserved in the Monk's House Papers at the University of Sussex (edited by Snaith and published in *Woolf Studies Annual* 6) as "evidence of the currency of her ideas and the circulation of her arguments" (128), contradicting the criticism in several contemporary reviews, including Q. D. Leavis's, that Woolf was elitist and impractical. Snaith finds, instead, that working-class as well as professional women and men wrote to Woolf and that Woolf's idea of the Outsiders' Society "creates a non-prescriptive model for diversity within commonality" (128). As in the discussion of Bloomsbury, the use of primary sources creates a Woolf in touch with and a part of a contemporary feminist debate, rather than either a distant, apolitical ivory tower dweller or a singular, radical theorist/genius. Other examples of Snaith's use of primary sources to contextualize Woolf's thinking can be found in the final chapter, "'With this odd mix up of public & private I left off': War, Audience, and Artist 1938-1942." Snaith goes to the London and Sussex newspapers of the time to explain and corroborate Woolf's preoccupation with and fear of a German invasion that was constantly being predicted and then put off: "a constant deferral of what was felt to be the inevitable, which generated the paralysing uncertainty Woolf was to portray in *Between the Acts*" (131). And she offers a fascinating discussion of the lesbian feminist director and actress, Edith Craig (daughter of Ellen Terry), as a source for Miss La Trobe. Snaith finds that, as in *The Years*, Woolf combines women's history and fiction, making LaTrobe a more marginal figure than Craig actually was so as to express her (Woolf's) own concerns about war, the loss of her audience, and the role of art.

But what of Snaith's pursuit of the notions of "public" and "private" through Woolf's writing life? Each chapter traces a different aspect of Woolf's ongoing negotiation of these terms. Chapter two, "Representing Women's Lives," discusses how "for Virginia Woolf, writing itself was a crucial part of women's movement from the private to the public sphere" (42) and how Woolf experimented with fiction, biography, autobiography, and history as ways of writing women's lives, of bringing the "lives of the obscure" into the public realm. Chapter three, perhaps the most successful and interesting, offers a helpful and insightful analysis of Woolf's narrative strategies, particularly her use of free indirect discourse. Snaith carefully defines free indirect discourse, which Woolf uses in eight of her nine novels, distinguishing it from direct interior monologue. Direct interior monologue presents the character's subjectivity in the first person and thus represents the character's stream of consciousness. In free indirect discourse, a third-person narrator reports the character's thoughts verbatim using the past tense and thus combines a "public" voice (the third-person narrator's) and a "private" voice (the character's inner thoughts). Free indirect discourse allows Woolf to combine the inner and the outer, the public and the private, and to unsettle the authority of the omniscient narrator without settling in to the unrelieved subjectivity of one character's mind. "Her use of multiple voices through free indirect discourse acknowledges the variety, fragmentation and situatedness of subjectivity: it cannot be totalized or contained. Through its continual reworking of the relationship between public and private, free indirect discourse breaks down any notion of a fixed binary opposition" (82). This analysis of narrative strategy allows Snaith to make important distinctions between Woolf's and James Joyce's techniques and insightful arguments about narration in *Jacob's Room* and *The Waves* in particular which help clarify difficult critical debates on these two novels.

Chapter four, "Negotiating Genre: Re-visioning History in *The Pargiters*," takes up Woolf's interest in the fact/fiction distinction which, Snaith argues, Woolf conceived of in terms of public/private and which she "retained in order that it might be transgressed" (90). Most of this chapter focuses on *The Years* and the 1930s when the fact/fiction division was most salient for Woolf. Snaith again goes to the primary sources, in this case the biographies, autobiographies, and memoirs Woolf read in researching *The Pargiters*. Snaith disagrees with critics such as Hoffman, Leaska, and Radin who argue that *The Years* is flawed because Woolf was unable to reconcile fact and fiction and thus had to split *The Pargiters* into *The Years* and *Three Guineas*, leaving *The Years* too diffuse, insufficiently unified. Tracing Woolf's incorporation of her research into *The Years*, Snaith argues that "it was the conjunction of *genres* which she could not maintain rather than the fact/fiction conjunction" (93). "*The Years* was her own experiment, her own way of conveying her feminism, preventing it from being propaganda, while incorporating the evidence which she had accumulated" (110). Snaith also makes the point that most of Woolf's sources for *The Pargiters* and *The Years* are biographies and autobiographies, works that deal with facts but are also private and subjective. "Woolf is returning, then, to a question she raised as early as 1906 in 'The Journal of Mistress Joan Martyn,' namely the importance in women's history of private and individual experience, and of women's recounting of that experience" (110-111). "Private" narratives must be validated as historical and political evidence for women's history to be possible; Woolf redefines history as discourse. While most of this discussion is instructive and insightful, it seems to me that Snaith pushes the "equal validity" of biography/autobiography and fiction too far, without considering the material distinctions between them, their different ontological statuses. And to say that in Woolf's notion of history "the priority is not accuracy, but rather the recognition of history as discourse itself" (111) disregards Woolf's stated goal of being as factual and accurate as possible and undermines Snaith's own argument that Woolf bases *The Years* carefully in historical research. It seems to me that Snaith misses an opportunity here to continue her analysis of the complexity and flexibility of Woolf's thinking; Woolf develops an understanding of history as discourse without giving up the possibility of making judgements about truth and accuracy. In this way, Woolf's epistemological stance is not simply an anticipation of postmodernism, but something more nuanced and complex.

Finally, in the last chapter, Snaith argues from Woolf's diary as well as her more "public" writing, that WWII constituted a literal and metaphoric invasion of the private by the public, and Woolf experienced a continual oscillation between public and private realms, a collapse and redefinition of the terms ("the public/private split between genres is collapsed by the public/private division between war and writing, politics and art" [139]), and a recognition of the temporary nature of any public cohesion or community. Snaith reads *Between the Acts* as "undo[ing] the term 'public' and disclos[ing] the heterogeneity it conceals. Rarely do critics see either the extent and importance of the oscillation between plurality and unity or Woolf's use of heterogeneity and refusal of closure as a stay against, rather than a symptom of, fascism" (147). "Woolf's preoccupation with the 'public' realm at this time, as well as her own disagreement with public opinion, resulted in her seeing even more clearly the problems with notions of collectivity and unity" (156).

Virginia Woolf: Public and Private Negotiations is an important contribution to Woolf studies, particularly in its discussions of Woolf's feminism and pacifism, her narrative strategies, her attitudes about gender and class, and her views on history, fact, and fiction. Snaith has indeed made the case that "to ignore distinctions, contradictions and complexity is to ignore the ways in which Woolf responded to historical and cultural contexts. It is also to ignore the multifariousness of her own thought and her commitment to flexibility of ideas. Tracing the public and private through certain aspects of her work illustrates this flexibility. . . . Ideas of public and private . . . were central to so many areas of her writing and thinking, just as they are crucial to the changing situation of women during her lifetime, and to the ways in which she has been represented by critics" (165).

—Diana L. Swanson, *Northern Illinois University*

The Measure of Life: Virginia Woolf's Last Years
Herbert Marder (Ithaca, NY: Cornell U P, 2000) 416 pp.

When I first began reviewing books about Virginia Woolf (on Jean Guiguet in 1964 for *Comparative Literature*), I complained about the vague titles used for these big books, i.e. they were all titled simply "Virginia Woolf," as if they could hand her to us on the half shell.... That trend has continued over all these decades and therefore, my ears pricked up when, at a recent Virginia Woolf Conference, Herbert Marder told us that his present project had as its primary focus just the last period of Woolf's life and career. At last someone willing to not try to do it all, and the more piquant that it should be Herbert Marder whose first book on Woolf, way back in 1968, had the groundbreaking and even earthshattering title, *Feminism and Art: A Study of Virginia Woolf*! I am grateful to Mr. Marder for both books, of course.

What a change just in the acknowledgment sections, where from Aileen Pippett and some excerpts from the diaries and letters available in 1968, the biographer blends, in Mr. Marder's charming simile, "like a nesting quail, into the dense underbrush of documents, transcripts and commentaries" (2). Of course, when the microscope focuses in on a slice of life, "the complexities of things become more close," as Bernard says in the college section of *The Waves* and Marder's book is full to the brim with the by now extraordinary amount of material available on Virginia Woolf, her friends and family, and the historical period. To these treasures, he adds his own rich range of reference, with apt commentary from Schopenhauer, Camus, etc. It all adds up to a book only Herbert Marder could have written and is therefore in itself interesting.

A daunting task, it took commitment; it took being grounded in oneself as well as being grounded in Woolf's works. Marder's educational background is closer to Woolf's own than that of many Woolf scholars and his prose less given to jargon. Were there nevertheless moments when I wished Carolyn Heilbrun (of *Writing Women's Lives*, etc.) had undertaken the project instead? Yes, when I felt his reading differing from mine, turning away from "the really interesting questions," missing something which I thought Heilbrun might have caught. There are times when the book feels the way it must have felt for Virginia Woolf living it, when we are turning and turning in a widening gyre way out past the falconer's voice. It is recursive by nature, but to those of us who know the material so well, it sometimes reads tediously repetitive, as if we are waiting for the other shoe to drop.

However, like David McCullough's biography of Truman, Marder's historical background offers a valuable review of the times some of us have lived through. It is a study of the period, a study of what happens to artists and other sensitive people with feelers out in to the collective unconscious, when a golem comes up from the depths of the pool. I had forgotten, for example, that Mark Gertler, the fine Jewish painter and erstwhile swain in vain for Carrington's favors, had suicided in that hideous waiting period of precarious peace. Isota Tucker Epes, who has been reading Woolf longer than any of us (as she says, back in the halcyon days before it was known that Woolf would commit suicide), wrote me recently of two young men she had known during this period who died directly or indirectly because of the horrors ahead. Marder's book reminds us of the toll World War II took on the 20th century, as well as on Virginia Woolf herself.

Again, as I move toward the end of my word allotment for this brief review/preview, I want to applaud Marder for his focus on the end of Woolf's years. It is hard to stare down that pipe with the mad beggar gibbering from it. Most books on Woolf rush toward the end (with the important exception of Panthea Reid's *Art and Affection*, which gives close literary detective attention to the puzzle of the several suicide notes). I have noticed that my students, not surprisingly, prefer to identify with the Virginia Stephen of the Dreadnought Hoax and the Beresford profile rather than with Gisèle Freund's rather repressed, Emily Dickinson-like later photographs. Herbert Marder has no fears here and has not looked away.

He is to be thanked too for publishing the whole of the miraculously preserved Wilberforce letters to Elizabeth Robins which chronicle closely though somewhat obtusely Woolf's last weeks. I remember reading them at the University of Sussex with the helpless sensation of watching that riderless horse running through the park in *Jacob's Room*. With the best will in the world, the good doctor could not get close enough to Virginia Woolf to slow down those pounding hooves. Nowadays, of course, there would be the ubiquitous medications but in those days, diet, doing embroidery, and what Virginia Woolf saw as the threat of the rest home was all anyone could think of. Leonard's giving her a feather duster for therapy is emblematically futile.

In one of his many useful sortings-out of these issues, Marder says:

> Virginia's death was not caused by any sudden dementia or wild aberration. She had thought it through and written her letters to Leonard and Vanessa in advance. In a sense, she had prepared for this all her life. But it was not predetermined either—she chose the time on the spur of the moment, and was making plans shortly before her death to revise *Between the Acts* as well as to see her friends in April. Her last few days were colored by this incongruity, this

> permeable skin between two realities, since she had already decided to kill herself, and still went on as if she had an indefinite amount of time ahead of her. Then the warning signs—the disorientation, voices—coupled with the hopelessness she felt in Octavia's office, carried her over a threshold. At that point, she put her plan into action, leaving the two letters she had prepared, and scribbling a third that Leonard later found on her writing tablet, in which she said another good-bye and added a hasty response to Octavia's arguments. "I know that I shall never get over this... Nothing anyone says can persuade me." The last sentence expressed her defiance of all professional advice and claimed the right to judge for herself, regardless of the cost. (341-2)

We'd all put together differently the pieces of the puzzle in this countdown. To my ears, Marder skates too quickly past the March 21 sisterly "pull up your socks" letter from Vanessa, which Panthea Reid and I both are sure contributed significantly to Virginia Woolf's decision to go through with her suicide plans. Maybe to the gentlemanly Mr. Marder it is just too "calling blame and naming names." I do "blame" Vanessa, Octavia, and yes, even Leonard Woolf, and I say also good for John Lehmann who, alerted by Leonard's warning note, telegraphed to Virginia about *Between the Acts*. Fortunately, it is Marder who has written this dispassionately passionate book as a careful observer of human nature and of the divine comedy of life in a secular age. We all do regret the books and essays and letters and diary entries not written because of Virginia Woolf's premature and by no means inevitable death, but what I find myself regretting was "that simple and profound paper upon suicide which I see myself leaving for my friends."

—J. J. Wilson, *Sonoma State University*

Granite and Rainbow: The Hidden Life of Virginia Woolf
Mitchell Leaska (NY: Farrar Straus & Giroux, 1998) xii + 513 pp.

Mitchell Leaska's title, words written by Woolf herself in 1927, serves as an ideal metaphor for the life of Virginia Woolf, as well as her work, for it implies the hard reality beneath her luminous imagination. Woolf privileged always the goal to "discover real things beneath the show," (7) a formula Leaska follows in his work on her life. And as the "real things" of her life running "beneath the show" were consistently linked, Leaska's careful work illustrates the continuous relationship between her life and her work. He writes in the introduction, "The familiar separation of life and work upon which most literary biography depends does not apply to Virginia Woolf. Her life and work were inseparable, and part of her life was inscribed in every novel she wrote" (16). He offers a clear-headed acknowledgment of the fact that any biography is necessarily an act of interpretation. For the many works (Leaska acknowledges seven or eight) written on Woolf's life, there seem to be endless stories, but even a "factual" rendering, such as in the biography as a form, leaves out and/or emphasizes points which then shape that life in the mind of both writer and reader.

With so much fine biographical work available on Woolf, many of the details here are already familiar; however, Leaska carefully profiles Leslie Stephen and Julia Duckworth as the parents who eventually became the Ramsays in fine poetic fashion as well as, later, the Pargiters in a more overt and, perhaps, heavy-handed way. Of particular value are the deep psychological and emotional connections Leaska makes, showing, through Woolf's own responses, what the works meant to her. Although *Jacob's Room*, her third novel, was the first in which Woolf really felt she'd begun to "say something in [her] own voice" (221), *To the Lighthouse* was the first widespread success as well as the definitive work exemplifying her unique style. But again, Leaska clearly reveals her own perceptions. Woolf was satisfied with *To the Lighthouse*, despite mixed reviews and an ambivalent public, because in it she grappled successfully with many of the aesthetic issues at the heart of her life's work. The difference between this and the way she felt about *The Years* is critical in understanding the trajectory of all those three prongs which cannot (and, for full understanding according to Leaska, should not) be separated: her life, her work, and her often troubled perception of those. When *The Years* received acclaim, even became a best-seller, she lost faith in her public because she was convinced that the work was a failure. She struggled with *The Years* for nearly five years, at the same time writing

Roger Fry's biography as well as *Three Guineas*. It was late in a life whose undoing is painfully familiar, and Leaska deftly shows us how her struggles with the relationship between fact and fiction became an increasingly dizzying swirl from which she could not extricate herself, either in her work or her life.

Leaska loops back to the parents, particularly the father who "haunted" her, repeatedly throughout his work. While he makes it clear that the effects of her childhood followed her relentlessly through her life, at times he seems to understate the effects that George and Gerald Duckworth had on her sexuality and what he often calls her "unnatural love of her father." Leaska provides ample evidence of the desperate and incestuous bond between Woolf and her father, through both her private and public writing, but he misses the opportunity to attach more significance to the unreality created by the continuous presence of abuse. Such acts as the molestation Woolf suffered at the age of six from one step-brother (Gerald) and the uninvited and repeated "sharing" of her bed with the other (George) on whom she depended in the emotional absence of her father, grief-stricken at the loss of his wife, must have weighed more heavily on her convoluted perceptions of Leslie Stephen than Leaska allows. Specifically, as he chronicles Woolf's major breakdown (and suicide attempt) in 1913, Leaska carefully enumerates the reasons, from her brother Thoby's death to her sister Vanessa's sudden marriage to Clive Bell, to the physiological-hormonal (as well as genetic) basis for her life-long manic-depressive psychosis as it was so diagnosed. He anchors death and loss to Leslie Stephen's ever-present ghost, a ghost who grew in stature and significance as Woolf aged. But the absence of the Duckworths at the juncture of her breakdown seems an omission, particularly since he has already acknowledged some of its impact earlier in the text. Wouldn't Woolf's ambivalence toward her father have been tied to her early experiences with male dominance and sex? Wouldn't some of her disappointment and anger be based on the fury she must have felt at being so unprotected by both parents in her own home?

Granite and Rainbow proves to be a careful work, despite the above limitation. Leaska consistently shows how extraordinarily personal writing was for Woolf. Her private life, illustrated by her diaries and letters, was conversant with her public writing life. Even her several emotional breakdowns occurred in concert with, or in reaction to, the completion, struggles with, or perceived rejection of her work as it reached publication. At the same time that she disclaimed public response as unimportant, she was tormented at the thought of each of her works becoming public, as Leaska tells us, "[T]hough she was forever saying she didn't care, Virginia did care very much," and goes on to say she "faced the ordeal" when each of her seventeen books was published (232-33).

Of great value, also, is the detailed and lucid way in which Leaska shows Woolf's path toward style, that is, how she developed as the experimental and deeply intellectual writer she was. Her struggles, both aesthetic and emotional, with *Jacob's Room* both shook her deeply and paved the way for the even more successful (in her own as well as critics' eyes) works, *Mrs. Dalloway* and *To the Lighthouse*. She wrestled with some highly significant aesthetic problems of time and space in the written word. Because writing is sequential, and therefore linear, she found a great challenge in rendering genuine human experience as it occurs simultaneously, awkwardly, sometimes absurdly, with itself. It was from her attempts to solve this aesthetic problem that she developed what she called "tunneling" into her characters' pasts, as she believed it was here that they became individualized. She always valued the past over the present because of the perspective it offered, even went so far as to say that "the past is beautiful because one never realizes an emotion at the time. It expands later and thus we don't have complete emotions about the present , only about the past" (244). Therefore, the pasts of her characters, their memories and perspectives, however elusive, identified them more than any other trait.

In addition to the aesthetic ground she broke, Woolf also pioneered the frontier of what we now might call reader response criticism, almost to an extreme. She believed, and placed great value in, the importance of the emotional and individual experience of the reader; in fact it seems its significance could not be overstated. In response to criticism (more often acclaim) for *To the Lighthouse*, Leaska quotes her as saying she "meant *nothing* by The Lighthouse," adding that she saw that "all sorts of feelings would accrue to [it] but I refused to think them out, and trusted that people would make it the deposit for their own emotions" (266). Clearly she gives the reader a great deal of freedom as well as responsibility for participation in the creative process. She is admittedly far less interested in a reader grasping what *she* meant than in that reader's deciding for oneself. In writing *The Waves*, she addressed her own questions of time and space as thoroughly as she ever would, and she left the gaps which would confer upon her readers their greatest responsibilities as well. *The Waves* was received with a good deal of public ambivalence: it sold well because by its publication, following *To the Lighthouse*, *Mrs. Dalloway*, and *Orlando*, Woolf had established an audience. However, even some of her close contemporaries disagreed as to its value, and some were baffled. E. M. Forster found it brilliant, even called it a "classic" whereas Lytton Strachey deemed it "perfectly fearful."

Leaska illuminates Woolf's own history, her creative process, and the several significant relationships of her life with sympathy and scholarship. Other than a slight tendency to repeat a few specific examples, for instance the relationship which is established between the characters of Clarissa Dalloway and Septimus

Warren Smith by the the imagery of the coin being tossed into the Serpentine, this is an engaging and thorough work. Details about Vanessa, Clive Bell, Leonard Woolf and Vita Sackville-West, among many others too numerous to name, all contribute to quite a complete portrait of Woolf. In fact, it is a huge work in scope and content: 440 pages accompanied by a complete chronology, a family tree, and comprehensive notes. Woolf students and fans will find an intriguing and dramatic account while scholars will benefit from some of Leaska's lucid and thorough interpretation of both life and work.

Despite its few flaws, this is a lively narrative and an informative resource. I read with much interest. The story of Virginia Woolf, by its very combination of the Victorian and the Modern, the aesthetic and the intellectual, the public and the private, is one that fascinates us, it seems, endlessly. For just as Leaska has admittedly rendered his own interpretation of that story, the complex and variegated text that was her life offers that individual experience she so valued in the interpretation of her many works.

—Stephanie Zappa, *Chabot College*

The Feminist Aesthetics of Virginia Woolf: Modernism, Post-Impressionism and the Politics of the Visual
Jane Goldman (Cambridge: Cambridge U P, 1998) 243 pp.

In *The Feminist Aesthetics of Virginia Woolf: Modernism, Post-Impressionism and the Politics of the Visual*, Jane Goldman examines references to specific colors and to light and dark contrasts in selected works by Virginia Woolf in order to understand the link between Woolf's feminism and her Modernist aesthetics. She identifies "a new feminist language of color" (168) operating in Woolf's work, what Goldman calls *feminist prismatics*, which she sees as central to understanding this link between Woolf's political and artistic sensibilities. This language of color, Goldman explains, originates in two early twentieth-century social movements: women's suffrage and Post-Impressionist art. Woolf, inspired by the unconventional use of color and light in women's suffrage art and in Post-Impressionist painting, appropriates for literature specific colors associated with feminism and certain metaphors associated with male sovereignty, specifically light and the sun. The book's central claim is that Woolf uses such colors, shading, and references to the sun and other solar phenomena as metaphors to assert a feminist vision in her writing. This vision counters patriarchal notions of the human subject as singular, stable, and masculine while appropriating Enlightenment claims of human rationality for women.

Goldman develops her thesis through detailed close readings of a few lesser-known Woolfian texts and, in the final chapters, applies her theory of *feminist prismatics* to two of Woolf's most celebrated novels: *To the Lighthouse* and *The Waves*. The book is divided into two parts: *Eclipse* and *Prismatics*. Part one takes as its starting point Woolf's experience in 1927 of witnessing a complete solar eclipse, which she wrote about in her diary and in a 1928 essay "The Sun and the Fish." The entire first half of Goldman's book is devoted to a meticulous analysis of these two minor, though as we discover not insignificant, texts. These two "eclipse narratives" form the basis of Goldman's argument. If, as Goldman explains, "the sun may be read as the pinnacle emblem of patriarchy, the metaphor of male reason and subjectivity" (72), then Woolf's description of the sun's disappearance during the solar eclipse may be read "as a feminist allegory" (75). Goldman compares the diary and essay versions of the eclipse in order to demonstrate how Woolf deliberately "uses colour [in 'The Sun and the Fish'] as an indication of plural subjectivity, and she decentres the notion of one light by the creation of multiple points of enlightenment" (50) indicative of a new feminist order. Goldman contextualizes her reading of "The Sun and the Fish" through an analysis of the iconography used by the Women's Social and Political Union and other women's suffrage groups in their propaganda campaigns. She focuses in particular on the use of specific colors, light and dark contrasts, and sun imagery in posters and banners promoting feminism. As Goldman explains, "[t]he most startling difference between this [the essay's description of the eclipse] and the diary account is the range of colours mentioned. [. . .] Purple, white, and green [. . .] are the colours Woolf selects [in the essay] to accompany 'the defeat of the sun'. [. . .] These colours were linked with the militant Women's Social and Political Union in particular and 'the cause' [for women's rights] in general" (68).

Part two offers a broader range of texts and contexts. In addition to the analyses of *To the Lighthouse* and *The Waves* in which the study culminates, the second half of the book investigates Woolf's connection to her contemporaries' experiments in the visual arts. Goldman draws on several texts by Woolf concerned with painting or color: *Walter Sickert: A Conversation*, *Kew Gardens*, the essays "Pictures" and "Pictures and Portraits," passages from Woolf's diaries and letters, and the forewords she wrote to catalogues accompanying exhibitions of paintings by her sister, Vanessa Bell. Goldman compares Woolf's approach to color expressed in her writing to that of the painters and art critics of her day, including Vanessa Bell, Roger Fry, Clive Bell, Julius Meier-Graefe, and Maurice Denis.

She rejects what she calls the "orthodox view" in Woolf studies that Woolf was most influenced by Roger Fry and Clive Bell. By the second Post-Impressionist Exhibition of 1912, their theories of art valued form above all else, considered form as transcending human experience, and treated color as merely an element of form. Goldman, acknowledging her debt to Diane Gillespie's *The Sisters' Arts*, which establishes the aesthetic connection between Woolf and her sister, argues instead that Woolf's approach to color corresponds to that of the artists of the first Post-Impressionist Exhibition of 1910 and to the work of Vanessa Bell. As Goldman explains: "they [Woolf and Bell] both try to show non-physical experiences as formal realities, at the same time emphasizing and illuminating feminine experience. Both show communication between people as material events. Both relate this to colour" (150). Goldman calls Bell's approach to color "iconographic colourism" (163), in which, according to Woolf, colors function materially as "characters" interacting with one another. What distinguishes Woolf's use of color from Bell's, Goldman asserts, is the fact that Woolf combines this formal approach with an explicitly feminist use of color, originating in political activism.

Goldman's precision in delineating Woolf's place among changing theories and practices of visual art that swept early twentieth-century Britain makes *The Feminist Aesthetics of Virginia Woolf* valuable to anyone interested in Modernism and the relationship between the visual and verbal arts. Her study joins many in recent years that have politicized Woolf's aesthetics, overturning the once dominant idea of Woolf as the quintessential apolitical Modernist. The book contributes to these ongoing debates by connecting one element of the artist's formal practice—her use of color—to a collective material reality. *The Feminist Aesthetics of Virginia Woolf* does not merely bring together Woolf's feminist and aesthetic concerns; it shows how these concerns are themselves bound together historically by social movements in which uses of color signified the prospect of political change. As Goldman explains, in London in 1910, Post-Impressionism was "associated [. . .] with [. . .] manifold degeneracy, the revolutionary overthrow of the social and political status quo, suffragism, and riotous colour" (122). At the first Post-Impressionist Exhibition, an outraged public "gazed in horror at the paintings of Gauguin," Matisse, and others, whose unconventional use of color was considered an obscene distortion of the human form. In the streets, the same public was shocked by "an equally colourful spectacle" made by the militant suffragists (117, 118). Goldman demonstrates convincingly that Woolf was aware of this association among Post-Impressionism, feminism, vibrant color, and social upheaval, and that she exploited it in her writing.

The Feminist Aesthetics of Virginia Woolf is directed to an audience well versed in feminist and poststructuralist literary theories and in the intricate scholarly debates over Woolf's aesthetic influences, particularly those associated with the visual arts of the period. The experience of reading this book might be compared to that of viewing a Post-Impressionist painting. Up close (the perspective offered in *Eclipse*), one sees an exhaustive array of details, repetition, and layering. Stepping back (with the help of the broader perspective offered in *Prismatics*), one notices the harmony of the total composition, whose elements work together in surprising and satisfying ways.

—Janet Winston, *Virginia Commonwealth University*

Notes On Contributors

Kristina Busse is a PhD student at Tulane University finishing her doctoral dissertation entitled "Imagining Auschwitz: Postmodern Representations of the Holocaust," which examines the relationship between historical and psychoanalytic approaches to the Holocaust. She teaches at the University of South Alabama.

Catherine Craft-Fairchild is an Associate Professor of English at the University of St. Thomas, St. Paul, Minnesota. She teaches film studies, women's studies, and British literature. As well as her book, *Masquerade and Gender: Disguise and Female Identity in Eighteenth-Century Fictions by Women* (Pennsylvania State UP, 1993), she has published articles and reviews in *Eighteenth-Century Fiction, 1650-1850: Ideas, Aesthetics, and Inquiries in the Early Modern Era*, and in *Modern Language Review*.

Judith Greenberg is currently completing a manuscript on the role of the echo in the writing of trauma. Her work concentrates primarily on modern French and British texts.

David Porter is Harry C. Payne Visiting Professor of Liberal Arts at Williams College. From 1962-1987 he taught in both the classics and music departments at Carleton College prior to becoming president of Carleton (1986-87) and then of Skidmore College (1987-99). He is the author of books on Horace and on Greek tragedy, and of numerous articles in classical and musical journals; he is also coeditor, with Gunther Schuller and Clara Steuermann, of a book on pianist Edward Steuermann. His most recent articles have been on Willa Cather, Edith Wharton, and the Hogarth Press.

Anca Vlasopolos is a professor of English at Wayne State University, has directed the Program in Women's Studies and is Director of the Program in Comparative Literature. She is the author of *No Return Address: A Memoir of Displacement* (Columbia University Press, 2000), *The Symbolic Method of Coleridge, Baudelaire, and Yeats* (Wayne University Press, 1983) and of numerous essays. She has also published a poetry collection, *Through the Straits, At Large*, and a detective novel, *Missing Members*.

Policy

Woolf **S**tudies **A**nnual invites articles on the work and life of Virginia Woolf and her milieu. The *Annual* intends to represent the breadth and eclecticism of critical approaches to Woolf, and particularly welcomes new perspectives and contexts of inquiry. Articles discussing relations between Woolf and other writers and artists are also welcome.

Articles are sent for review anonymously to a member of the Editorial Board and at least one other reader. Manuscripts should not be under consideration elsewhere or have been previously published. Final decisions are made by the Editorial Board.

Preparation of Copy

1. Articles are typically between 25 and 30 pages, and do not exceed 8000 words.

2. A separate page should include the article's title, author's name, address, telephone & fax numbers, and e-mail address. The author's name and identifying references should not appear on the manuscript.

3. A photocopy of any illustrations should accompany the manuscript. (Black-and-white photographs will be required for accepted work.)

4. Manuscripts should be prepared according to most recent MLA style.

5. Three copies of the manuscript and an abstract of up to 150 words should be sent to: Mark Hussey, English Dept., Pace University, One Pace Plaza, New York NY 10038-1598. Only materials accompanied by a self-addressed, stamped envelope (or international reply coupon) will be returned.

6. Authors of accepted manuscripts will be asked to submit two hard copies and an electronic version. Authors are responsible for all necessary permissions fees.

Please address inquiries to: Mark Hussey, English Department, Pace University, One Pace Plaza, New York NY 10038. mhussey@pace.edu Fax: (212) 346-1754.

www.ingramcontent.com/pod-product-compliance
Lightning Source LLC
Chambersburg PA
CBHW020912020526
44114CB00039B/392